# THE WILD WEST

Time-Life Books is a division
of Time Life Incorporated.

PRESIDENT and CEO, TIME LIFE INC.,
John M. Fahey, Jr.

## TIME-LIFE BOOKS

PRESIDENT, Time-Life Books:
John D. Hall
EDITOR-IN-CHIEF: Thomas H.
Flaherty
*Director of Editorial Resources:* Elise D.
Ritter-Clough
*Executive Art Director:* Ellen Robling
*Director of Photography and Research:*
John Conrad Weiser

### EDITORIAL OPERATIONS
*Production:* Celia Beattie
*Library:* Louise D. Forstall
*Computer Composition:* Deborah G. Tait
(Manager), Monika D. Thayer, Janet
Barnes Syring, Lillian Daniels

 A Time Warner Company

Printed in the United States of America
First Printing: March 1993
10 9 8 7 6 5 4 3 2 1
ISBN: 0-446-51761-5
LC: 92-50880

TIME-LIFE is a trademark of Time Warner Inc.
U.S.A.

This book was created by Time-Life
Custom Publishing in partnership with
Rattlesnake Productions, Telepictures
Productions, and Warner Bros. Domestic
Television Distribution.

## TIME-LIFE CUSTOM PUBLISHING

VICE-PRESIDENT AND PUBLISHER:
Susan J. Maruyama
*Marketing Director:* Frances C. Mangan
*Production Manager:* Prudence G. Harris
*Operations Manager:* Phyllis Gardner
*Promotion Manager:* Gary Stoiber
*Financial Manager:* Dana Coleman

*The television miniseries was created for
Telepictures Productions by Rattlesnake
Productions.*

## RATTLESNAKE PRODUCTIONS

*Executive Producer:* Douglas Netter
*Producer:* John Copeland
*Producer, Director:* Kieth W. Merrill
*Co-Producer:* Jamie L. Smith

## TELEPICTURES PRODUCTIONS

*President:* Jim Paratore
*Senior Vice President:* Bruce Rosenblum
*Vice President:* David Auerbach
*Production Executive:* Michael S. McLean

## WARNER BROS. DOMESTIC
## TELEVISION DISTRIBUTION

*President:* Richard T. Robertson

## EDITORIAL STAFF FOR THE WILD WEST

*Editor:* Roberta Conlan
*Editorial Administrator:* Myrna Traylor-
Herndon
*Senior Art Directors:* Robert K. Herndon,
Thomas S. Heustis, Raymond G. Ripper
*Picture Editor:* Charlotte Marine Ful-
lerton
*Art Director:* Fatima Taylor
*Text Editors:* Jim Hicks, Paul Mathless
*Associate Editors/Research:* Gwen C.
Mullen, Quentin Gaines Story
*Writers:* Mark Galan, Charles J. Hagner
*Assistant Art Director:* Kathleen Mallow
*Senior Copy Coordinator:* Colette M.
Stockum
*Copy Coordinator:* Donna D. Carey
(principal)
*Picture Coordinators:* Jennifer Iker, Greg
S. Johnson (principal)
*Editorial Intern:* T. Nieta Wigginton

*Special Contributors:* Amy Aldrich,
Peter A. Pocock, Brian Pohanka, David
S. Thomson, Jim Watson (text); Cheryl
G. Binkley, John Leigh, Maureen Leni-
han, Katharine G. Loving, Barbara Jones
Smith, Wendi Maloney, Tanya Nádas
(research); Barbara Fairchild Quarmby
(copy); Mel Ingber (index).

*Correspondents:* Elisabeth Kraemer-
Singh (Bonn), Christine Hinze (Lon-
don), Christina Lieberman (New York),
Maria Vincenza Aloisi (Paris), Ann
Natanson (Rome). Valuable assistance
was also provided by Elizabeth Brown
(New York).

## CONSULTANTS FOR THE WILD WEST

*Alan Axelrod* (Chroniclers) holds a Ph.D. in American culture from the University of Iowa and is the author of *Art of the Golden West* and *A Chronicle of the Indian Wars: From Colonial Times to Wounded Knee*.

*Dee Brown* (Foreword) has written more than 25 works of fiction and non-fiction, most notably the history *Bury My Heart at Wounded Knee*. He lives in Little Rock, Arkansas.

*Brian Dippie* (Mythmakers) is a professor of American history at the University of Victoria in British Columbia, Canada.

*William Gwaltney* (Soldiers) is a staff historian for the National Park Service in New Mexico.

*Frederick Hoxie* (Indians) is director of the D'Arcy McNickle Center for the History of the American Indian at the Newberry Library in Chicago.

*William Turrentine Jackson* (Dreamers and Wayfarers) is a professor of American history at the University of California, Davis.

*Albro Martin* (Dreamers and Wayfarers) recently retired as a professor of history at Bradley University in Peoria, Illinois. His research specialty is American business history.

*Brian Pohanka* (Soldiers) is a historian specializing in the Civil War and frontier subjects. He has written extensively on the battle of the Little Bighorn.

*Byron Price* (Cowboys) is the executive director of the National Cowboy Hall of Fame and Western Heritage Center in Oklahoma City, Oklahoma.

*Glenda Riley* (Settlers) is the Alexander M. Bracken Professor of History at Ball State University in Muncie, Indiana.

*Elliott West* (The Way West, Settlers, Townspeople) is a professor at the University of Arkansas, where he specializes in American social history.

# CONTENTS

# FOREWORD

To bring the vast saga of America's Wild West into one volume is an awesome task. The makers of the television series *The Wild West* succeeded in encompassing virtually the whole of this mighty epic in 10 hours. And this published companion to the series completes a parallel sweep across the tale that spanned roughly the last three decades of the 19th century.

The West is a scenic place and requires pictures to supplement words in telling its story. The Westerners—natives and emigrants alike—require portraits to match their own words, or the words of others that describe their deeds. Those images are here in one of the most superb collections ever assembled on this subject. The people of the old Wild West came from every continent, representing many races and nationalities. We need to study their faces and read their words to comprehend how they dealt with forces almost incomprehensible to modern human beings. We have never spent weeks in ox-drawn wagons crossing the Great Plains and the Rockies, or lived in tipis with soldiers threatening our lives, or endured in sod houses without adequate water, fuel, or medical assistance. As the result of deep research we can now experience vicariously the fatigue and joy and pain and triumph the Westerners felt long ago.

Out of the frontier West the American character was formed—a people audacious and self-reliant and naive, generous and stubborn, righteous but forgiving, humorous in a folksy way, violent, hospitable, contradictory. Examples of all those traits are within these pages, in depictions that avoid the clichés that mar many overall accounts of this part of our history.

From well-chosen quotations out of diaries and letters, we listen to the real words of people who dared face the wildness of the West. In one sentence an irrepressible homesteader in Kansas tells more than could be said in a page of expository prose: "This is such a healthy country, if they want to start a grave yard, they would have to shoot some one." A traveler crossing the Great Plains on a slow-moving railway train is mesmerized by the vastness of the land: "It was a world almost without feature. An empty sky, an empty earth; front and back, the line of railway stretched from horizon to horizon.

On either hand, the green plain ran till it touched the skirts of heaven." A cowboy on a trail drive complains at a river crossing about the herd muddying the water before he could drink: "I ain't kicking, but I had to chew that water before I could swallow it." Words like these are the real stuff of the Western past.

We read of the scouts, former trappers who learned skills of survival and tracking by cooperating and living with Native Americans—skills later employed against those same people. We learn of the tragedy of the Indian wars, a dark stain upon our past resulting from inept government policies, arrogant army officers, and corrupt Indian agents. We see the magnificent faces of Indian leaders who guided their people in treaty councils and led them in desperate defiance against intrusions upon their homelands. We are told of the hard life of soldiers who were sent to keep the peace in the Wild West, and how their leaders sometimes led them into deadly peril.

Running parallel with the Indian wars was the rise of that premier symbol of the American West—the cowboy. Here we discover what a cowboy's life was truly like, why he used the costume and gear that he did. We go along on a trail drive to a cattle-shipping town and find that although life was boisterous at the end of a cattle drive, it was not a continuous gunfight as depicted in the movies.

One sublime development in the Wild West, often overlooked in other histories of the period, is the story of how the women who went west shook off the shackles of customs and laws to become independent. They staked their own claims, ran their own newspapers, and, having proved they were the equals of their male counterparts, were the first women in the United States to win the right to vote.

Oh, yes, the West was wild for a time, ruthless and tragic, but it was glorious, too, the greatest and swiftest movement of mass settlement across a continent in the world's history, resulting in clashes between good and evil forces that reverberate to this day.

Americans know neither their country nor themselves unless they know the story of the old Wild West.

Dee Brown

# The Way West

Dwarfed by surrounding mountains, covered wagons ford Wyoming's Medicine Bow River, bringing white settlers west along the Oregon Trail.

# To Journalist John Louis O'Sullivan, the Westward Expansion of

the United States was a God-given right, pure and simple, needing no legal or diplomatic justification. "The American claim is by right of our manifest destiny to overspread and to possess the whole of the continent which Providence has given us," he wrote in 1845. "It is a right such as that of the tree to the space of air and earth suitable for the full expansion of its principle and destiny of growth."

*Manifest destiny!* O'Sullivan's ringing and original phrase leaped from his article into the public imagination, marking with moral approval what American expansionism had already done and was doing. Since the beginning of the 19th century, the United States and its citizens—driven by democratic ideals, a thirst for adventure, aspirations of a better life, and corporate and individual greed—had been bulling their way across the continent, taking the land by negotiation, theft, trickery, war, and sheer force of will. By the time O'Sullivan's article appeared, the United States was on the verge of completing its acquisition of all the territory that later would come to be known as the Wild West. Appropriately enough, the region would be memorialized in accounts of courage and endurance and skulduggery, of peaceful settlement and dreadful violence, of outsize heroes and murderous villains—the same qualities and character types that distinguished the acquiring of it.

In that very year, 1845, American settlers threatened to attack British posts in Oregon country, compelling Britain to yield to the United States what are now Washington, Oregon, and Idaho. Soon American armies would be invading Mexico in a trumped-up war that would cost that country its vast northern half, reaching from Texas to the Pacific shores of California. And not just rivals and neighbors suffered at the hands of the vigorous young nation. The Native Americans who had inhabited all that territory long before any white people showed up saw their institutions shattered and their lives transformed, their loved ones swept by the thousands into untimely graves, victims of European diseases to which they had no inborn resistance.

The Indians had suffered plenty before the U.S. started moving into the West in the early 1800s. By then, the Spanish had been in the Southwest for more than two centuries. Under their rule, pestilence and slavery, along with raids by other Indians, had reduced the population of New Mexico's once stable and prosperous Pueblo communities from at least 60,000 Indians to about 9,000. The death toll in California was equally dire. By 1800, a string of Spanish missions had converted some Indians, enslaved others, and by means accidental and intended managed to kill off a lot more, perhaps up to 90 percent of the indigenous population.

Horses, which Spaniards had introduced to America, also profoundly altered Indian existence. Hunting buffalo from horseback

Symbol of unabashed American expansionism, Manifest Destiny bears steadily westward, bringing settlers and miners in her wake as Indians and buffalo flee. The telegraph wire she trails from one hand will, along with the coming railroad, render the Pony Express rider and the overland stagecoach obsolete.

and trading the skins to whites for weapons and other goods proved so profitable that a few previously agricultural nations, such as the Cheyenne and the Crow, gave up their permanent settlements for the nomadic life. Meanwhile, Indians who were pushed onto the Plains by westward-moving white Americans also embraced the horse and nomadism—the Sioux from Minnesota, for instance, and the Blackfeet, who were known as the Algonquian back East.

Before the arrival of the horse, settled Indian agricultural communities existed in the pueblos of the Rio Grande valley on the eastern edge of the Great Plains and in the Mandan, Hidatsa, and Arikara villages up the basins of the Mississippi and Missouri rivers. As decades passed, mounted nomads raided these farmers more and more often, seizing food, trade goods, women, and slaves to sell to the Spanish, who shipped them south to work in the Mexican silver mines. Along with the scourges of smallpox and other diseases introduced by whites, the raids devastated horticultural populations. By the beginning of the 19th century, their once thriving way of life was considerably endangered.

Up until that time, the United States seemed too absorbed in the business of settling the land that lay east of the Mississippi to take much interest, except for the fur trade, in the West. But in 1800 there occurred an event that upset the international applecart: France extracted from Spain control of the immense territory called Louisiana and, most important, the port at its southern extremity, New Orleans. New Orleans was the gateway to the world for the whole of the Mississippi Basin and all the American agricultural products that moved down the river.

President Thomas Jefferson, fearing that the French, a potent military force under Napoleon's then-unrivaled leadership, might be bold enough to interfere with U.S. trade through New Orleans, tried to buy the port city. To his surprise Napoleon made a counteroffer that amounted to one of the most astonishing real-estate bargains in all history: the whole of Louisiana for $15 million. With no real constitutional authority to do so, Jefferson concluded the deal in 1803, buying for the U.S. 800,000 square miles of land stretching from the Mississippi River to the Rocky Mountains, from the Gulf Coast to the Canadian border. In one stroke the Louisiana Purchase doubled the geographical extent of the young republic.

Bargain though it was, the Purchase was met with hoots of derision from some, chiefly Jefferson's political opponents. The nation already had enough trouble on its hands trying to settle the still-wild states and territories—Kentucky, Tennessee, Mississippi—of its present frontier. To spend 15 million good dollars on who knew what sort of worthless wasteland, howled one of Jefferson's enemies, was "the wildest chimera of a moonstruck brain."

Undeterred, the president immediately dispatched two extremely able U.S. Army officers, Meriwether Lewis and William Clark, on an expedition to explore the largely unknown realm and beyond— an expedition he had them preparing even before he bought the territory. Leaving St. Louis on May 14, 1804, with 28 soldiers, a half-Indian interpreter, and an African-American slave named York, Lewis and Clark set off up the treacherous, sand-bar-strewn Missouri River in three boats and by fall had reached today's North Dakota, where they wintered with the friendly Mandan Indians.

Here they took on a valuable addition to the party, a 16-year-old Shoshoni Indian woman named Sacajawea, pregnant wife of a French-Canadian trapper who also joined the expedition. Sacajawea gave birth before they set off the next spring. Carrying her infant son while climbing treacherous mountain trails and thrashing down roaring whitewater streams in fragile canoes, she guided Lewis and Clark over the Rockies and along the Columbia River to the Pacific. She interpreted for them, rescued their gear when a boat capsized, obtained horses from local Indians, and earned herself a place in legend as the Indian princess (her brother was a Shoshoni chief) who showed America the way west. Lewis and Clark, though grateful, recorded her in their journals as "the Indian woman," because they could not spell her name.

By the time Lewis and Clark got back, reaching a tiny farm village on the lower Missouri in September 1806, they had been gone two years, four months, and 10 days and had crossed 7,689 miles of wilderness. Their topographic sketches showed how people could reach the distant Pacific Ocean, and their report of the rich beaver supply in the Western rivers set off a rush by trappers such as Jim Bridger, Jedediah Smith, and the Sublette brothers, William and Milton. These rough mountain men explored large areas of the territory and blazed the vital early paths across the West, including the great Oregon Trail.

While explorers were finding ways west, pressure for new land to settle was building up east of the Mississippi. Population was growing in the Ohio and upper Mississippi regions and along the Gulf Coast. The farm frontier was moving west like an avalanche and had reached the edge of the Plains. Part of this advancing wave funneled into the Oregon Trail, producing first a trickle and later a flood of emigrants heading into the Northwest.

Few chose to settle on the Plains themselves. The huge expanse between Missouri and the Rockies—the bulk of the Louisiana Purchase—was scorned as a place to live. This view was crystallized by an army explorer, Major Stephen H. Long, who pronounced the great grasslands "almost totally unfit for cultivation" and virtually uninhabitable. He dubbed the region the "Great Desert," a label that, changed to the "Great American Desert," soon appeared on maps even in children's geography books. It was a place to be shunned, to be gotten through as fast as an emigrant wagon train's ox-drawn prairie schooners would go.

But what was then called Oregon country was something else, a quarter of a million square miles of snowcapped peaks and forests and lush valleys, a lovely, fertile demi-Eden. By that time, contact with whites had inflicted great damage on the peoples of this region, such as the Kwalhioqua and the Tilamook. Ever since British explorer Captain James Cook arrived at Vancouver Island in 1778 and learned that sea otter skins worth $100 each in China could be bought from the Indians for sixpence a pelt, fur traders had been flocking to the Pacific Northwest. Before long, the most affluent Indians in North America, whose societies were characterized by dense populations, high standards of living, and highly developed cultures, were dying by the thousands of smallpox and syphilis.

The wealth promised by the fur trade had the United States and Britain jostling for position in Oregon country. American John Jacob Astor's Pacific Fur Company established a post called Astoria at the mouth of the Columbia River in 1811. Britain's Hudson's Bay Company set up shop farther north at Fort Vancouver. In an 1818 compromise, the two nations agreed to an uneasy joint occupation, but the strife between them continued.

The newcomers heading overland for the Pacific Northwest, most of them would-be trappers or traders, were not fazed by any dispute over national possession. The adventuresome leader of one

The Shoshoni Indian guide Sacajawea signals to a party of Chinook Indians, as Meriwether Lewis *(standing)*, William Clark *(in cocked hat),* and York look on, in a romanticized depiction of a meeting that actually took place on land in 1805.

party that struck out for this promised land was a highly enterprising Boston businessman named Nathaniel Wyeth who by age 29 had made a small fortune in ice—cutting it from a frozen pond during the winter and shipping it to the West Indies. In 1832, Wyeth and 24 hopeful recruits started west across the Plains with wide-eyed optimism. Fortunately, they had engaged the veteran trapper William Sublette as scout. Without him "we must have perished," one member of the party noted, "for want of sustenance in the deserts of the Missouri." When they finally reached Fort Vancouver in October,

eight months after leaving Boston, disappointment waited. A ship Wyeth had sent ahead loaded with beaver traps and all manner of trade goods—everything this entrepreneurial dynamo needed for the business schemes he had cooked up—was reported lost at sea. Wyeth was no man to quit. He headed back to Boston and was soon signing up recruits for another journey. Again he made it all the way to Oregon and this time he stayed.

One member from Wyeth's second team of travelers was a tall, brawny Methodist clergyman named Jason Lee, who became Oregon's first American missionary. He was quickly followed by more men of God eager to reclaim the souls of the heathen Indians. One of these proselytizers was a New York physician and preacher, Marcus Whitman, who was determined to prove that both heavy wagons and women could endure the rough overland journey. He married a buoyant and brave young woman named Narcissa Prentiss, and by way of honeymoon, they hit the Oregon Trail in 1836.

The wagons were a bust. Two big ones had to be abandoned, and a lighter third vehicle caused endless trouble before it, too, was finally left behind. "Husband had a tedious time with the wagon today," wrote Narcissa. "Did not wonder at all this. It was a grater wonder that it was not turning a somerset continually." Narcissa not only survived the trail in fine shape but became pregnant along the way. After they reached their destination she delivered the first white American baby born in Oregon; unhappily, the child later drowned.

Whitman went on to found a mission in the eastern part of Oregon Territory, home of the Cayuse Indians. He encouraged white settlers to take over the land of the people he supposedly was serving, saying that since Indians were resisting conversion they deserved to lose their land and "ought not to complain at the results." After measles carried by the settlers killed numerous Cayuse children, the Indians attacked the mission, slaying about a dozen whites—including Marcus and Narcissa.

In the opposite, southeastern corner of the West, in the vast region called Texas, other American citizens were also making themselves at home on someone else's land, in this case with official invitations. As the giant, corrupt Spanish Empire crumbled around the edges, Mex-

Visionary Boston entrepreneur Nathaniel Wyeth led the first emigrants over the Oregon Trail in 1832, hoping to set up in trade out West.

ico wrested its independence from Spain in 1821. Americans were already moving into Texas in numbers that Mexicans found disturbing. However, in hopes that settlement would discourage raids by the Apache and the Comanche, and—more shortsightedly—that Americans would reward generosity with loyalty, the Mexican government began granting large tracts of land to bands of American colonists.

There were only about 3,000 Mexican settlers, called Tejanos, in Texas at the time. But these patricians ran a highly advanced ranching economy of long standing. Their huge haciendas enclosed whole towns of workers and families. By 1823, the Mexican numbers were already matched by 3,000 immigrants from the United States. By 1830, Americans totaled about 7,000—a number that had more than quadrupled, to 30,000, by 1835.

Far from feeling obliged because of the Mexican government's generosity to them, many of the American Texans were eager to overthrow their benefactors. A new president in Mexico City, General Antonio López de Santa Anna, provided the excuse when he marched north with several thousand soldiers to whip the Texans into line. Santa Anna's campaign had widespread support among a Mexican populace resentful of the American presence on land they regarded as their own. But the general did not know what he was up against: His enemy was fiercely stubborn, and as dangerous as a cornered mountain lion, even when vastly outnumbered. Santa Anna got a sharp lesson when his army of thousands confronted a mere 187 Texans holed up inside an old Spanish mission called the Alamo in San Antonio. The Texans could have escaped but instead fought to the death in a vicious battle on March 6, 1836.

The decision to defend the Alamo was militarily foolish, but losing heroes such as Davy Crockett and Jim Bowie steeled the resolve of the Texans, and accounts of the one-sided battle won worldwide sympathy for them. Both effects were magnified shortly afterward, when Santa Anna took 371 prisoners at Goliad, Texas, and cruelly massacred all of them. It was a vengeance-minded Texas army of 800 under General Samuel Houston that in April caught Santa Anna and 1,500 men off guard at the San Jacinto River in southeastern Texas. Charging to the battle cry of "Remember the Alamo!" the Texans routed the Mexicans in 18 minutes, killing hundreds of them. Santa Anna was forced to sign a treaty granting independence to what became the Republic of Texas.

Before long, Mexico would be challenged in California just as it had been in Texas, and for the same reason: an influx of settlers from the United States. Initially this was largely the doing of a sharp operator and booster named John Marsh. Marsh, pursued by federal authorities in Iowa for selling guns and ammunition to the Sioux (he was an Indian agent at the time), prudently made his way along the Santa Fe Trail to far-off California. There he at first passed himself off as a physician; officials in Los Angeles, unable to read Latin, accepted his Harvard bachelor's diploma as a medical degree. When he had grown sufficiently wealthy from his medical practice, he bought a 17,000-acre ranch in the San Joaquin Valley.

Hoping ultimately to transform the Mexican province into a U.S. territory, Marsh wanted more American citizens to settle in California. He wrote dozens of glowing letters about the place to folks in the Midwest. He praised the climate, the soil, the ease of getting there, and the availability of compliant labor. "When caught young," he wrote, Indians "manifest a great attitude to learn. They submit to flagallation with more humility than negroes." His letters were passed from hand to hand, and some were published in newspapers.

In 1841, a party of 69 hardy souls, many of them lured by Marsh's extravagant paeans, set out from Sapling Grove, Missouri. They headed up the Oregon Trail in their ox-drawn wagons, determined to be the first to make the passage on wheels. On the far side of the Rockies, those bound for California would take a turn in a southwesterly direction. Marsh, who himself had never been that far along the Oregon Trail, had written that they would find the fork somewhere vaguely in the vicinity of what is now Idaho. The rest of this first emigrant wagon train, meanwhile, would continue to Oregon.

The group was representative of all the pioneers to follow, including farmers and business people, scoundrels and missionaries, and at least one child. The organizer of the California-bound contingent, John Bartleson, was named the captain of the wagon train. But a 21-year-old Ohio schoolteacher named John Bidwell proved a better leader and was accepted by all as the real man in charge. One well-liked emigrant, traveling under the name of Talbot H. Green, was actually Paul Geddes, a bank embezzler. He struggled with the weight of a "lead" brick all the way to California—beneath a coating of lead was the gold he had stolen from his bank. Nancy Kelsey, 18 years of age, made the journey with her husband and year-old daughter, Ann,

whom she carried whenever the steep slopes made it impossible for the child to ride in the wagon.

Thirty-four people took the fork to California. It proved far different from the easy route Marsh had described. In the deserts of Utah and Nevada they "could see nothing before us but extensive arid plains," Bidwell recorded, "glimmering with heat and salt." Marsh had promised an abundance of water and grass for the animals; instead, the oxen verged on death. The pioneers had to eat many of the beasts anyway, in order to survive themselves. When they pushed into the forbidding and trackless Sierra Nevada range, Bidwell wondered "if there was any possibility of extricating ourselves from this place." Because of blisters, Nancy Kelsey clambered shoeless up the stony slopes as she carried her baby over the mountains. In the end, the long-suffering party survived and made their way into the San Joaquin Valley. The following year 200 pioneers headed west and in 1843 another 1,000, followed by 4,000 in 1844 and 5,000 in 1845.

By then, American expansionists led by President James K. Polk were inciting violence everywhere on the continent that U.S. interests collided with those of rivals. Polk, who wanted Texas, California, and all the territory in between, made his intentions clear; the U.S. would never be able to get along with the Mexicans, he declared, "until we have given them a good drubbing." Texas was annexed, and a clash near the Rio Grande provided an excuse for the drubbing to start in May 1846. By the autumn of 1847 American troops occupied Mexico City. In 1848, Mexico officially ceded California and New Mexico—the latter including what are today Arizona, Nevada, and Utah. Meanwhile, in June of 1846, Britain had agreed to give up to the Americans all of Oregon country below the 49th parallel; only the war with Mexico had prevented Polk from insisting on a border about 350 miles farther north.

Once the whole of the West was under U.S. control, emigration surged. The discovery of gold in California lured 30,000 people there in 1849 alone. Few of the pioneers were fully aware when they set out how exhausting the 2,000-mile trek would prove. They chronically ran low on food and water. Cholera, diphtheria, and other diseases took their toll. "The cowards never started," a saying went, "and the weak died on the way."

But the costs of the westward movement were never as high for

In the 1840s, booster John Marsh wrote extravagant letters in praise of the then-Mexican province of California, luring hundreds of hopeful American settlers to the promised land with the ultimate aim of making California into U.S. territory by sheer strength of numbers.

the whites as for the Indians they encountered along the way. Despite folklore to the contrary, the Indians rarely attacked the pioneers; in fact, many tribes went out of their way to be helpful. Their grimly ironic reward was often death by disease. The Cheyenne lost about half their population in a single year, 1849. The Sioux, too, suffered devastating losses that year. They died in droves—from cholera, whooping cough, influenza, typhus, and other epidemics left behind by passing wagon trains. Then and since then, white Americans seemed almost oblivious to this result of the move west. Perhaps understandably, they focused on their own hardships, which were plentiful enough. That such a prodigious tide of humanity kept moving on despite the difficulties, said one Oregon settler, "will be received by future generations as a legend on the borderland of myth."

As ever more of the best land in Oregon and, to a lesser extent, in California was settled, the westering urge at last found its object closer to home, on the much maligned grasslands of the Plains. Important to this shift was the Kansas-Nebraska Act of 1854 that turned the two future states into U.S. territories and opened them officially to settlers. And the settlers came. In the six years before the Civil War the non-Indian population rose from almost nothing to 136,000.

That massive conflict would be a watershed for the West. By the time the Civil War ended, Northern commerce and industry would be ready to reach across the plains and mountains to ensure not only transcontinental trade but commercial ties to the Orient as well. An obliging U.S. government would provide legislation to help visionary railroad builders such as Theodore Judah, who dreamed of spanning the West with shining rails, get on with the job. Federal homesteading boons, combined with railroad industry blandishments and outright lies, would draw to the West ever more farmers and would-be farmers whose interests often conflicted with those of cattle barons and dirt-poor cowboys such as Teddy Blue Abbott, who worked for them. Women came too, to raise children, labor alongside their husbands in the fields, or eke out a hardscrabble living in mining camps, as Anne Ellis did in Colorado. Into the mix would pour many honest small-businessmen seeking to get in on the ground floor of what they hoped would be boomtowns, a fair helping of drifters and adventurers, and a goodly number of dishonest scoundrels, some as charming as Talbot H. Green with his lead brick and others just plain wicked. Lots of them would be armed. It was going to be a Wild West indeed.

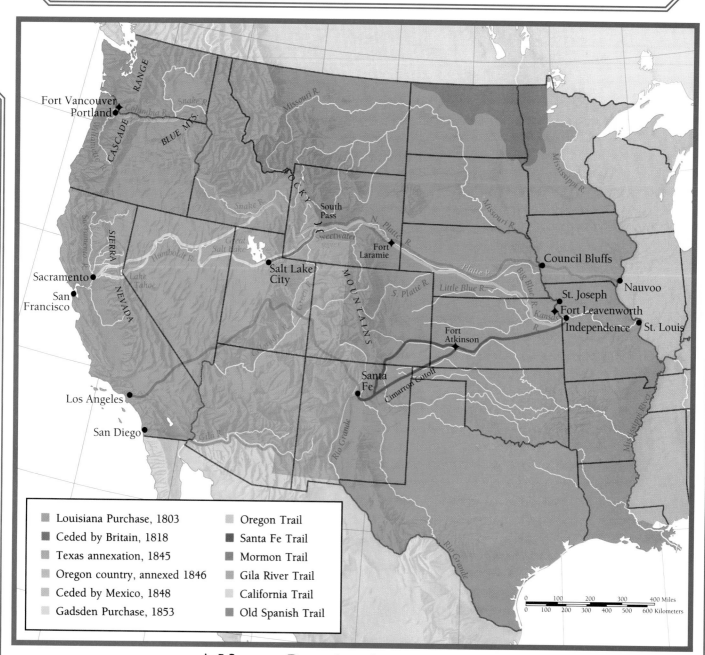

Legend:
- Louisiana Purchase, 1803
- Ceded by Britain, 1818
- Texas annexation, 1845
- Oregon country, annexed 1846
- Ceded by Mexico, 1848
- Gadsden Purchase, 1853
- Oregon Trail
- Santa Fe Trail
- Mormon Trail
- Gila River Trail
- California Trail
- Old Spanish Trail

# A Nation Complete from Sea to Sea

Starting with the Louisiana Purchase from France in 1803 and ending with the Gadsden Purchase from Mexico 50 years later, the United States bargained and bullied its way west to the Pacific Ocean, north to the 49th parallel, and south to the Rio Grande, thereby completing the nation's broad outline. As was typical of the period, the transactions involved in this expansion assumed the nation's right to buy, trade, and otherwise acquire land that had been occupied for thousands of years by other people; over the next 50 years, Native Americans would be relegated to ever-shrinking parcels of reservation land.

Even before the federal government took over land acquisition in the far West, emigrants from the East had been staking their own claims, struggling overland to California, Oregon, and Texas on well-used trails through the deserts and mountains. With the advent of coast-to-coast rail lines in the 1860s, the overland trails fell into disuse, but in their heyday they had opened the West to settlement—and thence to acquisition—by a flood of people in search of a better, richer life.

In a desolate land softened by the warm glow of sunset, a settler extends Western hospitality to two travelers—shelter in exchange for company.

# It had been marked "Great American Desert" on the maps of the first

wagon trains bound for Oregon Territory or California. And the label, though exaggerated, was not wholly unjust. Those pioneers striking out from western Missouri or Iowa in the 1840s and 1850s well remembered their passage through the flat, arid, wind-swept, treeless expanse of the Great Plains, a region that stretched from Canada to the Texas Panhandle, from the Missouri River to the Rocky Mountains. Few thought to stake a claim there.

But before long, most of the fertile lands of the Pacific Slope, throughout what are today's Oregon and California, were spoken for, and the nation's surge westward began to take a retrograde turn. The American idea of frontier folded back on itself; in the mind of the land-hungry settler, only the unbroken Plains, an endless sea of waving buffalo grass populated by "savages," still beckoned.

That hunger for land spread like wildfire in the restless times following the Civil War. Keturah Belknap, a 30-year-old Iowa woman, wrote, "There has been a strange fever raging here. Nothing seems to stop it but to tear up and take a six-month trip across the plains."

Returning Union army veterans, many of whom had never ventured outside their home counties before going off to fight in the war, now found home too cramped to hold them and life there unpromising. Former Rebels felt an even greater need of a fresh start. Many had come back from the war to find their homes destroyed, their livestock gone, their fields and orchards returned to the wild, their way of life lost, and their country in the hands of Yankee occupation forces and carpetbaggers.

From the Old South, too, came a new kind of American citizen, one who burned to be a landowner and farmer—the freed slave. Led in community groups by such forceful personalities as former slave Benjamin Singleton, thousands of African-American families moved west to make a new life.

And from across the Atlantic Ocean came thousands of northern European immigrants, driven out of their ancestral homes by poverty, political oppression, and religious persecution and lured to the

American prairie by railroad- and steamship-company advertisements promising land for the taking in what was trumpeted as a bounteous Eden.

The railroads, beneficiaries of the Transcontinental Railroad Act of 1862, had been granted vast stretches of government land running in wide strips on either side of the tracks they were building to bind the Pacific Coast with the eastern half of the country. They thus had two converging interests—turning the land into cash by selling it to settlers and filling up the country along their rights-of-way with farms and bustling towns that would engender profitable traffic in passengers and freight.

Another force behind the great migration onto the Plains was the Homestead Act, also passed in 1862, which offered grants of 160 acres to anyone 21 years of age or older. The homesteader had only to build a shelter on the land within the first six months and make improvements while residing on it for five years, after which he—or she, for unattached women made up a significant minority of the claimants—could "prove up" fulfillment of the legal requirements and gain full title to the land.

Emily Towell, who at age 52 was considerably older than most when she went homesteading with her husband, felt the call. "Every imagination," she wrote, "was fired with dreams and visions of new homes and fortunes to be made in the Fertile West."

Often, however, claiming a homestead was not the realization of a settler's dreams but the beginning of her worst troubles. In designating 160 acres, the U.S. Congress—made up mostly of Easterners familiar only with the fertile soil and abundant rainfall of Eastern farmlands—never considered that a grant of such size might not even provide a family's subsistence in the arid West. Nor did the gaudy railroad come-ons mention summer temperatures on the Great Plains that might reach past 110 degrees, with not a speck of shade for miles around, or winter temperatures of more than 40 degrees below zero, with blinding blizzards that could catch a farmer or a schoolchild out in the open and leave him lost and frozen 10 feet from his door.

Besides the extremes of heat and cold, nature offered a seemingly endless procession of other tests of body, spirit, and even sanity. Furious tornadoes, lightning, hailstones, and flash floods threatened crops, livestock, and human life itself. And the wind, unceasing and

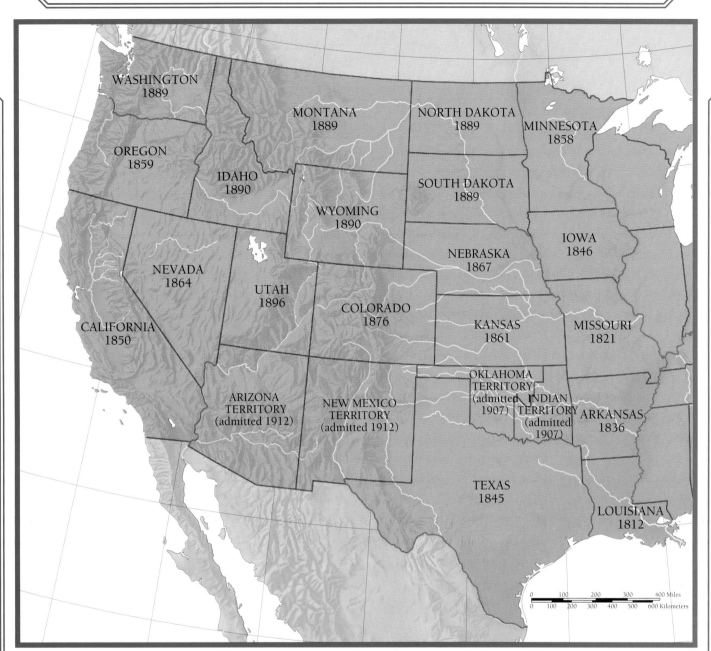

WASHINGTON
1889

OREGON
1859

IDAHO
1890

MONTANA
1889

NORTH DAKOTA
1889

MINNESOTA
1858

SOUTH DAKOTA
1889

WYOMING
1890

NEVADA
1864

UTAH
1896

NEBRASKA
1867

IOWA
1846

CALIFORNIA
1850

COLORADO
1876

KANSAS
1861

MISSOURI
1821

ARIZONA
TERRITORY
(admitted 1912)

NEW MEXICO
TERRITORY
(admitted 1912)

OKLAHOMA
TERRITORY
(admitted
1907)

INDIAN
TERRITORY
(admitted
1907)

ARKANSAS
1836

TEXAS
1845

LOUISIANA
1812

0    100    200    300    400 Miles
0  100  200  300  400  500  600 Kilometers

# A Growing Nation

Starting in the 1840s, as the numbers of westbound settlers jumped by hundreds and then thousands year by year, the map of the western United States underwent a series of transformations. Until then, the region was only lightly demarcated: Louisiana, Missouri, and Arkansas were states; Iowa was organized as a territory. The rest was unorganized, shared, or claimed by other countries (page 39). By 1900, as seen above, not only had the U.S. gained territory from Mexico and Britain, but those tracts had been subdivided and most of the subdivisions had been admitted to the Union as full-fledged states.

Statehood was not granted easily. A territory could elect its own assembly and a nonvoting representative to Congress when its population reached 5,000 free male voters. When the total population reached 60,000, it could petition Congress for admission to the Union, but the timing of admission often depended on the political balance of power in Washington. Still—and remarkably—almost all the Wild West made the transition from colonial rule to self-government in less than a century.

unbroken by any natural barrier, was enough to drive a solitary homesteader crazy.

But of all the difficulties the settlers had to face, the two most lethal were debt and the aridity of the Plains. Many emigrants had borrowed money for the train fare west or for their most basic farming needs—a yoke of oxen, a wagon, a plow, seed. They had to plant, raise, harvest, and sell a crop for a profit on their first try, because anything that went awry—from the loss of a draft animal to a collapse in grain prices in far-off Chicago or New York—could wipe them out for good.

The dry climate held the settlers hostage to fate. Although in the long run the annual rainfall on the prairie averaged about 12 inches, this average was the product of extremes—24 inches one year, 4 inches the next year, 8 inches the year after that. A farmer could watch his crops thrive—or shrivel.

Ultimately, fewer than half the settlers in some states stood up to the challenge. Yet for every tenderfoot who took one look at the desolate, featureless landscape and caught the next train east, there was another who was enraptured by the immense sky and the sweep of wildflowers. For every newcomer exhausted by cholera, ague, or typhoid fever or defeated by the death of a little son or daughter, there was one like the irrepressible Scottish homesteader in Kansas who was heard to say, "This is such a healthy country, if they want to start a grave yard, they would have to shoot some one." For every family that pulled up stakes after their bumper crop was obliterated by a visitation from nature's Pandora's Box of scourges, there was another who grittily dug in and waited for the better times to come. Of course, some of those who stuck it out and eventually prospered had stayed only because they were so destitute they could not afford to move anywhere else.

For most newly arrived families, the first priority was to get a crop in the ground. The work was slow and hard. Just breaking the soil involved a constant wrestling match with a plow pulled by mules or oxen. So tough was the earth that the cast-iron plow in use back East could make little headway against it; a sharp-edged plow of steel or tempered iron with a different curvature was needed. Weeding, haying, harvesting, threshing, and myriad other tasks kept farmers busy from early spring to late fall.

# WAGONLOADS OF TREASURES

Practicality often warred with homesickness on the trek west as settlers tried to balance what they needed to stay alive en route and to set up housekeeping at the end against the niceties of the civilized life they were leaving behind. The travelers' prairie schooners—so named because their protective canvas covers appeared on the horizon like a ship's canvas sails—were sturdy enough to hold as much as 2,500 pounds, and the optimistic pioneers tended to stuff them with the creature comforts and talismans they could not bear to leave behind. But as the animals hauling these burdens succumbed one after another to exhaustion, the travelers were forced to cast off excess weight. Beds, tables, and stoves littered the trail, along with such luxuries as fancy dresses and mirrors. But not every sentimental treasure was jettisoned; certain beloved objects, some shown here, occupied pride of place in their new homes.

—China—

These Went West ——
The articles shown here reflect the needs and wants of the families who picked up and moved themselves to the unknown land out West. On the practical side, they carried medicine kits, quilts, and frying pans—all essentials for the journey; a butter churn would be useful on arrival. Clocks and family Bibles were not practical but served as links to distant family and civilization. One woman safely transported a set of china by wrapping it in blankets and packing it in trunks (above).

—Prairie Schooner—

—Family Bible—

—Herbal Medicine Kit—

—Three-Legged Skillet—

—Clock with Brass Works—

—Butter Churn—

—Patchwork Quilt—

Farming was a family affair. Margaret Mitchell, who came with her family to a Kansas homestead in 1870 at the age of 15, wrote, "There were nine children in our family, six girls and three boys, and as the girls were older and my father not strong, the hard toil of the pioneer life fell to the girls. . . . There were unpleasant things to be done, but we never thought of shirking them." Another Kansas sodbuster, Joseph Reed, writing about his son, said proudly, "Little Baz can run all over, fetch up cows out of the stock fields, or oxen, carry in stove wood and climb in the corn crib and feed the hogs and go on errands down at his grandma's." This industrious, competent child was all of two years old.

For the woman of the house, having children was a mixed blessing. With conscious irony, homesteader Annie Greenwood observed, "The week Rhoda was born I cooked for fifteen men who had come to stack hay. And in the intervals of serving them I would creep into my bedroom to sink across my bed. I was so tired. Through my bedroom window I could see the mare and the cow, turned out to pasture for weeks because they were going to have their young."

Animals were precious to the settlers, who did their best to take good care of them, although blizzards, predators, locoweed, and disease inevitably took a toll. Of all the livestock that the homesteaders kept, oxen were probably the most useful and most unsung. They cost much less than horses or mules, plowed a straighter furrow, were more serene and docile, and could graze on anything. Abbie Bright, a Philadelphia-bred 21-year-old who followed her brother Philip out to Kansas in 1870 and staked a claim near his, loved her own ox: "He is quite a pet. . . . When I call him, he comes as far as the roap will let him. I was moving him to a new feeding place, and he put his nose on my shoulder."

Some homesteaders would live in a tent or in the wagon that brought them until the planting was over and they could build a house. Except along rivers and creeks, timber was almost nonexistent on the Plains, and few families could afford sawed lumber from town. So the sodbusters turned to the stuff that gave them their name—the earth beneath their feet, woven by a dense network of grass roots into a tough, ready-to-hand building material.

A house made of blocks of sod three inches thick, 12 to 18 inches wide, and two or three feet long was sturdy enough to prevail for a good six or seven years against any weather, even a tornado. It was

essentially fireproof, it remained cool in summer and warm in winter, and it could be put up in a few weeks for virtually nothing. Only the relative luxury of glass windows and a wooden door might run the cost up to $5 or $10.

But the "soddie," as it came affectionately to be called, had its drawbacks: The roof, usually of sod as well, leaked profusely during rain and dripped for days afterward. When dry, it issued a constant drizzle of earthen crumbs, which, if no cloth was tacked up to catch them, added a gritty texture to the family's meals and made cleanliness a relative matter. The space within was at best dimly lighted; stories are told of families who, after years of living in a sod house, could finally afford a wooden house with ample windows, only to find that the bright interior hurt their eyes.

Delbert Parnham, a young homesteader who came to Kansas in 1871, described another feature of life in a soddie: "Sometimes the bull snakes would get in the roof, and now and then one would lose

A determined-looking pair of settlers and their three small children make a visual record of their worldly goods by posing for a photograph in front of their wagon. The wagon not only served as shelter and vehicle on the trail, it also provided a temporary home when the family reached its destination.

By the 1890s wheat farmers on the Great Plains could deploy huge horse-drawn combines (*left*) to harvest their crops. Technological advances in farm equipment nearly tripled annual crop yields in the quarter century after the Homestead Act opened up the Plains to settlement.

his hold and fall down on the bed, then off on the floor. Mother would grab the hoe, and there was something doing. After that fight was over, Mr. Bull Snake was dragged outside."

Vying for priority with putting in a crop and building a shelter was the need to find a reasonably handy supply of water for drinking, washing, and cooking. The fortunate early comers could choose a claim on a river or creek, which not only provided water but usually also included a good supply of wood for building or fuel. Later arrivals would have to dig a well.

Most of those who settled on bottom land away from a stream could count on finding water relatively close to the surface, but on the higher tablelands settlers might have to dig down several hundred feet before getting results, and even then some holes would remain dry. Many sodbusters enlisted the aid of a dowser, or water witch, who searched for underground water with a forked stick held in both hands that supposedly would vibrate and point downward when it was carried over water.

Well water might be clear and cold, or muddy and tepid. It also had to be shared. Said Delbert Parnham, "We had nothing with which to wall the well, so it was really just a hole in the ground. We . . . had to strain the water to get the crickets and bugs out in the summer and rabbits in the winter."

By the 1870s the life of the settler was beginning to be improved by technological advances. One of the first was an inexpensive, factory-made windmill designed to pivot so it always faced the shifting wind. Taking advantage of the one inexhaustible energy source on the prairie, store-bought windmills or homemade ones built to the same design ensured ample water for livestock and saved women the backbreaking toil of raising and carrying water for washing and cooking. Windmills became ubiquitous on the prairie.

Close in their wake came barbed wire, invented in 1873 by an Illinois farmer by the name of J. F. Glidden. Permitting the building of fences in a land lacking both wood and stone, barbed wire revolutionized life on the Plains, foreshadowing the end of open-range cattle ranching and giving homesteaders a cheap and surefire method of protecting their crops from destruction by hungry cows or the dwindling buffalo herds.

Technology came to farm work, too. Breaking the sod first with a simple plow pulled by two animals, the successful farmer slowly graduated to ganged plows pulled by larger teams. Reaping, binding, and threshing machines followed, powered first by great numbers of draft animals, then by stationary steam engines. Finally, steam tractors completed the mechanization of agriculture.

No technological advance, however, could help the sodbuster in the face of capricious nature, which often struck with a force that destroyed a family's crops and hopes at a stroke. The most awesome blow fell on a single day in the bone-dry midsummer of 1874, when farmers saw a dark cloud approaching from the west. Most thought at first that it might signify the coming of much-needed rain, but their anticipation turned to confusion and then to horror as the cloud blotted out the sun, making night of day, and descended with a whirring roar around and upon them, turning the landscape into a seething ocean of grasshoppers.

Said homesteader Mary Lyon, "When they came down they struck the ground so hard it sounded almost like hail. There was a watermelon patch in our garden and the melons were quite large and

long. They were not ripe so we could not save them, but by the evening of the second day they were all gone." The voracious insects stayed for several days, eating almost every growing thing in sight; they even devoured onions and turnips down to their roots, leaving odd holes in the ground.

Farmers who survived the grasshopper plagues, of which none before or since was ever as bad as the one of 1874, still had to put up with other terrors of summer, such as drought and hailstorms—one a slow death to the sodbuster's dream of a rich crop, the other a sudden blasting of his or her hopes. Stories were told of farmers working their fields when a storm would suddenly whip up, loosing torrents of hailstones as big as hens' eggs and forcing the farmer to hide beneath a wagon to keep from being battered, a fate the wheat and corn crops could not escape.

Susan Newcomb, who was 18 when she and her husband, Samuel, staked a claim in Texas, wrote in her diary on January 7, 1866, "This has been another cloudy, warm day and looks a little like we might have some rain before many days, but all signs of wet and dry weather fail sometimes in Texas. This part of Texas is very much subject to droughts, so much so that the largest streams often stop running." Drought in its turn was father to dreaded prairie fires, which ran before the unceasing wind and blackened everything in their path until rain or the massed efforts of the sodbusters stopped them.

Fighting prairie fires was one of the times during the growing season when homesteaders assembled from far and wide for the common good. Similar gatherings for happier purposes were anticipated with great excitement, as they gave settlers a rare break from the often bleak isolation of their lives out on the Plains.

Women suffered the most from the absence of sisterly companionship, since the wife and mother on a homestead was often the only adult female. A man could broaden his human contacts by working alongside a temporary hired hand, or hiring himself out to do some work for a neighbor, or going into town for supplies, which gave him a chance to compare notes about farm affairs and catch up on gossip and news. Thus, especially for the women, a husking or quilting bee, a wedding, the raising of a sod house for a new neighbor, a Fourth of July celebration—any of these was reason enough for a festive get-together. Perhaps the most exciting time of the entire year was the

long-awaited county fair or the state or territorial agricultural exposition. Beginning on the prairie around 1860, these annual events never lost their popularity.

In between times, homesteads generally welcomed visits from neighbors, and strangers passing through could usually count on a night's hospitality, for the arrival of company always brought a welcome reprieve from loneliness.

Gradually, though, the Great Plains began to fill up. As farm families became more numerous, towns grew up to meet their need for access to market facilities, gristmills, railroads, manufactured goods from back East, medical care, schooling, and religion.

Education was a high priority for most settlers, perhaps because more effort was required than just sending children off to school, as in the East. The first homesteaders, their homes scattered across the sparsely populated prairie, had to teach their offspring the basics at home. As soon as a community of settlers could raise enough money, however, they put up a one-room schoolhouse and hired a teacher.

Vera Pearson, a Kansas homesteader, recalled her school days: "The schoolhouses had a few bare benches, flat, without back, and so far off the floor that little legs, dangling high in the air, would ache cruelly before a change of position was possible." The teaching, she said, was conducted with "no charts, no maps, no pictures, no books but a Speller."

For all the importance homesteading families placed on education, their need for the children to help with the farm work made serious inroads into time available for them to attend school. Students might come to classes for a few months in a row, then drop out for a year or more. Many schoolteachers on the Plains were teenagers, only a step or two advanced in learning beyond the scholars in their charge, who might, indeed, be older than they.

Where there was a school there would soon be a church, followed by a Grange hall, a farm machinery dealership, a theater, and other amenities of civilization. The Great Plains were just as majestic—and sometimes as intimidating—as ever, but they were no longer the undisturbed realm of nomadic Indians, buffalo, prairie dogs, and grass. By untold struggle and immeasurable courage and grit, the women and men who came west had set a course for America's heartland that would make the Great American Desert the most productive agricultural land on earth.

# HEADING FOR THE PROMISED LAND

By and large, those heading west tended to be people of an optimistic and hopeful nature. But they were also often woefully naive about what lay in store. "October 1st saw us—a wagon, three horses and our humble household necessities—bound for the 'Promised Land,'" wrote one young woman. "My fears vanished as we traveled toward our Mecca."

As she would soon realize, however, Mecca was a long way off, and the wearisome journey would take a considerable toll in animal and human life. As the wagons slogged across the prairies and struggled over the mountains, food and water grew scarce and sometimes ran out. Animals died of exhaustion, and the settlers coped with the results of accidents and disease; cholera alone claimed thousands.

Even after a pioneer staked his claim and settled down, the struggle was far from over. To those accustomed to the wooded, hilly country back East, the flat expanse of prairie was dismaying. And the recurring fires and dust storms that leveled his crops and destroyed his house bludgeoned more than one would-be farmer into giving up. But most settlers stuck it out, forging new lives and communities in the vast land they now called home.

*"It was a very sad mother and father who saw their baby, their most treasured possession, taken away from them. There were many mounds at the side of the road, giving mute evidence of suffering and sorrow."*

◆

*Emily Towell*

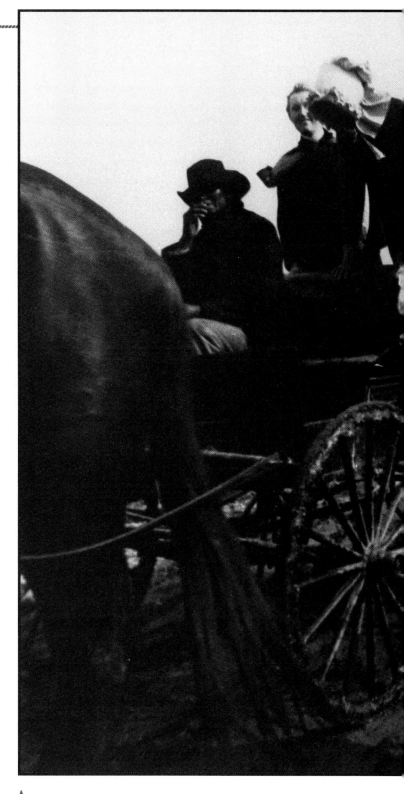

A Moment of Pleasure ——

Exhilarated by the adventure of traveling across the country—or perhaps by the prospect of a brief respite from the day's long walk—a young woman looks gleeful as the wagon comes to a halt. A resilient group, pioneers could find humor in the worst of times. A sudden downpour left one drenched woman in tears at first, but then she laughed at the thought of how comfortable her father's hogs were in the mud.

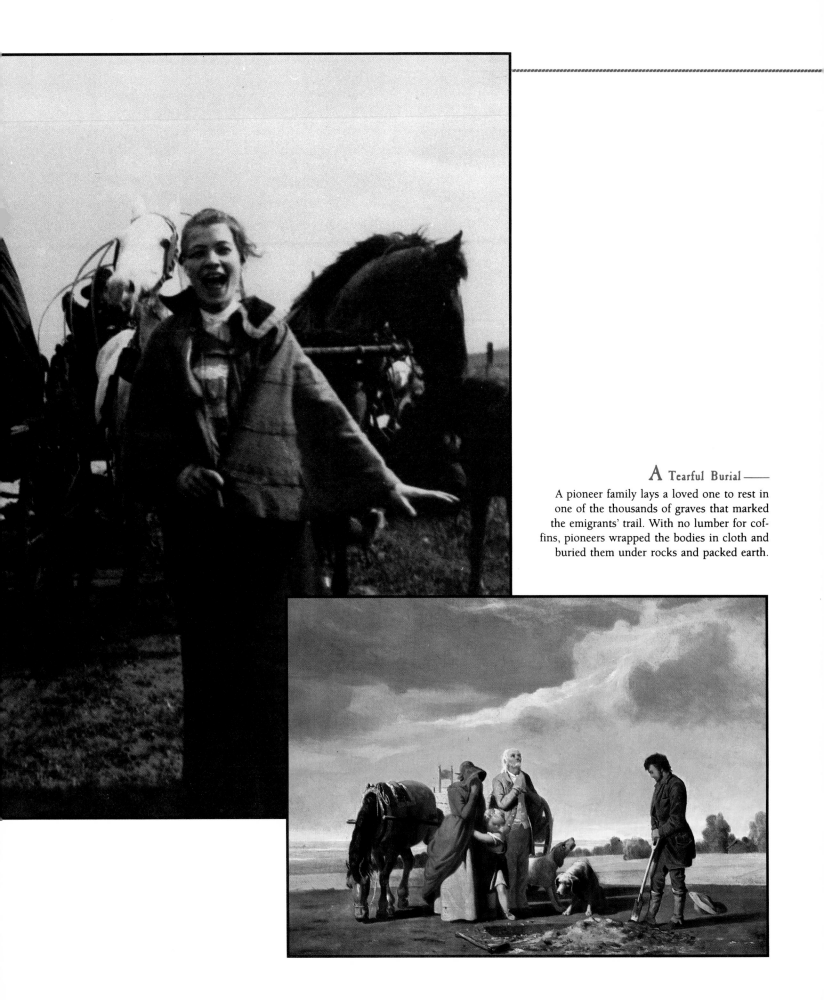

A Tearful Burial——
A pioneer family lays a loved one to rest in one of the thousands of graves that marked the emigrants' trail. With no lumber for coffins, pioneers wrapped the bodies in cloth and buried them under rocks and packed earth.

# House on the Treeless Prairie

Finding materials for a house was a challenge on the Plains, where the nearest lumber was many miles to the east. Instead, settlers found land that was, in the words of one new Kansan, "bare, treeless, wind-swept, sun scorched."

So the pioneers turned to the earth beneath their feet, hacking through the tough roots of prairie grasses to chop out heavy sod bricks. With bare ground as the floor, the sodbusters built up walls of sod, sometimes plastering them over to keep down the damp and dirt. A nearby river might supply willows or rushes to fashion a roof, but more often, a sod roof had to do. When it rained outside, rivulets of mud coursed inside, continuing long after the rain stopped.

*"Well, when I came everybody had taken a claim, or was going to. So brother said I should take one too. It was the fashion—and fashion has a great influence on people."*

◆

*Abbie Bright*

**R**oom for One———
Using a chair seat as a table, a bachelor frontiersman in Nebraska tucks into supper inside his snug sod house. This resourceful fellow seems to have covered his dirt walls with plaster.

**H**ome and Its Comforts———
Having dragged their possessions outside for the occasion, a pioneer couple stands for a photograph in front of their soddie, as such dwellings were nicknamed. The antlers stuck in the roof helped the sodbusters spot their homes from afar; without such signals, the grass-topped soddies virtually disappeared into the surrounding prairie.

A Nebraskan sodbuster slices earth into strips with a special plow, then cuts the strips into blocks for loading onto a wagon. To build an average soddie required about an acre of turf.

# Establishing a Real Homestead

Once crops were planted and a house built, homesteaders could think about making some needed improvements. With the advent of barbed wire in the early 1870s, for instance, a farmer could protect his crops from marauding cows and buffalo. But one of the most critical first tasks was to devise a ready supply of water, especially if no pond or river lay nearby. Digging a well by hand was hard labor, made harder if it proved a dry hole. "We dig a deep well and got nothing," recorded Emma Mitchell, who settled in Russell Springs, Kansas, in the late 1870s. "Many a time I walked a quarter of a mile down into a deep draw with pails and carried water to wash with." Indeed, the work of the homestead was so demanding that women performed grueling chores usually reserved for men, and children worked as hard as adults.

*"One of the first things to do was to dig a well. We had nothing with which to wall the well, so it was really just a hole in the ground. We drew water with a rope and pail, and in a short time, had to strain the water to get the crickets and bugs out in the summer and rabbits in the winter."*

◆

*Delbert Parnham*

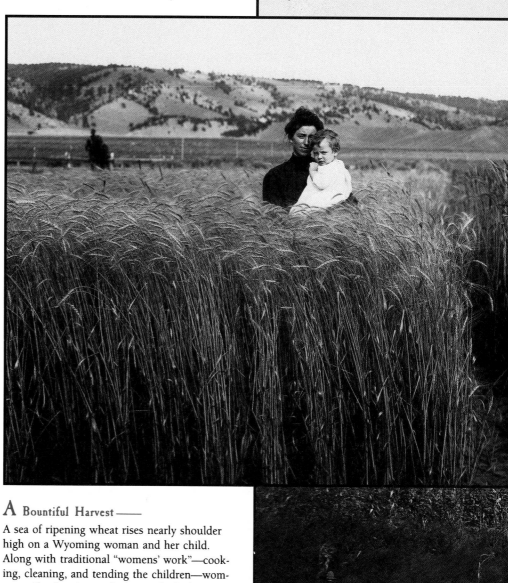

**A Bountiful Harvest** ——

A sea of ripening wheat rises nearly shoulder high on a Wyoming woman and her child. Along with traditional "womens' work"—cooking, cleaning, and tending the children—women on the frontier pitched in with the heavy labor of plowing and planting to grow crops to feed their families.

**Harnessing the Wind** ——

Water was scarce on the arid Plains, but with a windmill like the one that dominates this Wyoming homestead, the incessant prairie wind could be used to pump hundreds of gallons a day for drinking, cooking, and washing. Farmers generally had to find some other method for irrigating their fields.

Straight from the Source——

A well-trained farm cat—one member of the menagerie of animals on a typical homestead—intercepts the stream of milk her laughing mistress aims directly from the cow's udder.

### A Young Hunter

A proud boy, with his faithful dog, shows off the rifle he uses to hunt game near his family's Idaho farm, one of the more enjoyable chores that frontier children performed when they were not working in the fields.

# Coping in the Face of Disaster

Nature was the sodbuster's sometime friend and ofttime foe on the plains of Kansas and Nebraska. "It snowed all day and blew so that we could not see the river," wrote Luna Warner *(below)* of Solomon, Kansas, about one blizzard. "Our chickens were all frozen into the woodpile." Dust storms *(bottom right)* carried acres of soil away, hailstorms could flatten crops, and tornadoes *(top right)* could rip homesteads to pieces. Perhaps the most constant adversary was drought. Peering skyward for signs of rain, a farmer might as easily spy the terrifying, telltale columns of smoke rising from a prairie fire. When the grass was like tinder, a spark from a campfire or the discharge of a gun could set the whole world ablaze.

*"The wind blew very hard today and made the dust very disagreeable in this place. Sand storms are very common here. They are heavy winds that come from across the plains—something like the sandstorms in Africa that we read about."*

◆

**Samuel Newcomb, Texas**

Luna Warner ———

Luna Warner, 15, arrived in Kansas with her family in spring 1871. Her lively journals described not only the hardships of frontier life but also her teenage passion for dancing.

# The Birth of Communities

With their farms often separated by tens of miles, homesteaders combated loneliness and isolation by finding many excuses to get together. Sometimes the reasons were serious—as when a neighbor needed to rebuild a house or barn that had burned down—but just as often, gatherings were purely social. Quilting bees offered women a chance to sit and talk; dances gave young people an opportunity to meet and mix with the opposite sex.

As far-flung communities grew in size, the increased sense of social kinship and shared values among their members gave rise to permanent institutions such as schools and churches. Many of the first schoolteachers were male, as they were back East. But by the latter part of the century, women had come to dominate the teaching profession in the West.

*"Don't think that all our time and thoughts were taken up with the problems of living. We were a social people. We never waited for an introduction or an invitation to be neighborly."*

◆

*Mary Lyon*

A Barn Raising——

Balancing on beams and rafters, a veritable barnful of settlers pause for posterity in the midst of helping a neighbor erect his new farm building. Barn raisings were not just work; they were also an excuse for a party.

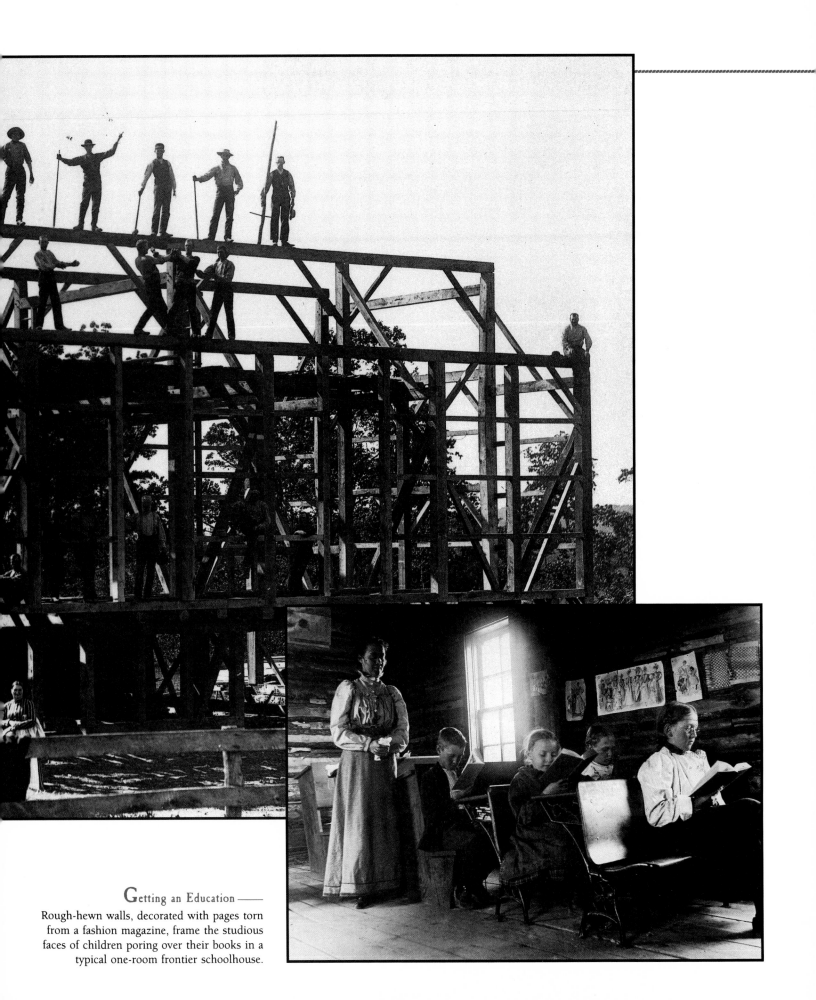

Getting an Education ——
Rough-hewn walls, decorated with pages torn
from a fashion magazine, frame the studious
faces of children poring over their books in a
typical one-room frontier schoolhouse.

A Quilting Bee———

A group of women in Pendroy, North Dakota, stitch while they chat at a quilting bee hosted by the postmaster's wife *(above, right)* in 1890. With little time for recreation, women welcomed the chance to socialize even as they worked to produce something necessary.

**P**icnic High Jinks ———
Their Sunday outfits notwithstanding, two boys perch atop a crude merry-go-round during a picnic held by the Methodist Episcopal church in Junction City, Kansas, in 1896. Though they ministered to the spiritual needs of their congregations, churches also sponsored a variety of secular activities.

**T**ime to Dance ———
Frontier finery is on display at a dance in Colorado in 1895. Dances were a popular and inexpensive way for young men and women to meet one another. As one admirer noted, "Most of the girls, beating time with their little feet in jigs, reels, and hornpipes, were pretty enough to chain to the spot any worshipper of natural beauty."

# "Farewell to America!"

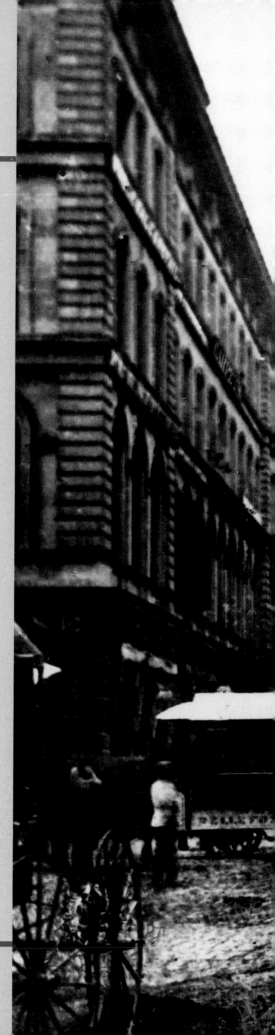

In 1843, as his wagon lumbered westward onto the Kansas plains, former Missourian John East looked back and shouted, "Farewell to America!" The cry reflected a common sentiment about the vast, unknown land that lay ahead. Though occupied for thousands of years by Native Americans and for more than two centuries by Spanish colonists, the West was alien country to mid-19th century emigrants, whether they came from Missouri or from as far away as Europe and Asia.

The notion of the West as virtually uninhabited wilderness persisted nearly to the end of the century, in large part due to the difficulty of traveling there. Even by 1876, when a dense network of some 50,000 miles of railroad track linked bustling Eastern cities such as New York, Chicago, and St. Louis, only a solitary line crossed the continent to the Pacific Coast. Understandably, past the first tier of states beyond the Mississippi River, scarcely a handful of towns had populations of more than 5,000, and even these places were often thrown up haphazardly, in the heat of a land or mineral rush. Isolated by huge distances, these and other, smaller, outposts lacked most of the familiar graces of civilization. The photographs here and on the following pages illustrate the jolting dislocation many wayfarers experienced as they ventured out from St. Louis and across Kansas—onto the foreign soil of the Wild West.

St. Louis, Missouri, 1876 ———
Last stop for sophistication on the way west, St. Louis in 1876 rivals its more easterly sister cities for amenities such as complex architecture, street lamps, sidewalks, and a rail system for horse-drawn streetcars.

**M**ullinville, Kansas, 1880 ———
Five hundred miles southwest of St. Louis,
the frontier begins at Mullinville, and the signs
of habitation are sparse. In the middle of the
one and only street is the town well—an absolutely vital municipal feature for citizens on
the arid Plains.

**S**outhwestern Kansas, 1897 ——

Even three years from the turn of the century, the emptiness and monotony of the Kansas landscape overwhelms the lonely house on the horizon some 80 miles west of Mullinville. Though rail lines crisscrossed Kansas, many areas remained sparsely settled.

# DREAMERS
# AND
# WAYFARERS

A train puffs into an idealized Western town complete with river and picturesque mountain range in a Currier and Ives print exalting the new railroads.

# IN 1860 THE UNITED STATES WERE UNITED IN NAME ONLY. BESIDES THE NATION'S

growing split over slavery, the young states of California and Oregon lay divided from the rest of the U.S. by a vast sweep of wilderness populated mainly by Indians, Mexicans, and a few buffalo hunters, prospectors, and pioneering farmers. For many Americans, this territory was the unfinished business of "manifest destiny"; they dreamed of conquering the wilderness and spreading American civilization throughout the West.

One of the most practical of the dreamers, though his contemporaries would hardly have called him so, was a 35-year-old civil engineer from Connecticut named Theodore Judah. Already an experienced railroad builder while still in his twenties, Judah had the vision to see a time in the near future when an American could ride a train from New York to California in a matter of days. For his passionate pursuit of the dream of creating a railroad to link the West Coast to the East, he was saddled with the epithet Crazy Judah. But he knew he was the man to make that dream a reality. To his wife, Anna, he said, "It will be built, and I am going to have something to do with it."

At the time, traveling across the country was a daunting task. Between the Missouri River and California's settled coast lay some 1,600 miles of intimidating prairie, desert, and mountains. Wayfarers had only a few ways of making the trip, none of which could be anticipated with a light heart.

They could travel by steamboat up the Missouri River, which joins the Mississippi just north of St. Louis, having carved a winding passage of almost 3,000 miles from its source in the Montana Rockies. Navigating the Missouri's sinuous curves and capricious currents was a challenge for even the most skilled steamboat pilots. One of them, Steamboat Bill Heckman, wryly described the river as "too thick to navigate and not thick enough to cultivate." Samuel Clemens, yet to gain fame as Mark Twain, went west with his brother in 1861, making the first leg of the trip by Missouri River steamboat from St. Louis to St. Joseph, Missouri. "The boat might almost have gone to St. Joe by land," he wrote, "for she was walking most of the

time—climbing over reefs and clambering over snags all day long."

Westbound travelers unwilling to face the steamboat's considerable perils—wreck, fire, boiler explosion—could make the grueling trek overland, joining a wagon train if they had a wagon and a team. What this choice might mean was articulated by Susan Magoffin, a woman who made the journey: "Worse and worse the road!" she wrote in her diary. "Half a dozen men by bodily exertions are pulling the wagons down the hills. We came to camp about an hour and a half after dusk, having accomplished the great travel of *six or eight hundred yards during the day.*"

By 1860, however, the stagecoach had become the primary means of land transportation between Missouri and the West Coast. Wells, Fargo & Company, which got its start in California in 1852 by transporting pay dirt and mail for forty-niners, was the largest stagecoach outfit in the West. Although the company dominated the stage business west of Salt Lake City, for a long time it could make little progress east of that point, because it kept running head-on into a man named Ben Holladay, one of the West's larger-than-life figures.

Holladay ran a virtual stagecoach monopoly between Missouri and Salt Lake City and operated other routes all the way to Oregon. A crude, boisterous man who built a multimillion-dollar empire of stage lines, steamships, packing plants, gold mines, gristmills, and land, he lived an ostentatious lifestyle and hobnobbed with high-ranking government officials—some of whom were in his pay.

In business, Holladay was ruthless and rapacious, continually expanding his stagecoach empire by attacking smaller companies. His technique was to establish a rival service along a given route and carry passengers for one-tenth the going fare. After he had grabbed all the business along the route, and the competition had folded, he would raise his fares higher than ever, take his best coaches off the line, and cut back on the schedule of runs.

Many coaches were notoriously uncomfortable—crude wagons with canvas sides and roofs and hard benches to sit on. Most coaches had no suspension system, so the ride was a bone-jarring ordeal. Passengers also had to endure bad weather, bad food, mechanical breakdowns, Indian attacks, and the occasional drunk driver. One man described his trip as "the hardest two weeks' work I ever did."

Holladay cared nothing for the comfort of his passengers. His orders to his drivers were "Pack 'em in! Pack 'em in like sardines!"

Leland Stanford

Charles Crocker

These four worked perfectly together to create the Central Pacific Railroad. Stanford, a grocer turned governor, was adept at using political oil. Crocker, noted for roaring "like a mad bull," drove ahead the construction.

His stagecoaches often got underway with nine adults jammed inside and an equal or greater number hanging on for dear life on the roof.

For all his brutish ways with competitors and his boorish manner, Holladay was a shrewd businessman. Long before the dream of a transcontinental railroad was realized, he foresaw the railroad's lethal impact on the stagecoach business. Coolly reversing his longtime expansionist policies, he shocked the staid and sober officers of his chief rival, Wells, Fargo, by abruptly offering in 1866 to sell out to them, lock, stock, and barrel. The offer was accepted, and Ben Holladay, the one-time Stagecoach King, walked away from the business forever with $1.8 million for his troubles.

If the discomforts and perils of cross-country stagecoach travel were too much for the westward wayfarer to contemplate, the only remaining possibility was to go by ship. That could be done one of two ways. From New York, vessels sailed or steamed south to the tip of South America, made the often treacherous passage around frigid, stormy Cape Horn, and then headed north for San Francisco. The 13,600-mile voyage might take six months. The second option was to sail south to the Isthmus of Panama, take a mule caravan across 50 miles of fetid, steamy, disease-ridden, bandit-plagued jungle to the Pacific shore, and board a second ship for passage up the coast to California, a route totaling 5,450 miles. The reward for brooking these hazards was a relatively brief travel time of five weeks—assuming a northbound ship was waiting on Panama's Pacific side and had room for more passengers.

Theodore Judah's dream of putting an end to all of that was rooted in California, where stood the greatest obstacle to the building of a transcontinental railroad—the Sierra Nevada. Running almost the entire length of the state and isolating the populous coastal cities from the rest of the continent, the Sierra was held by conventional wisdom to be impassable to trains. The locomotives of the day could not negotiate a rise steeper than 116 feet in a mile, an incline hardly perceptible to the eye, and all known routes across the Sierra exceeded that rate of climb. Judah was one of the few who had faith that a suitable pass would be found.

A job building a short-line railroad from Sacramento to the gold-mining country of the Sierra foothills had brought Judah to California. Once there, he spent much of his free time looking for a way

Mark Hopkins

Collis P. Huntington

Hopkins was the money man, always poring over the books. Huntington, a bold, unscrupulous schemer, lobbied Washington for favorable laws and federal aid and plotted devious strategies his collaborators carried out.

through the mountains. Finally, in late 1860, he was contacted by one Daniel Strong, a pharmacist in the foothill town of Dutch Flat who had discovered a gradually rising passage through the mountains. With growing excitement, the two men surveyed a practical route through the pass, and Judah rushed back to Sacramento, where he founded a Central Pacific Railroad Company in June 1861.

Judah then set about finding financial backing. After a lengthy struggle against the skepticism of California business people, he finally rounded up a small number of supporters, including a cabal from Sacramento who came to be known as the Big Four: Collis P. Huntington and Mark Hopkins, partners in a hardware store; Leland Stanford, a wholesale grocer; and Charles Crocker, a dry-goods dealer. Together with Judah they incorporated the Central Pacific.

Judah hurried off to Washington to lobby for a government charter for the CP. By then the Civil War had begun, and Congress was eager to see a railroad extended to California to help bind the Western states to the Union. In the summer of 1862, it passed and President Abraham Lincoln signed the Pacific Railroad Act, which authorized the building of a transcontinental line and chartered two railroad companies to do the job, Judah's Central Pacific and a company based at the eastern end, to be called the Union Pacific.

The Central Pacific would start construction from the West Coast, the Union Pacific from the Missouri River; they would meet approximately at California's eastern boundary. For every mile of track each railroad laid, it would receive a government grant of 10 square miles of land in alternate sections on either side of its right of way. The government would also bestow a loan of $16,000 per mile of track built on the Plains, $32,000 per mile through the desert country of the Great Basin, and $48,000 per mile through the Rockies and the Sierra Nevada. To qualify for the money, each company had to finance and lay the first 40 miles of track on its own.

Shortly after the Central Pacific broke ground in January 1863, Judah found himself at odds with the Big Four, who were in a hurry to throw down 40 miles of slapdash track and collect the first installment of government money. Judah wanted the line to be soundly constructed, regardless of how long it took. Disillusioned by the emerging greed and lack of principle of his colleagues, he once again set out for the East in October 1863, this time to find other investors.

Traveling by the Panama route, Judah and his wife could antici-

pate a somewhat easier and faster journey than previously, as the isthmus was now traversed by a railroad. Ironically, however, Judah contracted yellow fever during the crossing. He died within a week of reaching New York, at the age of 37. With the voice of the Central Pacific's honest, single-minded engineer stilled, the financiers of the CP were free to resort to the kinds of maneuvers that Judah had deplored. Still, their high-handed ways not only lined their pockets but also enabled them to ramrod the gargantuan work of building a railroad through some of the most inhospitable terrain in the world.

While Judah was dreaming of crossing the Sierra Nevada with a railroad, another young, idealistic, New England-born engineer harbored a similar dream—this one about building a railroad westward from mid-continent. Grenville M. Dodge, in a letter to his sister, wrote, "Soon you'll be whirled along by steam never dreaming that four years before was a wild open country inhabited only by wild beasts and the Red Man." Dodge, a surveyor for the Rock Island line, had an advantage over Judah: No one considered his dream crazy. He worked for railroad executive Thomas C. Durant, who had his own hardheaded intention to build a transcontinental railroad.

## Flying across the West at Horseback Level

The Pony Express rider in this Frederic Remington painting charges out of a station on the fabled mail route from Missouri to California. Riders leaped onto a fresh horse every 12 to 15 miles, exhausting as many as six mounts before passing the mail pouch to the next rider. The Express covered the 1,966 miles between St. Joseph and San Francisco in 10 days, an astonishing speed for the era. The daring riders became legendary figures. But the service that began in April 1860 ended only 20 months later, made obsolete by the telegraph.

Durant would become the driving force behind the Union Pacific Railroad, but Dodge would not sign on until three years later. He had joined the Union army at the outbreak of the Civil War and within two years would win general's stars.

Before the UP could break ground, the starting point for the line had to be designated. President Lincoln finally selected Omaha, Nebraska, as the UP's eastern terminus. Construction began in December 1863. Both companies ran into trouble almost immediately. Although they were authorized to raise funds by selling stocks and bonds, few investors cared to risk capital on a will-o'-the-wisp scheme like a transcontinental railroad when there was easy money to be made in war industries. Supplies were as scarce as money. The iron needed to make rails was all going into weapons and munitions, and the Union army had first call on locomotives, rolling stock, and almost anything else a new railroad might require. And even if equipment had been plentiful and cheap, there was no one to build the line; most able-bodied men were off fighting.

When the lack of money became critical in 1864, Collis Huntington and Thomas Durant both descended on Washington. Wielding tongues of silver and purses of gold, they soon won ample numbers of congressmen and senators over to the railroad cause. The result was a series of amendments to the Pacific Railroad Act that doubled, to 20 square miles, the grants of land per mile of track and reduced the unsubsidized start-up requirement from 40 miles of track laid to 20 miles of roadbed graded. The revised legislation also directed the Central Pacific to build 150 miles into Nevada, where it would link up with the Union Pacific. Despite Congress's bounty, however, labor and supplies remained scarce, and construction proceeded slowly.

The end of the war in April 1865 eased the supply problem and created a pool of veterans looking for work. The majority of these men mustered out in the East, where most of the fighting had taken place, so the Union Pacific's manpower problem was solved. But out West the CP work force was still far too small, and when some Irish workers threatened construction boss Charlie Crocker with a strike, he decided to buck the prevailing race prejudice and hire 50 men from among the thousands of Chinese who had poured into California during the gold rush. Surprised and impressed by the sobriety and industriousness they showed on the job, Crocker soon emptied the Chinatowns of Sacramento and San Francisco of capable workers

# DRIVING THE RAILS THROUGH WILD, MEAN, AND STUBBORN COUNTRY

Seldom has any human undertaking presented more difficult and dangerous natural obstacles than those faced by the surveyors, engineers, and tracklaying gangs of the Union Pacific and Central Pacific railroads as they built the first rail line across the West. They had to construct bridges long enough to span the wide flood plains of great rivers and high enough for steamboat smokestacks to pass underneath. They risked their lives working 100 feet or more above canyon floors to build spidery wooden trestles. And they sweated and died carving ledges to carry tracks high along sheer canyon walls and cutting their way through miles of heavy rock, especially to get across the Rockies. Toughest of all were the many tunnels that had to be driven straight through mountains, such as the Summit Tunnel beneath Donner Pass in the Sierras—a 20-foot-high bore drilled and blasted a few inches a day through 1,659 feet of solid granite. All in all, the construction of this first trans-Western railroad and the other lines that followed ranks as the greatest technological triumph of their day.

With two engines pulling, an early passenger train inches along a narrow shelf cut into the side of a granite gorge in the Rockies. Ledges like this had to be blasted out, the workers drilling holes in the rockface and stuffing them with black powder.

Raised high on a spidery bridge over Canyon Diablo in Arizona Territory, a three-car passenger train is out of harm's way in case of flash flooding, which could turn the dry canyons and arroyos of the Southwest into destructive torrents.

A locomotive steams into the far end of Bloomer Cut, an 800-foot-long slash through solid shale dug by Central Pacific work crews in the Sierras. A mistimed explosion during the excavation cost James Strobridge, the tough, driving chief of the CP gangs, the sight of one eye.

and even sent agents to China to recruit more. Eventually, the Central Pacific's construction work force was 90 percent Chinese.

In the fall of 1865 Grenville Dodge left the army and became chief engineer of the Union Pacific. Up to that time, the UP had not even managed to lay track from its beginnings at the Omaha terminal to the city limit. Dodge plotted a simple and direct course; it would carry the UP line west from Omaha, across Nebraska, over the Laramie Mountains, and across the Wyoming Basin to the Wasatch Range and the Great Salt Lake. To oversee the work crews, Dodge hired John Stephen Casement, a former Union army general. Casement drilled his motley collection of laborers—Irish immigrants, veterans, freed slaves, failed farmers, and disillusioned prospectors—until they could lay a rail and spike it down with military efficiency.

They were almost equally proficient in defending themselves against marauding Indians. Although federal troops patrolled the Union Pacific's route, workers frequently had to drop their rails and pick up rifles to fend off attacks by Cheyenne and Sioux warriors, who correctly saw the advancing railroad as ringing the death knell of their way of life. Despite these attacks, the UP was able to lay track 40 miles west into Nebraska by the end of 1865.

The pace of construction quickened when the Pacific Railroad Act was amended a third time in 1866—this time without specifying a meeting point for the two lines. Congress simply provided that the railroads might build until they met. The two outfits pitched into a stirring competition to lay the most track, drawing the excited attention of the nation and energizing the rival crews to outdo themselves. The UP laid 425 miles of track in 1868; the CP, having bored no less than 15 tunnels through the solid granite of the Sierra, was nonetheless slowed by backups of supplies on the far side of the snowed-in peaks and managed only 360 miles.

As the ends of the two tracks neared each other, the race took on a ludicrous quality. Each company adopted the questionable theory that it could claim a sort of squatter's rights to lay track as far as it had prepared roadbed—without regard to where the other company's railhead was. Each dispatched teams of road graders far in advance of its tracklaying crews. As a result, the rival crews overlapped each other for almost 200 miles in Utah and Nevada, often working side by side. The death rate from accidents skyrocketed as workers set off blasting powder charges without warning their rivals.

Finally, in January 1869, the federal government put a stop to the madness. A committee of civil engineers was dispatched out West to look over the situation. They selected a spot in Utah called Promontory Summit, 53 miles east of Ogden in the hills north of the Great Salt Lake, as the place where the iron band binding West to East would be completed. On May 10, 1869, to great hoopla on the site and wild rejoicing throughout the country, Leland Stanford of the CP and Thomas Durant of the UP drove ceremonial golden spikes to hold down the last rail, and UP and CP locomotives loaded with dignitaries touched cowcatchers, completing a 2,000-mile-long line spanning the Wild West from Omaha to Sacramento.

Theodore Judah's dream had been realized in glorious fashion, though he was not there to savor the plaudits of the nation. His widow, Anna, sat alone and forgotten in her home back in Massachusetts. "The last rail of the Pacific Railroad was laid on the anniversary of our wedding day," she wrote. "It seemed as though the spirit of my brave husband descended on me and together we were there."

In 1870, its first full year of operation, nearly 150,000 passengers rode the transcontinental line. A dozen years later, the number soared to almost a million. Wealthy travelers could pay $100 and make the four-day journey in first-class Pullman accommodations; a well-upholstered upper berth in each compartment folded down from the ceiling, and hinged seat backs could be flattened to make a lower berth. For an extra four dollars a day, first-class passengers could ride the once-a-week Pacific Hotel Express and dine on meals that equaled those served in the finest restaurants.

Second-class passengers making the complete run traveled at the same speed as those in first class, but for their $80 they had to sleep sitting up. Most second-class travelers did not complain, however, since they were only going from point to point and therefore not paying the entire fare. Cowboys, farmers, miners, and Indians, the permanent residents of the West, typically rode only a few hundred miles one way or the other. By the early 1880s, short-haul travelers outnumbered through passengers six to one.

Third-class passengers paid $40 for a transcontinental trip—the lowest fare for the worst accommodations. Most were emigrants from the East or from Europe who hoped to homestead in the West. Their cars, fitted with rows of narrow wooden benches, were often coupled

to freight cars, and they were routinely shunted onto sidings to wait while express trains clattered past. For an emigrant train, the trip from Omaha to Sacramento could take 9 or 10 days.

Many who settled in the West were lured there by colorful handbills promising fertile land along the railroad's right of way. The railroad, which had not yet taken formal title to the land, demanded no payment from the arriving settlers; it expected to profit by carrying their crops to market. The land offered, however, was often swampy or, according to one visitor, "dry, decomposed and incapable of cultivation." If a farmer did manage, with backbreaking labor, to turn an unpromising parcel of land into a fertile, productive farm, the railroad could, and often did, simply come and practically steal the land back by demanding an outrageous price for it.

By 1893, five railroads spanned the West, ranging from the Great Northern, which ran cross-country between Minneapolis and Seattle just south of the Canadian border, to the New Orleans-Los Angeles route of the Southern Pacific. As people followed the rails, the West grew. Except for Utah, Oklahoma, Arizona, and New Mexico, every territory in the once daunting land between the Missouri River and California became a state during the three decades of transcontinental railroad building.

The transcontinental lines, product of enormous physical labor and swashbuckling financial enterprise, were much more than mere transportation. They embodied the hope of a new beginning for settlers and offered mystery and adventure to wayfarers. In 1879 Scottish author Robert Louis Stevenson kept a journal of his ride from Omaha to San Francisco. He complained of the cramped third-class cars with their hard wooden seats, but he found the Plains strangely mesmerizing. "It was a world almost without feature," he wrote. "An empty sky; an empty earth; front and back, the line of the railway stretched from horizon to horizon. On either hand, the green plain ran till it touched the skirts of heaven."

For most Americans, the railroads meant the transformation of the West from forbidding wilderness to land of opportunity. The haunting train whistle calling across the endless prairie symbolized commerce, safety, speed—civilization. It created the somehow soothing feeling that the Wild West and the cultured East were finally, truly, the *United* States.

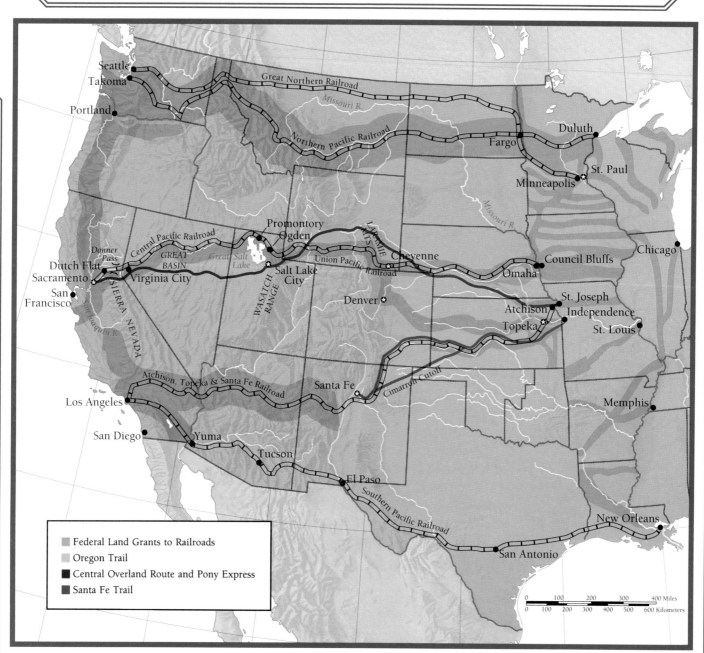

The map shows the following labels:

Seattle
Takoma
Portland
Great Northern Railroad
Missouri R.
Duluth
Fargo
Northern Pacific Railroad
St. Paul
Minneapolis
Missouri R.
Chicago
Promontory
Ogden
LA RAMIE MTS.
Central Pacific Railroad
Cheyenne
Donner Pass
GREAT BASIN
Great Salt Lake
Union Pacific Railroad
Council Bluffs
Dutch Flat
Virginia City
WASATCH RANGE
Salt Lake City
Omaha
Sacramento
Denver
St. Joseph
Independence
San Francisco
Atchison
Topeka
St. Louis
SIERRA NEVADA
San Joaquin R.
Atchison, Topeka & Santa Fe Railroad
Santa Fe
Cimarron Cutoff
Memphis
Los Angeles
San Diego
Yuma
Tucson
El Paso
Southern Pacific Railroad
New Orleans
San Antonio

Federal Land Grants to Railroads
Oregon Trail
Central Overland Route and Pony Express
Santa Fe Trail

0  100  200  300  400 Miles
0  100  200  300  400  500  600 Kilometers

# Winning the West with Railroads

The American West saw two great periods of railroad building. The first was during the 1860s, when government land grants spurred the construction of the first transcontinental railroad. The second, and more significant, burst began in the 1880s, when four other country-crossing lines and thousands of miles of subsidiary track were laid down. By 1893, the year the Great Northern linked St. Paul to Seattle, most of the track that would ever span the West was already in place.

The railroads were a tremendous economic boon. Their construction created jobs and fueled a prodigious demand for raw materials. Once completed, they gave Western resources easy access to Eastern and European markets. As soldiers and settlers rode the rails west, the trains returned to the East laden with timber, minerals, and cattle.

But the ascendancy of railroads meant the decline of the stagecoach. Since people and freight traveled faster and far more efficiently by rail, famous coach routes such as the Central Overland and the Oregon Trail soon became obsolete.

# VISIONARIES OF THE IRON HIGHWAY WEST

The two hardheaded, practical visionaries who more than any others realized the stupendous dream of pushing a railroad across the West were the remarkable pair of New England-born engineers shown here, Theodore Judah *(right)* and Grenville M. Dodge *(opposite)*. Judah talked so incessantly about the railroad he wanted to build that many thought him crazy, as his wife, Anna *(below)*, observed. But ignoring the clamor of the doubters who cried that rails could never be laid across the West's terrifying mountains, Judah pushed ahead, single-handedly surveying a usable route from California eastward over the Sierras. He then helped put together the financial combine that made the tracklaying possible.

Dodge, equally dedicated and tireless, spent almost five years alone on the Western Plains surveying a rail route westward from Missouri to the Rockies before fighting in the Civil War. Afterward he conducted more surveys, then bossed the army of construction workers that thrust the Union Pacific tracks to a meeting with the line that Ted Judah a decade before had planned and foreseen.

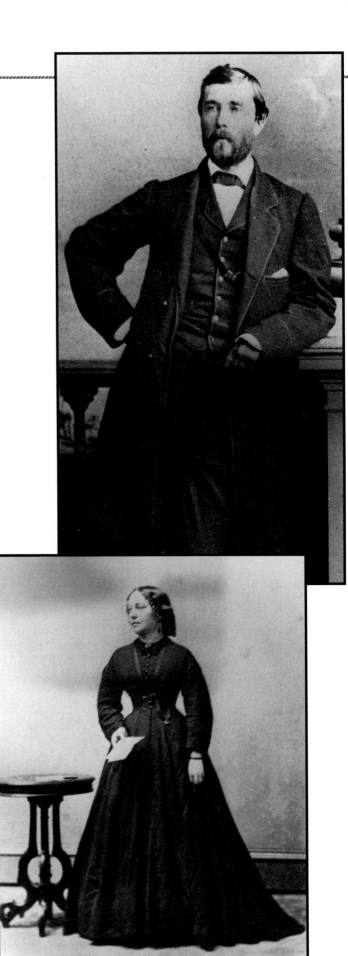

*"He had always talked, read and studied the problem of a continental railway, and would say 'It will be built, and I am going to have something to do with it.' Many a laugh have his friends had at his 'air castles.'"*

◆

*Anna Judah*

### An Ill-Fated Dreamer ———

Theodore Judah died, in effect, for lack of the transcontinental railroad he longed to build. Traveling east on a business trip in 1863 by the old, tortuous ship route that included a trek across the jungles of Panama, he contracted the yellow fever that killed him at age 37.

### The Hard-Fighting Hero ———

Grenville Dodge served the Union brilliantly during the Civil War, rising to major general and gaining the respect of two top officers who later had crucial influence on the railroads' affairs: President U. S. Grant and the postwar army chief, General Sherman.

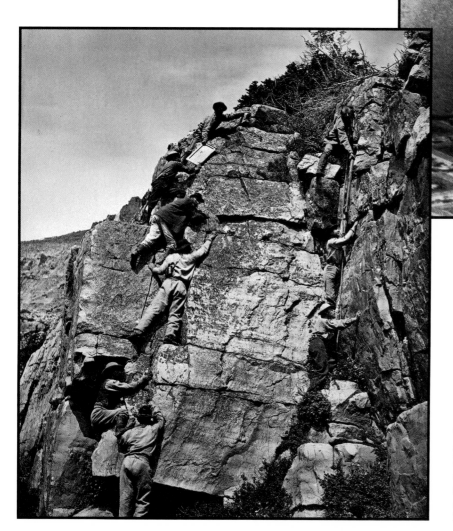

### A Defiant Terrain ———

An undaunted team of Union Pacific surveyors hand up their instruments one at a time to colleagues clinging to crevices and perched on scant inches of ledge in a steep cliff. Sometimes—in truly rough terrain—they had to hoist their pack mules with block and tackle.

# Rough Going before the Railroad

Travelers in the prerailroad West had three modes of commercial transportation—steamboat, stagecoach, and rickety wagon. All were slow, rough, dirty, and dangerous. Western rivers abounded in snags that could rip a steamboat's hull, and the boilers often exploded, blowing boat and passengers to smithereens. Trips on the crowded Overland Stages were bone rattling and exhausting at best, and could be far worse if the coach turned over or if outlaws more lethal than the poetic Black Bart (*below*) attacked. As for wagons, most broke down eventually, leaving travelers to go the rest of the way on foot.

*"I've labored long and hard
for bread,
For honor and for riches,
But on my corns too long
you've tread,
You fine-haired sons of
bitches."*

◆

*Charles E. Boles (Black Bart)*

A Legendary Coach Driver ——
Hank Monk was celebrated for his casual artistry with the reins. "The stage-driver was a hero," Mark Twain wrote, "a great and shining dignitary" who was "above being familiar with such rubbish as passengers."

K ing of the Coach Lines ——
The imperious Ben Holladay ran the Overland Stage as a near monopoly, ruthlessly forcing out competitors. He then cannily sold his company shortly before the railroads eliminated most coach travel forever.

A Jam-Packed Concord Coach ——
Concord coaches, meant to carry nine passengers, were often stuffed beyond capacity. Indeed, the Overland's Ben Holladay was infamous for urging drivers to "Pack 'em in like sardines." Overcrowding was lightly borne for brief jaunts—this coach holds friends on a Sunday outing—but on long overland journeys the practice was miserably uncomfortable, and downright dangerous.

A Wrecked Stage ——
Passengers scramble to escape an overturned coach in the painting at right by Western artist Charles Russell. Treacherously steep and rough trails caused many such crashes. So did runaway teams of half-tamed horses—and, occasionally, a more than half-drunk driver.

## Final Port of Call ——

The riverboat *Benton* draws a curious crowd as it lies in shallows near Sioux City, Iowa, its back broken and chimneys askew after hitting submerged pilings and then slamming into a sturdy Missouri River bridge. Sunk twice before, the *Benton* had been refloated and put back in service—until this final calamity reduced the steamer to a hopeless hulk.

## Running on Muscle Power ——

An overloaded freight wagon gets a mighty heave-ho from three teamsters while a pair of horses struggles frantically to drag the vehicle up an embankment. The wagon trains of long-haul freight lines were usually drawn by oxen or mules. Which animal was better for the job was a constant source of debate for tough bullwhackers and mule skinners.

# The Wild Race to Lay the Rails

Work began slowly at both ends of the line. But when Congress failed to name a point where the rails should meet, a race soon developed between the Union Pacific moving westward and the Central Pacific pushing toward the east, since the company that laid the most miles of track would be rewarded with the most government bonds and federal land. The bosses drove the gangs with determined fury through cave-ins, rockslides, and horrendous blizzards. The work forces grew as large as armies, at least 13,000 men laboring for the CP and 10,000 for the UP. They were Irish immigrants and German, Southern Civil War veterans and Yankees, and especially in the CP gangs, thousands of Chinese whose stoic courage formed an epic in itself.

At the Starting Post——

Charles Crocker gestures from the grandstand while Leland Stanford (*center*) wields a shovel during groundbreaking ceremonies for the Central Pacific at Sacramento on January 9, 1863. The Union Pacific held similar ceremonies at Omaha at about the same time.

Deadly Weather——

CP workers try to clear the snow-choked right of way in the High Sierra during the savage winter of 1866-1867, which saw 14 blizzards, one lasting 13 days. Men were buried alive in 40-foot drifts, and roaring avalanches carried away entire workers' camps, killing hundreds of Chinese laborers.

### Braving the Heights ——

Daring Chinese workers wrestle a rail onto a high trestle while others dangle in wicker baskets to drill holes and plant explosives in a sheer rockface. After they lit the fuses, they would be killed if not pulled up quickly enough. The risky work gave rise to the phrase "a Chinaman's chance"—which means very little chance at all.

### "The Best in the World" ——

Lee Wong Sang signed on with Central Pacific agents at age 19 in his native village near Canton and, with boatloads of other recruits, was shipped across the Pacific to California. Chinese laborers were "the best in the world," said the CP's mercilessly demanding work boss, James Strobridge, and they tackled the most perilous jobs without complaint.

## Laying Track ——

A Union Pacific crew lugs rails into position at the railhead in Nebraska. Carried to within half a mile on flatcars, the iron was brought farther forward by a horse-drawn cart. Then began the hard, sweaty work of hauling the rails off the cart, up the roadbed, and into position—a task that the UP workers carried out with military precision, by one account: "Less than 30 seconds to a rail for each gang, and so four rails go down to the minute."

## Racing Past the Finish Line ——

While an explosion hurls rock behind them, furiously competing CP and UP gangs meet in Utah—but do not stop. Incredibly, each went on laying rails alongside the other's completed track and without warning set off blasts that killed numbers of their rivals.

L inked at Last ────

Rival chief engineers Grenville Dodge and Samuel Montague shake hands moments after the last spike was driven and the tracks joined at Promontory Summit. Behind them the CP's locomotive Jupiter and the UP's Engine 119, both festooned with bottle-waving celebrants, touch cowcatchers, marking the end of what has been called the greatest race of all time.

# Caught Up in Railroad Madness

News that the rails had been joined set off wild celebrations across the country, followed by a rush of avid rail travelers. In 1870, the first full year of operation, 150,000 people rode trains across the West, and the number soon rose to a million annually. Many were poor immigrants seeking a new life in the West. They rode the bone-bruising wooden benches in third-class coaches. Others were rich folk lusting for the thrill of crossing the Western expanses. For them the railroad laid on parlor cars, diners, and sleepers produced by that mogul of luxurious travel, George Pullman. Even with Pullman's comforts, though, there were still dangers of accidents, robbers, and—occasionally—Indians. The rails were through but the West was still wild enough.

**P**ainful Ride for a Writer ———
Robert Louis Stevenson, yet to be famous and almost penniless, rode a cheap, slow third-class train across the West in 1879. It was an agonizingly uncomfortable trip. "Few people," he wrote when he reached California at last, "have praised God more happily than I did."

**G**oing Privileged Class ———
Passengers dine in a Pullman "Palace Car," which served meals featuring such elegant fare as stuffed roast quail and antelope steak. A conductor, one grande dame noted, stood "at the wine closet" ministering "to the parched palates of the guests."

The Huddled Masses——

Russian immigrants wait in a small North Dakota town to board a mixed train of coaches and freight cars. Third-class travelers were often rudely herded about by train crews—"sorted and boxed," Robert Louis Stevenson mordantly noted—but at $40, the fare was the lowest for a transcontinental trip.

Luxurious Privacy——

Plush furniture in the ornate Victorian mode crowds the sitting room of a handsomely paneled Pullman car. The extra charge for such deluxe private accommodations was a then hefty $50 a day.

Highballing Up the Line——

Throwing a plume of coal smoke, the engine of a passenger train thunders past an Idaho farm in the 1880s. At best, locomotives managed 40 miles an hour, but that moved a train from Omaha to California in four days, delirious speed in the West of the horse and wagon.

### Notorious Desperados

Butch Cassidy *(seated right)* and his "Wild Bunch" that included Harry Longbaugh, "the Sundance Kid" *(seated left),* try to look respectable in their city duds in a photograph taken in 1901. They turned to train robbery after warming up with bank heists and cattle rustling.

### Forcible Entry

A rifled safe sits empty in a Union Pacific express car blasted open with dynamite by Cassidy's Wild Bunch after they stopped the Overland Limited near Wilcox, Wyoming. Cassidy studiously avoided gunplay and claimed he had never shot a man.

**S**etting a Trap ——

A posse gets ready to board a train with its horses in order to surprise the bandits when they attack. Cassidy and his sidekick Long-baugh evaded capture and escaped to South America, where they robbed more banks before coming to an unknown end.

*"Sleeping Rabbit said, 'If we could bend the track up and spread it out the train might fall off. . . . When the train came to this place it wrecked. . . . One man came running along on back carrying a light and they killed him. They killed all of them."*

◆

**John Stands-in-Timber, Cheyenne**

# The Huge Impact of the Railroads

"Cheap lands!" "Easily cultivated!" "Inexhaustible fertility," trumpeted the land promoters. Crowds of people responded, some literally galloping into huge areas opened up by the original railroad across the West and by four more built by 1893. Vast tracts were owned by the railroads themselves, courtesy of Congress, which handed them millions of acres along the rights of way. Selling land to settlers made the railroad money men, already rich, richer still. More lastingly, the railroads made huge granaries of the once forbidding wilderness. Tragically, the coming of the rails put the final iron nail in the coffin of the Indians' way of life.

*"I hate all the white people. . . . You are thieves and liars. You have taken away our lands and made us outcasts."*

◆

**Chief Sitting Bull, speaking in Ogalala Sioux to uncomprehending officials at 1883 dedication of the Northern Pacific.**

A Race for Real Estate ——
Exploding across the landscape, horses, wagons, and people dash forward to claim homesteads on former Cherokee land after the firing of a gun begins the great Oklahoma land rush of 1893.

A Railroad Baron's Fancy ——
Charles Crocker lavished $2.3 million on his enormous mansion *(below)* on San Francisco's Nob Hill. Crocker's colleagues in the Central Pacific spent with equal abandon on themselves but also put some of their money to worthier use. Leland Stanford started and bankrolled Stanford University; Collis Huntington founded the great Huntington Library.

**M**aking the Wilderness Bloom ——

A Western farmer and his family stand proudly behind a table overflowing with carrots and
cabbages, corn and potatoes. Set down in the
West by the railroads, farmers continued to
rely on the rails to take their produce to market—and in a rich collaboration the railroads
flourished doing just that.

# COWBOYS

A frenzied herd of wild mustangs churns up a hillside to escape capture by a trio of cowboys, one of whom has lassoed a black stallion.

# THOUGH THE COWBOY IS NOW AN AMERICAN ARCHE-TYPE, THE FIRST OF THEIR

kind were a far cry from the taciturn fellows portrayed in Hollywood horse operas. They were cowboys, yes, but they spoke Spanish, not English. Decked out in colorful costumes, they did their riding, roping, and branding in the Mexican provinces of Upper California and Texas and called themselves vaqueros, from *vaca,* the Spanish word for cow. The cattle they herded and the horses they rode were the descendants of animals introduced to the New World by the Spanish conquistadors in the 16th century.

The vaqueros crafted a legacy of skills, language, and style that would live on in the cowboy, a new American character that would become famous around the world after humble beginnings on the Texas frontier. There the Spanish cattle had mixed occasionally with the cows of the American settlers and had become identifiable over time as a rambunctious breed of wild bovine—lean, slab-sided, tough, and ornery—called the Texas longhorn.

The youths handling the longhorns had to get on horseback to round up and herd these large, cantankerous animals. They soon honed skills learned from the vaqueros—or "buckaroos," as the cowboys pronounced the word—to become superb horsemen, unexcelled ropers, and the stoic, honor-bound heroes of Western legend.

At first the longhorns were rounded up for their hides and tallow, but by 1860 they were being driven to St. Louis, Chicago, and other big cities to satisfy the growing taste for beef among Easterners. Hardly had the novel practice of collecting cattle and driving them to distant markets begun, however, than the Civil War stopped it in its tracks. The men of Texas went off to fight for the Confederacy, and the cattle were left to their own devices.

One of their chief devices was breeding. When defeated Texans straggled back to their run-down farms in 1865, they found the landscape teeming with wild longhorns—estimated at between five and six million. A longhorn steer—a castrated male—worth four dollars in Texas might fetch $40 up north, where the postwar increase in industrial workers and a flood of immigrants had created an insatia-

ble demand for beef. Markets for the longhorns also developed in the West; cattle were needed to feed army troops and railroad construction crews, and the federal government had to begin providing beef for Indians newly confined to reservations, where they could no longer hunt buffalo for sustenance. A new Western industry was about to boom, and the cowboy would be its working class.

Most cowboys were young—between their late teens and late twenties—but otherwise they were a varied lot. Ex-Confederate soldiers, mostly Texans, made up the largest group. Many Union veterans also joined the fraternity, having found the routine of life on the farm a dull letdown after the war. Perhaps 15 percent of the cowboys were African-Americans, some having acquired their cow-handling skills while slaves on Texas ranches. A somewhat larger portion were Mexican-Americans, inheritors of the venerable arts of the vaqueros.

Although most cowboys came from farms or workmen's homes, the heroic and adventurous aura of the life also attracted a small contingent of "swells." A few were younger sons of English nobles: With no prospect of inheriting land or title, they had been banished to the American West to find some useful outlet for their energies. A few others were graduates of or dropouts from Eastern universities, looking for excitement and challenge.

A cowboy's past was understood to be a private matter, for a new hand was as likely to have his name on a wanted poster as to be a churchgoing preacher's son. As rancher Flan Rogers put it, "We take a man here and ask no questions. We know when he throws a saddle on his horse whether he understands his business or not." Admitting that "a good many of our useful men have made their mistakes," Rogers added, "all we care about is, will they stand the gaff?"

Despite his youth, a cowboy thought of himself as being more than a mere farm hand. He was, he knew, admired by men who went about on foot and who hadn't the wherewithal to subdue a truculent 1,000-pound steer. And with his self-awareness came an unspoken pride that expressed itself in a polite reserve with anyone outside the cowboy clan. It also showed up in his dress; when it came to clothing, the cowboy could be a bit of a dandy—within, of course, the limits of what his mates would tolerate without making raucous fun of him.

The cowboy's getup combined the utilitarian and the decorative. In the rough, dangerous work he did every day, he needed protection

from the elements and from the unpredictable behavior of cow or horse. His hat, for example, however handsome and fine it might be when new, also had to serve to fan a fire or scoop up water; and it required a broad brim to shield him from both sun and rain. His brightly colored bandanna became a dust mask when he was trailing a herd or a tourniquet in case of injury or rattlesnake bite. He wore chaps—heavy leather coverings over his pant legs to save him from the penetrating thorns of mesquite brush and from rope burns. His boots, often expensive and custom-made of tooled leather, had high heels to hook a stirrup when he stood to counterbalance the weight of a roped steer. That the boots were awkward for walking meant little; a cowboy on foot was a cowboy out of place. His spurs were sometimes made of fancy worked silver and sported metal weights called jinglebobs, whose sole purpose was to announce his presence.

His six-gun, less a piece of essential equipment than a potent plaything and an advertisement for manliness, tended to stay in his bedroll when he was busy with serious ranch work. The gun occasionally came in handy on a trail drive or while he was riding fence, when he might need to kill a rattler, make noise to turn a stampeding herd, or signal his comrades if he was down and unable to move. But it came most into its own as a celebratory noisemaker. Firing a few shots into the air or at a saloon mirror added to the fun of whooping it up when the young cowpuncher hit town at the end of a trail drive.

Despite his lapses into juvenile high jinks, the cowboy came honestly by his fame. He worked at a brutally hard job, tackled tasks requiring agility, strength, and courage, nursed injuries without complaint, and plied his trade in the choking dust of 110-degree days and the slashing sleet of frigid nights—for a salary of $25 a month.

When he was at work, particularly on a trail drive, he might go for months without seeing a woman, let alone being near or touching one. At times, the only women he could hope to meet on equal terms were prostitutes, the "soiled doves" awaiting his arrival when his outfit finally made it to the railhead. Toward respectable women his attitude was primly Victorian and chastely worshipful; no proper lady ever needed fear the proximity of even the scruffiest, most disreputable-looking cowboy. One nervous ranch hand, sent by his boss to purchase a bull from a female ranch owner, approached her with a request to buy, as he put it, "a gentleman cow."

His low social status, his penury, his nomadic life—all combined

to deny the cowboy the possibility of marrying and having a family as long as he remained in that line of work. If chance placed him in the company of a young lady, however, he would go to any lengths to make the most of it. When a Texas ranch held a dance one rainy evening, the owners of a distant spread came with their newly hired governess, who forgot her overshoes when she and her employers left for home. An eager cowboy showed up the following Sunday and presented the young lady, whose name was Anne, with a parcel containing one overshoe. "But there were two," she said. "Yes, I know it," answered her visitor. "I'll bring the other one next Sunday, if you don't mind—and, Miss Anne, I sure wish you was a centerpede."

The cowboy came into his own during the spring and fall roundups. In the spring, the hands had to search every draw and hollow on the boss's range to collect all the cattle and drive them in so the calves could be branded and the young bulls castrated if they were not to be used for breeding. For the fall roundup, the biggest job was cutting marketable steers out of the herd. Essential to either season's work was the cowboy's saddle. Unlike the horses he rode, which were usually supplied by the ranch, the cowboy owned his own saddle. It cost him a month's pay or more, and he depended on it for a comfortable seat that would let him stay on horseback from predawn to nightfall and sometimes through the night as well.

When it was time to separate a calf from its mother or muscle a touchy steer away from the herd, the cowboy, working in harmony with his well-trained cutting horse, anticipated the cow's moves and blocked all attempts to return to the herd. Here, too, he called on his talent with a rope, neatly tossing a loop of his lariat—from the Spanish *la riata*—over the head of a calf in full flight or around its hind legs so that it could be thrown and the branding iron applied.

The hot, dusty atmosphere of the roundup camp was a scene of seeming pandemonium, the air split by the bawl of anxious mothers when their calves were cut out, the roar of steers forced from the bunch, the whinny of horses, the shouts and whistles and cries of the cowboys, the hiss of branding irons against hair and skin, the wails of the hurt and frightened calves.

One purpose of the fall roundup was to assemble a herd of steers—females were kept for breeding—to be driven to market, a trek of perhaps 1,500 miles north to the nearest Kansas railhead. The

A cowboy's saddle did double duty—as a comfortable seat during a long day on the trail and as a pillow at night. The leather Western stock saddle (*above*) gave the rider a good seat without rubbing sores in the horse's back. At the front, the duckbill-shaped horn, or pommel, held the cowboy's lariat; at the back, the high cantle gave support.

# The Rugged
# Art and Science
# of Busting a Wild Pony

Working cowboys needed at least six to eight mounts apiece to carry out the grueling demands of the cattle roundup and the long weeks on the trail drive. These cow ponies were drafted from the ranks of four-year-old mustangs that lived wild on the open range, surviving on grass and rarely topping 12 to 14 hands and 700 to 900 pounds. (A modern horse, by contrast, ranges from 14 to 16 hands high and weighs more than 1,000 pounds.) Once a year, usually in the late spring, the animals were rounded up and then subjected to a week of harsh treatment designed to do nothing less than break their spirits and teach them to obey their riders' every command.

Known, appropriately enough, as breaking, or busting, the procedure was often carried out by a roving specialist, a bronco rider who traveled from ranch to ranch, transforming wild mustangs into tractable cow ponies for five dollars a head. One such broncobuster was Lee Warren, whose battle with raw ponies at the Bow and Arrow Ranch in Montana at the turn of the century appears in the photographs shown here. Warren usually won these skirmishes, but he paid for victory with countless bruises and broken bones.

**Fighting Back**
Cross-hobbled by ropes entangling both forefeet and one hind foot, a horse struggles to throw off the unfamiliar weight of a saddle while Warren holds tight to the reins.

**Roping the Candidate**
Bronco rider Lee Warren loops a nicely balanced lariat over the neck of a bay gelding as it charges past him in the corral. Once snared, the horse will be snubbed to a post and bridled. Then the real breaking will begin.

## Mounting Up

Having unhobbled a now quiet horse, Warren scrambles into the saddle while twisting the pony's ear—a jolt of pain meant to distract the animal from the weight landing on its back.

## A Battle of Wills

Legs clamped around the horse's belly, Warren lowers a whip, or quirt, each time the animal bucks, driving home the key lesson to recalcitrant horses: Obey or else!

drive might be made by a rancher and his regular hands but more often was done by a drover, a contractor who took cattle on consignment or bought them from various ranchers to make up a trail herd.

The drover handled the business of buying and selling the stock; the man in charge of the drive was the trail boss. When all was ready, the trail boss started the herd moving north, stationing riders at the front, sides, and rear of the column. The herd was followed by a chuck wagon driven by the cook, a usually cranky jack-of-all-trades with whom the hands tried to keep on good terms, never knowing, for example, when they might have to call on his artistry with a needle and thread to sew up some torn cloth or skin. Bringing up the rear was the remuda, the herd of horses—four to six per man—that the outfit supplied for the drive. A wrangler tended the horses.

Each day on the trail began before dawn, when the cook would roust the hands for a breakfast of bacon, beans, and strong black coffee. The trail boss would set out to scout far ahead for good water and good grass for that night's camp. The men would select their horses from the remuda, saddle up, and mount just as the cattle were starting to struggle to their feet and look for grass. Soon the herd would be in motion, the trail hands at their posts and constantly on the move to chase uncooperative steers back into place.

The herd would be halted around noon so the cattle could graze and the men could get their lunch, eating in shifts. Then the northward movement would resume, the herd completing a day's progress of 10 to 15 miles before being watered and bedded down at nightfall. For the trail boss, the welfare of the steers came first, and as they approached a creek to drink he would drive them in an upstream direction, so that as each animal got to the creek it could drink clear water. Only then did the hands get their chance. One cowboy said to his trail boss, "Say, you go ahead and water the wagon and horses, and then you water the herd, and then we get a drink. I ain't kicking, but I had to chew that water before I could swallow it."

On the trail the cowboys were exposed to a multitude of dangers that could strike any time of day or night. As a Texas cowboy named Ad Spaugh later recalled, "Outfits had gaily started north, only to reach their destination months later with half of their cattle gone, some of their men lying in shallow graves along the trail or lost in the waters of angry rushing rivers."

Following the Chisholm Trail, which ran north through the Indi-

an Territory—present-day Oklahoma—the outfit might be forced to pay a toll ranging anywhere from $.10 to $1.00 a head to allow the cattle to cross tribal lands. Then, as a trail outfit entered Kansas, it had to get safely past marauding bands of brigands, remnants of murderous guerrilla gangs who fought on either side in the Civil War. It might then be met by angry groups of farmers determined to keep the longhorns, which carried a virus fatal to other breeds of cattle, away from their fields.

Violent weather was an ever-present threat, and it often led to one of the two worst hazards of a drive: rivers at flood. Cattle, horses, and cowboys stood in peril of their lives when crossing a raging river. Often a drive would have to wait weeks for the waters to drop.

Equally hazardous—to animal and man—was a stampede. Two or three thousand longhorn steers could be controlled only when they wanted to be. They were capable of erupting suddenly in mass hysteria, particularly at night and in bad weather—though they might also bolt at the flare of a match or the snap of a twig. No matter how cold, wet, tired, and deep in sleep a trail hand might be, he had to be ready to leap into the saddle when he heard the rumble that signaled cattle on the run. He would race headlong for miles to get in front of the herd. "Teddy Blue" Abbott, a Texas cowboy who became a rancher in Montana, said, "It was riding at a dead run in the dark, with cut banks and prairie dog holes all around you, not knowing if the next jump would land you in a shallow grave."

Shouting, yipping, firing their pistols, the cowboys had to slow and turn the lead steers till the momentum of the rush was blunted and the stampede converted to a churning, milling mass, which marked the end of the crisis. One trail hand, after staying awake all night chasing a stampeding herd, told his boss, "I am going to Greenland where the nights are six months long, and I ain't going to get up until ten o'clock next day."

When, in spite of all obstacles, the herd finally reached the railhead, the trail hands were ready to hit town and cut loose. As African-American cowboy Nat Love remembered it later, "It was our intention and ambition to paint the town a deep red color and drink up all the bad whiskey in the city. Our nearly two months journey over the dusty plains and ranges made us inordinately thirsty and wild." Their first stop would be for a shave, haircut, and bath. Then it was off to

the dry-goods store for new clothes to replace their filthy tatters.

While the hands were sprucing up, the drover or ranch owner was striking a deal with a cattle buyer, sealing a transaction of perhaps a hundred thousand dollars with a word and a handshake. More than just the cattle were sold; horses and equipment went as well. In a matter of hours, the trail outfit that had consumed the cowboy's total loyalty and for which he had endured immeasurable hardship might simply cease to exist, though drovers would often rehire the same hands to return to Texas and bring another herd north.

Decked out in his new duds, the cowboy would go in search of the cure for what ailed him. "We'd go in town and marry a girl for a week," said Teddy Blue Abbott, "take her to breakfast, dinner, and supper, be with her all the time. . . . I suppose those things would shock a lot of respectable people. But we wasn't respectable and we didn't pretend to be, which was the only way we was different from some others."

After the cowboy enjoyed a few hell-raising days of drinking, gambling, and consorting with soiled doves, his money was likely to be as much a thing of the past as the trail outfit he had come to town with. At that point, providing he didn't feel too old or too worn out and stove up to "stand the gaff," it was time to head back to Texas and start cowboying again. And he was more than ready.

Though Texas cattle ranchers did well in the years after the Civil War, the longhorn, in addition to being a handful to herd and drive, was not a prime beef animal. It was lean and its meat was tough, and it made money for ranchers mainly because they were able to establish large herds and fatten them on public land at virtually no cost except the small one of their cowboys' labor.

By the 1870s, increasing numbers of short-horned cattle were showing up on the Plains, brought from the Midwest or Oregon. Breeds such as Durham, Shorthorn, Devon, and Hereford made better beef cattle. They were blocky, heavy animals with a far higher fat-to-muscle ratio than longhorns, and they were easier to handle. Through selective breeding, the Plains beef animals of the 1870s and 1880s had almost all traces of longhorn squeezed out of them.

As Texas ranchers had done earlier, the Plains cattlemen laid claim to vast tracts of government rangeland—and the rivers, creeks, and springs found there—by means of a tenuous legal theory various-

Cowboy "Teddy Blue" Abbott outstares the camera, his new white Stetson cocked at the rakish angle befitting a 19-year-old just in off the trail in 1879. "We were the salt of the earth," Abbott later wrote of his fellows, "and we had the pride that went with it."

ly known as range privilege, possessory rights, accustomed range, or range rights. Generally recognized by other big ranchers but having no standing in law, these arrangements were based simply on the ranchers' having got there first—and on their ability to drive off any Indians, small ranchers, or homesteaders who trespassed.

With free land and a stock in trade that naturally multiplied on its own, the open-range cattle business was highly profitable in the 1870s and early 1880s. It attracted the attention of moneyed interests back East and in Europe, who not only poured millions of dollars into the large ranches but in some cases came out to run operations themselves. Thus it was that a ranch house might be a grandiose affair with European touches, and locals might read in the town newspaper of polo games and fox—or, more likely, coyote—hunts.

But the cattle barons faced a number of growing challenges to their autocratic style of doing business. The first problem was of their own making; heedless of the fundamental aridity of the Plains range-land, they allowed their herds to grow so big that the range became overgrazed. Furthermore, the huge cattle population on the range was a standing temptation to ne'er-do-wells, many of whom moved in and began making a full-time business of rustling.

Simultaneously, more and more of the range was being grazed by vast herds of sheep, which, if they remained for long in one place, nipped the blades of grass so short that nothing was left for cattle. Cattlemen in general had an almost visceral dislike of sheep and those who herded them—but some cattle ranchers hedged their bets with sheep for times when beef prices fell and wool sold at a premium.

Finally, the homestead movement was pressing westward. Homesteaders, contemptuously called "nesters" by the cattle ranch-ers, were staking claims without regard to the barons' sacred "posses-sory rights" and were marking their claims with barbed wire. What's more, some of the settlers were cowboys bent on having their own ranches—who sometimes started their herds with unbranded ani-mals of ambiguous ownership. The open range, economic bulwark of the big ranches and essential condition of the cowboy's occupation, was closing—no matter how hard the barons might resist the trend.

Although their most common reaction to encroachments on the range was to move farther west, some cattle ranchers turned to vio-lence in defense of their baronies. Blurring the distinction between small ranchers and out-and-out rustlers, a few big outfits hired

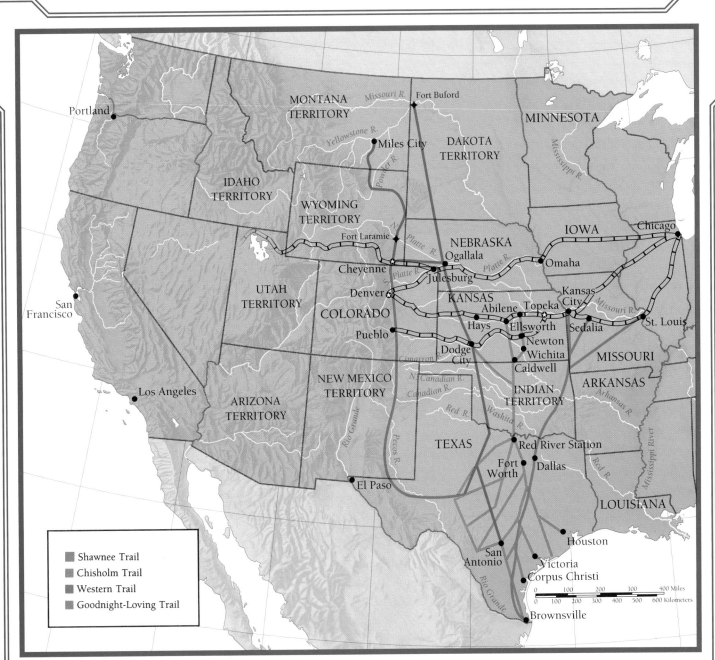

# Moving Longhorns to Market

During the four decades of the longhorn cattle drives, the main trails from the animals' breeding grounds in Texas to railheads in Kansas and Missouri shifted gradually west. The oldest trail, the Shawnee, opened in the 1840s and ran northeast to Missouri towns such as Kansas City and St. Louis. Already hampered by Missouri's quarantine on fever-bearing longhorns, the Shawnee was shut down by the time of the Civil War. After the war, Kansas ordered Texas herds to stay west of a special quarantine line, creating new cattle highways such as the Chisholm Trail. Fed by tributary trails, the Chisholm handled half the beef hoofing it from Texas.

The Western Trail—also called the Dodge City Trail for its original terminus— eventually extended north into Dakota Territory, with a northwest branch peeling off at Ogallala, Nebraska, to head into Wyoming and then to Montana. In 1866, Charles Goodnight and Oliver Loving opened the trail that bore their names, pioneering markets in the West by selling livestock to ranchers in Colorado and Wyoming and military posts in New Mexico.

gunslingers in the guise of stock inspectors with orders to stop any-one they caught with unbranded cows. In Montana, so-called vigilance committees were formed to hunt down suspected rustlers or horse thieves and burn them out or lynch them. When the small ranchers and farmers organized in self-defense, often with the backing of townspeople who resented the barons' high-handed ways, the result was a few well-publicized shootouts and all-out range wars.

Sheepherders, too, sometimes felt the barons' wrath. Masked night riders in the pay of the cattle ranchers slaughtered sheep thousands at a time, shot herders' beloved and highly trained sheepdogs, and sometimes killed the herders as well.

But despite all the barons' efforts to hold on, the erosion at the fringes of their empires continued. Then, in 1886, a severe drought that left the herds in poor condition by summer's end was followed by a series of blizzards that devastated livestock on the range. Some ranches lost 90 percent of their stock. When the first thaw came in the spring of 1887, cowboys all over the Great Plains shared the grim and noxious experience of riding out among the stinking piles of decaying carcasses to add up the losses. They were viewing the end of the open-range cowboy's heyday.

Typical of the aftermath was the reaction of Montana cattle baron Granville Stuart to the near-obliteration of his herds: "A business that had been fascinating to me before, suddenly became distasteful," he wrote later. "I never wanted to own again an animal that I could not feed and shelter." The hard but unarguable lesson the ranchers learned was that they could not safely leave cattle to winter on the range without providing a supplemental feed supply. The new order of the day in cattle ranching would be to maintain moderate-size herds on smaller parcels of pastureland and to grow or purchase forage crops to feed them over the winter.

A ranch hand still needed his cowboy skills, but he was a year-round employee now, and many of his tasks smacked of farming and were carried out on foot. Gone was the sense of freedom and individuality that defined the cowboy. To the range cowboys used to an unrestricted life on the Plains, the new ways were unappealing. As Nat Love put it, "Many of us became disgusted and quit the wild life for the pursuits of our more civilized brothers." Despite the hold the American cowboy has exercised on the world's imagination ever since, his golden age was over—scarcely 20 years after it had begun.

# HIS OWN BOSS

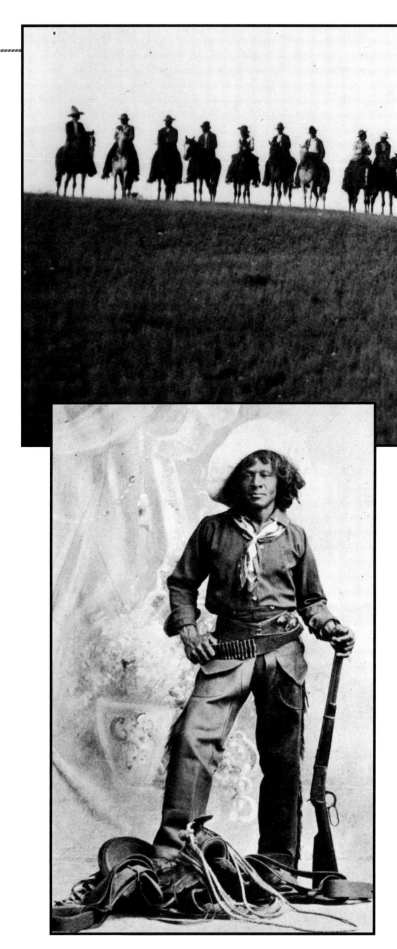

The cowboy of popular myth—the one who might have sung a plaintive "Don't fence me in" while guarding the trail herd at night—was actually a rather short-lived phenomenon. The era of open-range cattle ranching and the great cattle drives lasted barely two decades, its end hastened by increasing settlement and by the disastrous winter of 1886-1887, which killed as much as 90 percent of some ranchers' stock. During those 20 years, while cattle barons made and lost fortunes in beef, cowboys practiced a hard and lonesome trade.

The men who joined this fraternity shared three characteristics: youth, a lack of family, and a hankering for the freedom that comes of traveling light. Otherwise, they were a varied lot: Midwestern farm boys, Civil War veterans, Mexican-Americans, newly freed slaves. All endured considerable physical hardship for not much in the way of material gain. During roundup, they exercised their horsemanship, and calf-roping and branding skills. On the trail, they spent anywhere from two to six months at a time swallowing dust during the day, sleeping on the hard ground at night, eating son-of-a-bitch stew and vinegar pie. Tedium was relieved only by the heart-stopping excitement of trying to head off a stampede, which often as not happened at night, in a thunderstorm. But it was worth it. As one old trail hand put it, "A cowboy, if he knows his work, never gets no orders on the range. He's pretty well his own boss."

---

*"Armed to the teeth, booted and spurred, long-haired and covered with the broad-brimmed sombrero, his personal appearance proclaimed the sort of man he was."*

◆

*Harper's New Monthly magazine*

---

**N**at Love, Cowboy ——
Born a slave in Tennessee in 1854, the 15-year-old Love headed for Kansas in 1869 to begin life as a cowpuncher—one of scores of African-Americans who took up the trade after the Civil War. Love, shown here all spiffed up for a portrait, later became a rodeo celebrity.

**M**en of the Wide-Open Range———
An unbroken expanse of sky and rolling prairie as far as the eye could see were part of the attraction for restless young men like the mounted contingent seen here spanning the horizon in Pima County, Arizona.

**B**rothers in Trade———
In Denver, Colorado, a baker's dozen cowboys, some sporting fancy chaps, reflects a mix of races common to the West in the decades after the Civil War. The familiarity fostered by working together did not breed racial tolerance, however. Whites casually called African-Americans "niggers," and whites and blacks alike referred to Mexicans as "greasers."

**P**artners Taking a Break———
Lightly tethered to a bit of brush, a horse waits patiently while his human partner takes a breather on a scrubby hillock on the Texas plains. Over time, man and mount developed a wordless communication in the performance of their jobs—separating calves from the herd for branding and racing hell-for-leather to stop a mob of panicked cattle on the trail.

# The Hot, Dusty Chores of the Roundup

In any part of the West where open-range cattle ranching went on, the first greening of the grass in spring signaled the start of the cowboy's long season in the saddle. In spring, roundup hands fanned out to search for and gather up the boss's cattle, separating new calves from their mothers for branding. (Unbranded calves, or mavericks, were a sore temptation to rustlers.) On southern ranches, cowboys might also cut out mature beef for sale to drovers who would then trail the cattle north to market. On more northerly ranches, spring was a time for branding and for the good neighbor practice of returning strays to their owners; marketable steers were rounded up for shipment during the fall.

Cowboys who joined trail outfits for the cattle drives to railheads in Kansas and Missouri had many weeks of hard work and small comfort in store. Charged with keeping the herd intact, they spent wearisome hours in the saddle making sure no animals wandered off or got stolen and trying to keep the flighty creatures on the move but not run them to exhaustion. Indeed, exhaustion was more likely to strike the cowboy—living as he was on trail rations and snatches of sleep between turns at guard duty. Pleasures were few but real: the nightly camaraderie of the chuck-wagon campfire and the occasional chance to wash in a nearby river.

The Teamwork of a Roundup ———

Ranch hands on a Wyoming spread ride in from all points of the compass to drive steers, bulls, cows, and calves into a milling circle. Once the frenzied bawling of calves and bellowing of bulls had subsided, a few men could keep the calmly grazing herd together.

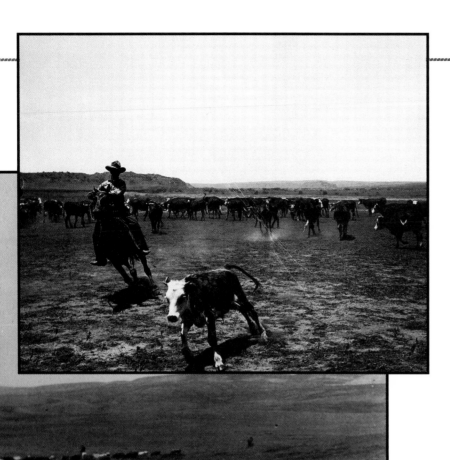

C atching a Maverick——
Galloping parallel to an unbranded calf, a skillful roper judges the right moment to bring the maverick down by snaring its hind feet with his lariat. The cowboy would then drag the animal to the branding fire.

A Female Branding Trio——
Two of Colorado rancher Fritz Becker's three daughters stretch a calf between them with their lariats while their sister applies the branding iron. This was usually man's work, but Becker fully expected his daughters to carry on after his death—and they did.

> *"Outfits had gaily started north, only to reach their destination months later with half their cattle gone, some of their men lying in shallow graves along the trail or lost in the waters of angry rushing rivers."*
>
> ◆
>
> *Ad Spaugh, cowboy*

### Negotiating a River Crossing ——

Cowboys coax a herd of cattle across the Powder River near Wyoming's N-Bar Ranch, one of the few ranches a trail drive might pass en route. Rivers could pose severe hazards to the drive: Even assuming the water was not running too high and fast to cross, the animals often panicked, either at the edge or in midstream, drowning themselves and others.

### Stampede! ——

Drenched and blinded by rain and darkness, a trail hand drives his wild-eyed horse toward the front of a herd stampeded by the storm as he tries desperately to head the animals off before they run over a cliff or into a ditch.

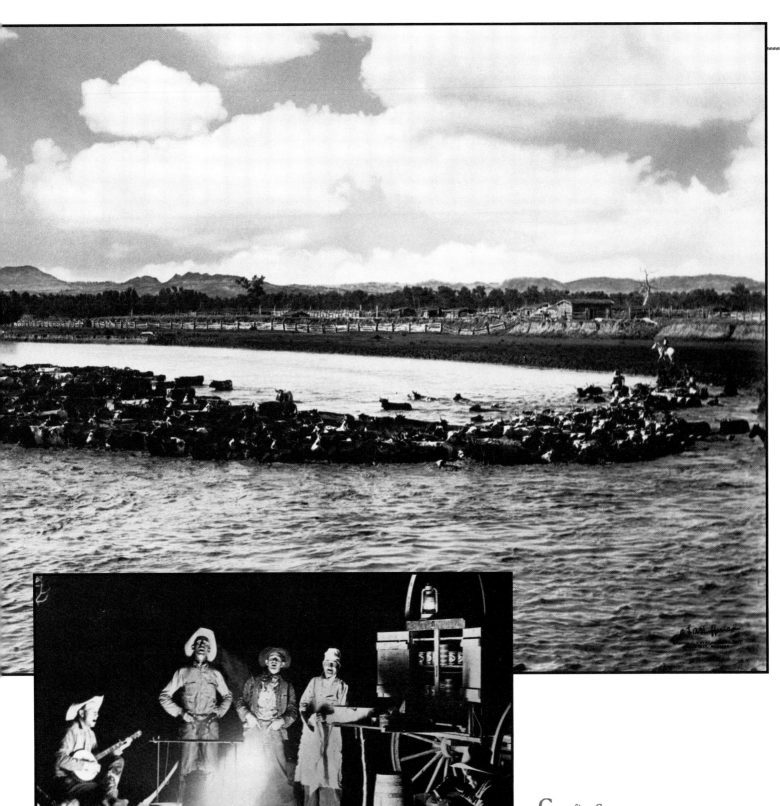

Campfire Songs ——

While one cowhand picks at a banjo, his pals and the cook join him in a full-throated song around the campfire. The cook was a jack-of-all-trades on the trail drive, serving as barber, seamstress, and doctor for the men in his outfit. The chuck wagon carried not only foodstuffs but guns, ammunition, and other supplies for the trail hands.

**D**estination, Kansas City ———
At the end of the drive, and until they were shipped to slaughterhouses back East, cattle were penned up in stockyards such as this one in Kansas City, Missouri. Teeming with more than 100 acres of beef on any given day, the Kansas City yard handled more than half a million head per year in the 1880s.

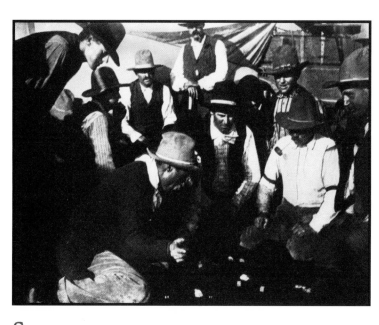

**S**even Come Eleven! ———
A game of chance after the midday break for chow offers a few minutes' diversion. Fearing fights and arguments, most cattle barons forbade gambling on the ranch but relaxed the rules for the duration of the trail drive.

**A** Quick Splash ———
Five cowhands cleaning up in an Oklahoma water hole pause long enough for a gypsy photographer to take a picture of them and some of their trail buddies. Itinerant photographers would sell prints like this to their subjects for 50¢ apiece.

Cattle On Board——
Using long prods to force steers up a chute and into a railroad car was the final, tedious chore for the trail hand—and gave him the lasting nickname "cowpoke."

# Drink, Women, and Whooping It Up

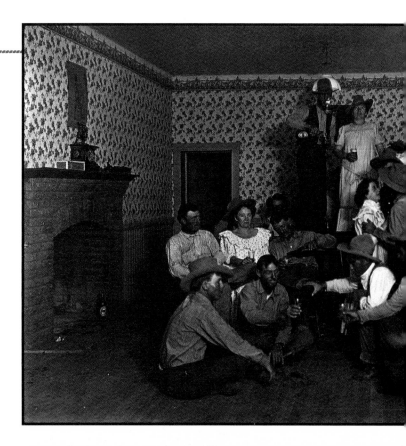

The first sight of the distant lights of town after months in the saddle sent cowboys into an agony of anticipation. Often the agony was prolonged, time off usually being granted in shifts since someone had to guard the herd outside of town until the cattle were sold.

But eventually his turn would come, and the trail hand hightailed it to civilization. Absolutely the first order of business was to wash off the accumulated trail grime. At a rooming house, or sometimes in a place adjoining a saloon, the cowpoke could get a bath, and maybe a shave and a haircut. Next stop was the haberdasher, to buy himself some new duds and toss out the dirt-stiff clothes he had lived in so long they were in tatters. Feeling like a new man, the cowboy was ready to take the town up on whatever pleasures it had to offer.

Galloping Up to the Bar — With pistols blazing and small regard for flailing hoofs and fallen mounts, five whooping trail hands crash through the doorway of a saloon—putting the world on notice that cowboys had come to town. Such antics actually were rare; some contrite offenders would reimburse the saloon owner for damages.

126

## Carousing with the Ladies ———

Cowboys and soiled doves raise convivial glasses in a gaily wallpapered room. "After six and eight months of seeing only leather-covered humans and none at all with skirts nor long hair," one cowboy wrote, "it was about time for a little change and some fun."

## Slaking a Powerful Thirst ———

Saloons were where most of the action was in the cattle towns that catered to the needs and wants of trail hands ready to whoop it up.

**O**pen for Business———

With saddles lined up along one side of his establishment and bridles gleaming in glass display cases, the proprietor of a saddle shop in Miles City, Montana, waits for trail hands who might want to replace worn riding gear or to splurge on an elegant new saddle.

**S**pruced Up———

Following a common practice, a trail hand named Billy Smith wears every stitch of his brand new clothes for a studio portrait. As one extravagant shopper recorded, "I outfitted myself in a heavy coat, a dozen plain white shirts, new hat, ties, a caddy of tobacco and cigarette papers, and other things, which all took a good hundred dollars from my wages."

**S**tarting the Long Trail Home———

Bottles tipped for a last snort, lucky trail hands bound for home climb aboard a caboose. Not all cowboys worked for a rancher willing to spring for their train fare back. Many had to make the return trip the same way they came—on horseback.

# The Story of a Frontier Romance

The daughters of cattle baron Granville Stuart and his Shoshoni wife, Awbonnie, were in great demand among eligible bachelors in eastern Montana. As persistent suitor Teddy Blue Abbott recalled many years later, the girls "were pretty, well-dressed, good dancers, and very much sought after."

The 25-year-old Abbott had worked ranches from Texas to Canada when he signed on with Stuart in the winter of 1884-1885. He soon set his sights on Mary Stuart, the middle daughter. Mary's parents objected to the match. "If we walked out so we could have a little talk together," Abbott recalled, "her father would come to the door and call out, 'Children, it's time to go to bed!'" The two were finally married in 1889, and the former cowboy bought a small spread (right), making it prosper over the next 30 years.

**Awbonnie and Granville Stuart** ——
Awbonnie Tookanka (left), a Shoshoni, was the first wife of cattle rancher Granville Stuart (right). Despite a society hostile to interracial unions, their marriage lasted 26 years, until Awbonnie's death in 1888.

**Mary and Teddy Blue Abbott** ——
Mary Stuart (left), daughter of Granville and Awbonnie Stuart, married one of her father's cowboys, E. C. "Teddy Blue" Abbott (right). The couple courted under her parents' watchful eye for two years.

### The Three Deuce

Teddy Blue Abbott's ranch, the Three Deuce, sprawls over 2,000 acres in eastern Montana's Fergus County. By 1900, the decade-old ranch was prosperous, shipping about a railroad car full of beef per year.

### A Burgeoning Brood

By the time of this 1902 family portrait Teddy Blue and Mary Abbott had five children. (Mary's brother, Edward Stuart, is shown to her left.) The couple later had two more children—and 14 grandchildren.

# The Ranch Hand's Life in Winter

For cowboys, the long hiatus between the fall and spring roundups seemed even longer once the snow set in, especially on the Northern Plains, where winter temperatures could plunge to well below freezing. Cattle were left to fend for themselves on the range, and unemployed cowhands often roved from ranch to ranch doing odd jobs to make a living. Sometimes a cowboy was assigned to a line camp in a remote section of the ranch, to patrol the perimeter and make certain no cattle strayed. Animals sometimes had to be rescued in blinding snowstorms—dangerous work that could mean a full day in the saddle. At the end of the day, the cabin was a warm haven—but there was not much to do and a man could get mighty lonely and bored. Even back at the main ranch, indoor amusements were limited to gambling, dancing (with each other), and perhaps a mock hanging or two.

**The Rescue** —
Muffled to his eyes in the face of a Wyoming blizzard, a cowboy slings an orphan calf over his saddle as his horse labors up a hill. Rescuing stranded animals was one of the ranch hand's most demanding winter responsibilities.

**Another Day in the Snow** —
At a lonely line camp on the Pitchfork Ranch in Wyoming, a cowhand saddles up after a snowstorm, heading out to hunt for strays.

### Gentlemen's Jig

At the Lazy S Ranch in Texas, two men dance to a four-piece band while the boss's wife and baby look on. There were never enough women to go around, but one man usually volunteered to play the woman's role, donning an apron or tying a handkerchief around his arm.

### A Private Corner

It was only a bunk in a corner, but the cowboy who slept here could call it his own, and could keep his valued possessions nearby—a rifle, a shotgun, a pair of warm angora chaps, a new hat, and barbells.

# Small Ranchers and the End of an Era

As the century drew to a close, cattle barons—who up till then had treated government-owned open range as their private property, grazing their herds wherever they pleased—found themselves in head-to-head confrontation with an influx of homesteaders and small ranchers. Many of the new arrivals were sheepherders—anathema to the cattlemen. The small-time ranchers, for their part, were suspected (sometimes with good reason) of stealing mavericks from the larger spreads. Worse, these newcomers marked their claims with barbed wire or, in Kansas, with a plowed furrow. In furious desperation, some cattle barons formed vigilante groups to intimidate their perceived enemies. One especially brutal encounter made a folk hero of its victim, a small rancher named Nate Champion (*below, right*).

*"Boys, there is bullets coming in like hail. . . . Nick is dead. He died about 9 o'clock. I feel pretty lonesome just now."*

◆

**Diary of Nate Champion**

A Martyred Folk Hero ——
Nate Champion (*standing, far right*), owner of a ranch in Johnson County, Wyoming, was suspected of cattle rustling and ambushed and killed in his cabin with a friend, Nick Ray, in 1892. Seen here several years earlier, when he worked as a trail hand, Champion kept a diary during the daylong gun battle; his despairing words survived and made him a hero.

### A Homesteading Clan———

A two-room log cabin was home for the families of brothers Frank and Hyrum Tidwell on their small horse and cattle ranch in Sunnyside, Utah, in the 1890s. The men slept outdoors in lean-tos *(far left)*. Marginal ranchers like the Tidwells often gave up in the face of the harshness of the Plains or the antagonism of powerful cattle barons.

### Barbed Wire on the Range———

Four masked men reenact a wire cutting on a Nebraska ranch—an act carried out by both sides in the range wars. With the advent of barbed wire, settlers put up fences to protect their crops from free-ranging cattle; cattlemen, in turn, fenced off water holes.

# GUNFIGHTERS

Flashes of gunfire light up a frontier night in Charles Russell's painting *When Guns Speak, Death Settled Disputes*.

# ON SEPTEMBER 7, 1876, FIVE HORSEMEN GALLOPED INTO THE CENTER OF

Northfield, Minnesota, firing pistols into the air and whooping wildly. As frightened townspeople ran for cover, three other men in wide-brimmed hats and long, linen dusters strode up to the First National Bank, drew their revolvers, and burst through the doors. Inside, they vaulted over the counter and yelled at cashier Joseph Heywood and his two co-workers to put up their hands.

Heywood dashed toward the vault, which was standing open, but the outlaws reached it first. One of them, a 29-year-old Missourian with steely blue eyes and a closely clipped beard and mustache, spied the safe inside and commanded the cashier to open it. Heywood figured that any show of resistance would probably cost him his life. Nonetheless, he summoned all his courage and refused.

"It has a time lock," he said. "It can't be opened." This (as every reader of dime novels knew) was a daring bluff to make while staring into the muzzle of a gun held by Jesse James.

Perhaps the most famous outlaw ever to roam the West, James by then had been killing people for nearly half his young life. The son of a slaveholder in western Missouri, he had taken up the gun during the Civil War, after a harrowing incident in which federal troops whipped him, tortured his stepfather, and abused his pregnant mother. Determined to avenge these depredations and to protect his family's way of life, Jesse in 1864 joined his older brother, Frank, and 200 other young gunmen in a rebel guerrilla outfit headed by William "Bloody Bill" Anderson that conducted some of the most savage anti-Union raids of the entire war.

On one occasion the irregulars looted the town of Centralia, Missouri, and murdered nearly 30 passengers aboard a Wabash, St. Louis, and Pacific train, most of them unarmed federal soldiers. Then the guerrillas slaughtered the troops that rode out to bring them to justice and mutilated their corpses. Years later, Frank would remember the bloodletting as one of the great events of his life. "The only battles in the world's history to surpass Centralia are Thermopylae and the Alamo," he boasted.

After the war, most of the men who rode in the gang managed to take up peaceful lives again, and the James brothers may have tried to do the same—for a while. But on Valentine's Day in 1866, Jesse and nine other former guerrillas stormed into Liberty, Missouri, and stole nearly $60,000 from the Clay County Savings and Loan Bank. As they made their getaway, they wantonly shot down an unarmed 19-year-old college student.

Eight months later, they struck again, this time at a bank in Lexington. Over the next 10 years, the outlaws robbed two stagecoaches, four trains, and seven banks, and brutally killed dozens of lawmen, vigilantes, and other brave and foolish victims. Among them: a bank cashier in Gallatin, Missouri, shot through the head and heart after he—like Joseph Heywood—balked at opening the safe.

Jesse may have been considering dispatching Heywood as well, but before he could pull the trigger, teller A. E. Bunker ran for the back door of the bank. Charlie Pitts, one of James's accomplices, sent a quick shot after him but missed. Following Bunker to the door, he fired again. The bullet struck the teller in the shoulder, but he managed to stumble to safety.

At that moment, one of the horsemen on the street out front yelled that the gang had better make their break, as the residents of Northfield were no longer hiding but were beginning to return the bandits' fire. One of the gang, Clell Miller, had already been hit. Bloodied by a blast of stinging bird shot, Miller remained in the saddle and kept on shooting until a 19-year-old medical student with an old army carbine finally killed him with a shot to the chest.

Jesse, the last outlaw to leave the bank, knew he would have to move fast to avoid a similar fate, yet he found time to settle the score with Heywood: James turned and shot the cashier in the head, killing him instantly. Then the outlaw dashed into the street, where for once his gang was getting a taste of its own medicine.

By the time Jesse mounted his horse, a second member of the gang, Bill Chadwell, had been shot dead. Blinded by bird shot, Chadwell was riding slowly when the owner of a hardware store drilled him with a Remington repeating rifle. A witness said the merchant took aim "as cool as though he was picking off a squirrel."

Gunfire from the hardware man and other citizens rained down on the outlaws, hitting Frank James in the leg and nearly wiping out

The Winchester .44-40 was the 19th century's best-selling rifle. The addition of a rear sight made it also one of the most accurate.

three brothers who were Jesse's longtime partners in crime—Jim, Cole, and Bob Younger. A bullet carried away half of Jim's upper jaw, Cole was struck in the shoulder, and Bob's horse, a handsome bay, was cut down. Bob took shelter behind some boxes, but not before he was hit in the thigh by a shot from the medical student.

"We're beat," one of the outlaws shouted. "Let's go!" Those who still could spurred their horses and made their escape. Afraid of being left behind, Bob Younger limped into the center of the street after them. Just then, a shotgun blast tore apart his right elbow. "My God, boys, you're not deserting me?" he called. "I'm shot!" Cole heard his brother's plea and turned back. He hauled Bob onto the back of his horse, and together they hurried to catch up with the remaining members of the gang.

For two weeks, the group stayed one step ahead of an army of pursuers. But on September 21, a posse trapped Charlie Pitts and the Younger brothers in a wooded area about 70 miles southwest of Northfield. In the shootout that followed, Pitts was killed, Jim Younger was shot 5 times, and Cole was hit 11 times. Bob Younger, wounded twice, was the only one still standing when the outlaws surrendered. "The boys are all shot to pieces," he yelled. "For God's sake, don't kill me!"

Having decided days earlier to go their own way, Jesse and Frank eluded capture. They escaped to Dakota Territory on stolen horses and then fled south, some say as far as Mexico. In time, they settled in Nashville. There they lived under assumed names and assiduously shunned publicity—until October 1879, when they burst into the headlines once again. Riding with a new gang, they held up a train outside of Kansas City, making off with $35,000. Over the next year and a half, they also robbed a stagecoach, a bank, and two more trains. But as 1881 came to a close, the end drew perilously near for the James brothers as well, thanks to the governor of Missouri.

Outraged by the gang's resurgence, he issued a proclamation offering $10,000 for the arrest or capture, dead or alive, of either Jesse or Frank. One who was tempted by the money, a huge sum at the time, was a Missourian named Bob Ford. Because his sister was the lover of one of the gang members, Ford was able to work his way into Jesse's company and on April 3, 1882, shot him in the back of the head. Frank, weary of life on the run and scared that he, too, might be killed when his guard was down, turned himself in six months later.

The Colt .45—dubbed the "peacemaker"—was the most popular pistol in the West. When introduced in 1873 the basic version cost $17, but an engraved pair like the one above, with ivory handles and an embossed holster, fetched up to $100.

Explaining his decision to surrender, Frank described a bleak life in stark contrast to the romantic notions commonly associated with gunfighters: "I have been hunted for twenty-one years," he said. "I have literally lived in the saddle. I have never known a day of perfect peace. It was one long, anxious, inexorable, eternal vigil. When I slept, it was literally in the midst of an arsenal. If I heard dogs bark more fiercely than usual, or the feet of horses in a greater volume than usual, I stood to my arms. Have you any idea what a man must endure who leads such a life? No, you cannot." So great was Frank's torment that, as his wife put it, he could not "cut a stick of wood" without looking around to see whether there was someone behind him about to kill him.

The same dread was doubtless felt by a fair number of gunfighters, including those as well known as Wyatt Earp and Doc Holliday, who had to outrun a sheriff's posse following the famous shootout at the O.K. Corral *(pages 158-161),* and those as deranged as the killer Bill Longley. A white man wanted for the murder of a black lawman in Austin, Texas, he took it on the lam in 1866 at the tender age of 15 and drifted aimlessly through the states of Arkansas and Kansas and Indian, Wyoming, and Dakota territories. When he was finally brought to justice 11 years later, he claimed to have murdered a total of 32 men. Asked why he had never been killed, Longley said, "Because I never had any confidence in nobody."

This could probably be said for John Wesley Hardin, another prolific killer. He was born in Bonham, Texas, in 1853 and, like the Jameses, learned from the Civil War a bitter hatred for everything Yankee and a profound conviction that might makes right. He killed for the first time when he was 15 years old. The victim was a freed slave who, angry after being bloodied in a wrestling match, made the mistake of seizing the bridle of Hardin's horse. "I shot him loose," Hardin said later. "He kept coming back, and every time we would start, I would shoot him again and again until I shot him down."

Hardin's father, convinced that to be tried for killing a former slave "meant certain death at the hands of a court backed by Northern bayonets," gave his son a shotgun and sent him south to live with his older brother, a teacher in Trinity County. For a short time, it looked as though John Wesley would leave his troubles behind. But

In addition to conventional sidearms most gunfighters carried "pocket revolvers," which were compact and easily concealed. The Smith and Wesson pocket .32 was a favorite of Wild Bill Hickok's.

# THE VIGILANT EYE OF THE PINKERTONS

The most famous crime-fighting organization of the 19th century was Pinkerton's National Detective Agency. Founded in 1850 by Scottish emigrant and ex-Chicago police detective Allan Pinkerton, the agency first made its name by protecting railroads. Its biggest coup came 10 years later, when it foiled an assassination attempt on President-elect Abraham Lincoln. An impressed Lincoln soon had the Scot heading a counterespionage force during the Civil War.

After the war, Pinkerton returned to sleuthing. His agents pursued some of the most desperate gunslingers of the day, including the James gang and Butch Cassidy's Wild Bunch. And they almost always got their man, no matter how long it took; some investigations were successfully closed only after decades of work. So effective were the agents' methods that when the government formed the Federal Bureau of Investigation in 1908, it used Pinkerton's agency as its model.

The logo of the Pinkerton agency was an all-seeing eye accompanied by the motto "We never sleep." The familiar symbol eventually gave rise to the term "private eye."

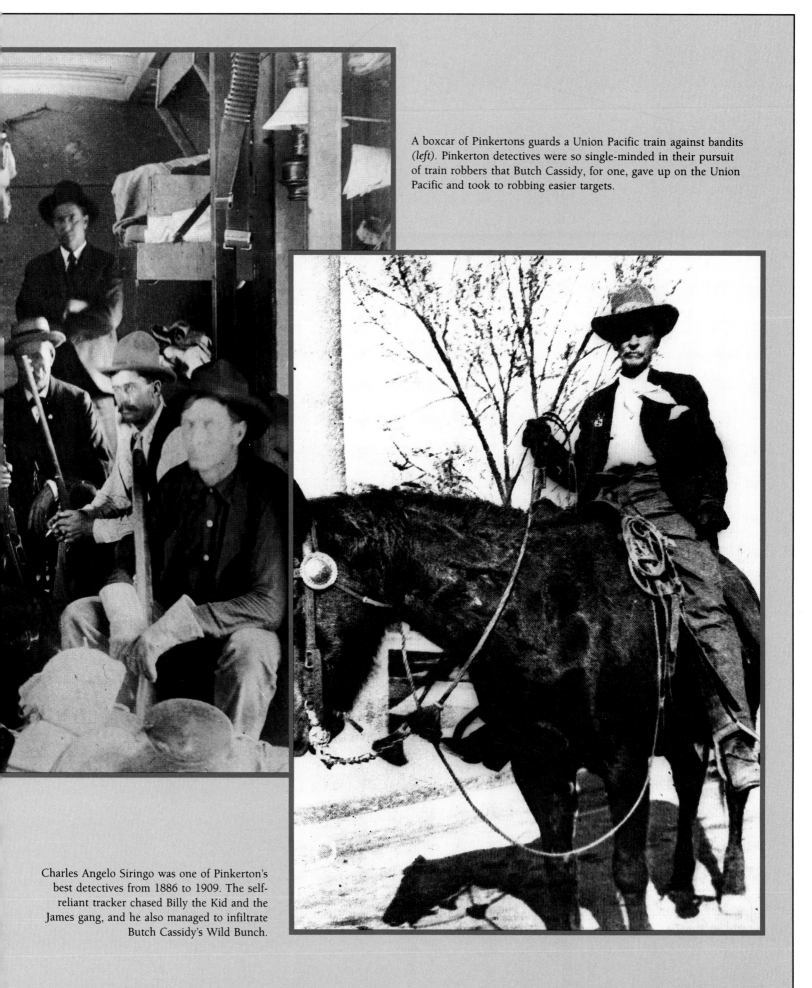

A boxcar of Pinkertons guards a Union Pacific train against bandits (*left*). Pinkerton detectives were so single-minded in their pursuit of train robbers that Butch Cassidy, for one, gave up on the Union Pacific and took to robbing easier targets.

Charles Angelo Siringo was one of Pinkerton's best detectives from 1886 to 1909. The self-reliant tracker chased Billy the Kid and the James gang, and he also managed to infiltrate Butch Cassidy's Wild Bunch.

then word came that three federal soldiers were riding his way. Commencing what he later called a "war to the knife" against the hated Yankees, Hardin ambushed the soldiers as they crossed a creek, killing two with the shotgun and one with his pistol.

Over the next year, Hardin's self-declared war would cost two more Union cavalrymen their lives and claim those of a gambler, a circus hand, and a con man as well. The killing spree would also earn Hardin a place on the wanted list of the Texas State Police. Forced to keep moving, he roamed throughout Texas, across Indian Territory, and into Kansas, coming into contact not only with Bill Longley, whom he met in Evergreen, Texas, but also with the famous scout and gunfighter Wild Bill Hickok *(pages 154-155),* then the marshal of Abilene, Kansas.

Hardin got along well enough with Hickok to be permitted the courtesy of wearing his guns in town but was forced to flee after an ugly incident at the hotel where he was staying. Annoyed one night by the snoring of a man in the next room, Hardin reportedly fired two shots into the wall separating them: The first woke the man up; the second killed him. When Hickok and four policemen arrived to investigate, Hardin took fright and jumped out a window clad only in an undershirt. "I believed," he said later, "that if Wild Bill found me in a defenseless condition, he would take no explanation, but would kill me to add to his reputation."

On the run again, Hardin continued to drift from place to place, killing wherever he went. By the spring of 1874, he was said to be the most wanted man in the West—an honor he earned in what may have been his fairest fight ever. On May 26, his 21st birthday, he met Deputy Sheriff Charles Webb in a Comanche, Texas, saloon and invited him to have a drink. Webb agreed and then apparently went for his gun while Hardin's back was turned. Alerted by someone's cry, the outlaw wheeled and jumped aside just as the lawman fired. Only grazed, Hardin quickly pulled his pistol and shot, fatally wounding Webb. According to one estimate, he was the killer's 39th victim.

Hardin was allowed to leave Comanche without interference, but large parties of men soon began systematically searching the countryside for him. And one night in early June, they found him, at a campsite in a valley several miles outside of the city. With more than 100 men in pursuit, Hardin and a friend hastily galloped into the darkness. But as they crested a hill, they discovered to their shock a

second posse waiting on the other side. The outlaws reversed course and dashed back up the hill, directly toward the crowd that had been nipping at their heels. In the confusion that followed, Hardin escaped—at least for a while.

Pursued relentlessly by other posses, he again departed Texas, heading first to New Orleans, then to Florida, where he lived under the pseudonym J. H. Swain, and finally to Alabama. But running only postponed the inevitable: Texas authorities were offering $4,000 for his capture, dead or alive, and detectives were trailing him from state to state. He was captured at Pensacola Junction, Florida, in the summer of 1877, while he was playing poker in the smoking car of a train.

Hardin was returned to Comanche, where he was found guilty of murdering Deputy Sheriff Charles Webb and sentenced to 25 years at hard labor. Pardoned 15 years later, he settled in El Paso and—strange as it seems—opened a law office. But try as he might to be a good neighbor, the former outlaw met an end similar to that of Jesse James. In August of 1895, a local constable sneaked up behind him in a saloon and blew his brains out. Hardin had reportedly quarreled

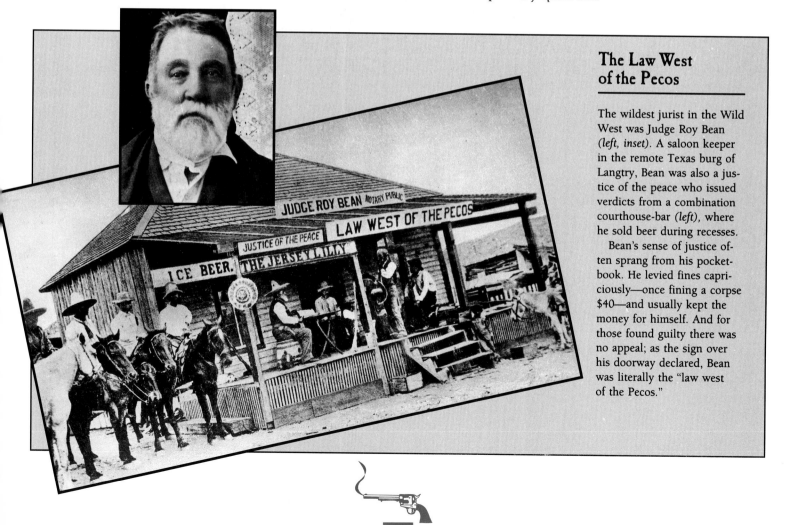

## The Law West of the Pecos

The wildest jurist in the Wild West was Judge Roy Bean (left, inset). A saloon keeper in the remote Texas burg of Langtry, Bean was also a justice of the peace who issued verdicts from a combination courthouse-bar (left), where he sold beer during recesses.

Bean's sense of justice often sprang from his pocketbook. He levied fines capriciously—once fining a corpse $40—and usually kept the money for himself. And for those found guilty there was no appeal; as the sign over his doorway declared, Bean was literally the "law west of the Pecos."

with the lawman earlier. The gunfighter never knew what hit him.

While he was in prison, Hardin had promised his wife that he would hang up his guns for good once he got out. But on the day he died, investigators found two pistols concealed in his vest pockets. Apparently, the transition from desperado to law-abiding citizen was more difficult than he had bargained. This was a hard truth learned many times by many gunfighters—including one Henry Brown, who rode into Caldwell, Kansas, in July 1882 packing two ivory-handled six-shooters and a well-worn Winchester rifle.

A gambler, a horse thief, and a gunman of some repute in Texas and New Mexico Territory, Brown had ridden with Billy the Kid during the bloody Lincoln County War four years earlier *(pages 150-151)*. Such an individual would seem a poor candidate for the position of Caldwell's marshal, which was vacant at the time. But when Brown volunteered for the job, the mayor hired him on the spot. "All right," he reportedly said, "It's your funeral."

The mayor's readiness may have had less to do with Brown's qualifications than with the town's recent history. The previous three marshals had all died on the job: The first was ambushed while patrolling late at night, the second was gunned down by rampaging cowboys, and the third was shot dead by a thug in a dance hall. The mayor feared the killings would scare away potential settlers by making Caldwell appear "incapable of self-government," as the *Dodge City Times* put it. If the newest marshal had no fear of gunplay, so much the better.

Anything but afraid, Brown wasted no time serving notice that he was a lawman to be reckoned with. He promptly killed two men in the line of duty—one for resisting arrest, the other because he foolishly challenged the gunfighter to a shootout—and calm returned to the streets of Caldwell. Delighted and grateful, the townspeople replaced Brown's old rifle with an elegantly engraved, gold-mounted Winchester bearing the inscription "For valuable services rendered the citizens of Caldwell."

By all appearances, Brown had succeeded where Hardin, a dozen years later, would fail. Brown no longer gambled, did not drink, and was never seen smoking or chewing tobacco. He even married a local woman, Maude Levagood, and took the neighborly step of buying a house. But then, just as he seemed to have earned widespread love

and respect in town, he inexplicably decided to turn outlaw again.

Early one morning toward the end of April 1884, he and his deputy, Ben Wheeler, met up with two cowboy friends on the open range outside of town and headed west. Their destination was Medicine Lodge, a tiny town with a small bank and no one like Henry Brown to protect it. The four men arrived shortly after opening time.

While one of the cowboys stood guard on the street, Brown and the two others went inside with guns at the ready. Minutes later, they came running out empty-handed and bloody, having mortally wounded the bank president and killed the cashier, who managed to lock the vault before collapsing. Brown and his men jumped on their horses and made their getaway into the surrounding countryside but soon boxed themselves in a blind canyon, where a posse captured them and brought them back to Medicine Lodge.

In jail with the others, Brown could only ponder why he had given up so much to gain so little. Uncertain what that night might bring, he hurriedly wrote the following letter:

> *Darling Wife:*
> *—I am in jail here. I want you to come and see me as soon as you can. I will send you all of my things, and you can sell them, but keep the Winchester. This is hard for me to write this letter but, it was all for you, my sweet wife, and for the love I have for you. Do not go back on me; if you do it will kill me. If a mob does not kill us we will come out all right after awhile. Maude, I did not shoot anyone, and did not want the others to kill anyone; but they did, and that is all there is about it. Now, good-bye, my darling wife.*
>
> H. N. Brown

A few hours later, Brown's worst fears were made real: An angry mob overpowered the sheriff and his men and broke into the jail, demanding their own kind of justice. In a panic, the prisoners made a break for it, but Ben Wheeler and the cowboys were quickly apprehended. They were hanged later that night from an elm tree east of town.

Brown, by contrast, died the death of an authentic gunfighter: Unarmed, he ran only a few yards, then the vigilantes let loose with their rifles and handguns. The fusillade of bullets and buckshot struck him from behind.

# THE WAY OF
# THE GUNFIGHTER

The West's most notorious gunfighters had much in common beyond quick reflexes. Almost to a man, their initiations to violence came very early in life. John Wesley Hardin, for example, killed his first victim at the tender age of 15. And as the authorities eventually closed in, he had to keep killing to evade capture, thus fixing his destiny as a shootist. A similar fate befell Billy the Kid *(pages 150-151)*, who first drew blood when he was 16 years old.

Most of these killers were molded by the Civil War. In border states such as Missouri, Southern sympathies ran high and Confederate guerillas tormented federal troops by raiding pro-Union towns. William Clarke Quantrill, for instance, mercilessly sacked the town of Lawrence, Kansas *(right)*. The savagery of these raids so appalled the federal government that it denied the guerillas the amnesty offered Confederate regulars at the end of the war. Made outlaws in their own homes, many—including Frank and Jesse James—turned to crime as both a livelihood and a means for exacting revenge on all things Yankee.

John Wesley Hardin —————
Killer of 44 men—one for the offense of snoring in an adjacent hotel room—Hardin spent 15 years in prison for his crimes. He then tried to go straight and became a lawyer. But his fiery temper made the transition difficult, and in 1895 he was shot in the back by a police officer with whom he had quarreled.

## The Lawrence, Kansas, Raid ——

In 1863, Quantrill's raiders—450 of them, including Frank James—rode into Lawrence,
Kansas. The marauders killed some 150 civilians, many of them children, burned down
their homes, then proceeded to get drunk.

## Clay Allison ——

An honest, upstanding citizen when sober, Alli-
son flew into murderous rages when drunk.
The bandages he wears here cover a gunshot
wound, accidentally self-inflicted while he was
trying to rustle some army mules.

# The Making of Legends

When it comes to the gunfighting legends, truth is usually much less sensational and romantic than fiction. Henry McCarty, for example, otherwise known as William Bonney, or Billy the Kid, has been credited by Western mythmakers with some 21 kills; the actual number may be just 4—a modest tally for such a notorious figure. Most of the deaths occurred in the vicious 1877 range war in Lincoln County, New Mexico, where Billy and John Tunstall, an honest rancher and businessman, were allied against wealthier—and thoroughly corrupt—cattle ranchers and merchants.

Jesse James, by contrast, got the better of history. Theodore Roosevelt referred to him as "America's Robin Hood," a champion of the downtrodden. But Jesse was a callous killer whose criminal tendencies sprang from simple greed and a lingering resentment of the North. He and his gang wantonly killed innocent bystanders to their raids, and James himself went out of his way during the Northfield, Minnesota, bank heist *(page 152)* to gun down a clerk.

Billy the Kid——
A well-known portrait of the Kid reinforces his reputation as a swaggering, vain killer. The real Billy, though clearly capable of murder, was also a literate, intelligent young man.

The Kid's Rough Justice ——
In this Charlie Russell sketch, Billy has coolly
shot the two sheriff's deputies who murdered
John Tunstall, for whom he worked as a ranch
hand. Part of a posse sent to capture the pair,
the Kid claimed they had tried to escape. Others believed he simply shot them out of hand.

The James Gang ———

In the 1870s, an arrogant Jesse James *(below, far left)* invited a visitor to photograph his gang in their hideout. James was a popular figure in the postwar South, and his fellow Missourians often helped him evade capture.

**Bob Younger** ——
In a shootout with the Northfield posse, Bob Younger was wounded twice. Along with his two brothers, he was captured and sentenced to 25 years in jail—of which he served only 13 before dying of tuberculosis.

**Jim Younger** ——
Like his brother Cole *(right)* and Frank James, Jim Younger had been a member of Quantrill's raiders during the Civil War. Shortly after serving his 25 years for the Northfield robbery, he committed suicide.

**Cole Younger** ——
Thomas Coleman Younger was shot 11 times during the Northfield job, most seriously under the right eye, as seen in this postcapture photograph. He survived his wounds and served out his full quarter-century sentence.

# Switching to the Side of Law and Order

*"That I have killed men, I admit, but never unless in absolute self-defense, or in the performance of official duty. I never took mean advantage of an enemy. Yet, understand, I never allowed a man to get the drop on me."*

◆

*James B. "Wild Bill" Hickok*

Because a quick draw was useful on both sides of the law, many erstwhile gunfighters found work as peace officers. Towns tended to overlook a potential lawman's checkered past, often counting on it, in fact, since a fearsome reputation could be a marshal's best weapon. A man would think twice before making a ruckus in a town policed by Wild Bill Hickok or Bat Masterson.

Law enforcement was a three-tiered affair out West. At the national level, each region had a marshal, whose jurisdiction was limited to federal crimes. Within the individual states and territories, every county had a sheriff. Finally, each town had its own marshal, the lowest paying and probably the most thankless job of the three. Not only were towns the magnets that attracted troublemakers, but when things were quiet, marshals were handed such unglamorous duties as shooting stray dogs and clearing trash.

Wild Bill Hickok——
A former buffalo hunter and scout for General George A. Custer, Hickok served as sheriff of Ellis County, Kansas, and later as marshal of Abilene. He was a fantastic marksman, allegedly able to shoot a straight row of holes in a target at 25 paces—with either hand.

### Hays City, Kansas

Hickok's days as Ellis County sheriff came to a sudden end in 1870, when, during a brawl in Hays City, he killed one soldier and wounded another. Fearing reprisals, the sheriff hopped a train at the local depot *(left)*.

### Henry Brown

Having switched sides once to become the marshal of Caldwell, Kansas, Brown turned outlaw again and robbed a bank in 1884. Shown below *(second from right)* with his three partners, he was dragged from his cell the day of his capture by a mob intent on a hanging. He was shot while trying to flee.

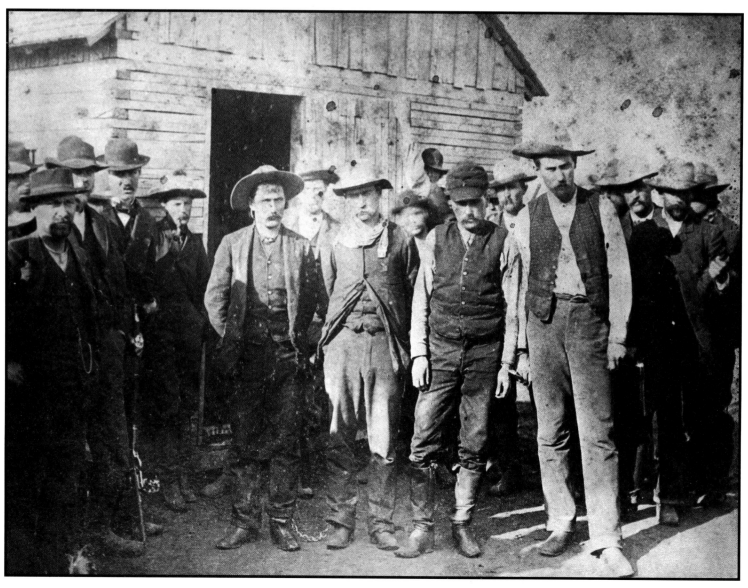

### Bat Masterson

Though something of a dandy, Bartholomew "Bat" Masterson *(right)* earned a reputation as a formidable gunfighter before being elected sheriff of Ford County, Kansas, in 1877, one of three brothers in law enforcement. Older brother Ed served as marshal in the county seat of Dodge City, a post later filled by brother Jim. Dodge City *(below)* was the quintessential Wild West town. This 1876 photo shows Front Street with the notorious Long Branch Saloon *(left of center)* and the Beatty and Kelley Saloon *(behind the barber pole),* frequented by Wyatt Earp.

**Ben Thompson** ——
Marshal of Austin, Texas, between 1880 and 1882, Thompson *(above)* claimed to have killed 32 men—"openly and manly," according to Bat Masterson—before trying his hand at law enforcement.

**Pat Garrett** ——
As sheriff of Lincoln County, New Mexico, the six-foot-four Garrett *(above)* tracked down and killed Billy the Kid in 1881. Afterward, he wrote *An Authentic Life of Billy the Kid,* a heavily embellished account of the outlaw's exploits.

**Dave Mather** ——
"Mysterious Dave" *(left),* a friend of both Bat Masterson's and Wyatt Earp's, served as marshal in a number of Western towns. He claimed to be a descendant of Puritan clergyman and author Cotton Mather.

# Showdown in Tombstone

Perhaps the most legendary gunfight in the Wild West took place in Tombstone, Arizona, on October 26, 1881. On the side of law and order—if in name only—were the Earp brothers: Virgil, the town marshal; and Wyatt and Morgan, who served on the police force. Allied with the Earps was John "Doc" Holliday, an itinerant dentist who specialized in gambling and gunplay. Facing the Earps were two sets of brothers, all cattle ranchers: Ike and Billy Clanton, and Frank and Tom McLaury. The Clantons and McLaurys also dabbled in horse rustling—an activity that aroused the interest of Virgil Earp. But the marshal could do little because the thieves were protected by Cochise County sheriff Johnny Behan. Adding to the volatile mixture was a love triangle (*right*) involving Johnny Behan, Wyatt Earp, and a young woman.

The feud finally ignited when a drunken Ike Clanton exchanged threats with the Earps and Holliday late one night in several Tombstone saloons. The shootout the next day, which took place near the O.K. Corral, left Billy Clanton and both McLaurys dead, and Morgan Earp, Virgil Earp, and Doc Holliday wounded. Months later, Clanton partisans avenged their friends' deaths, shooting Virgil Earp on a Tombstone street. Though his left arm was permanently crippled, he survived the attack. Morgan Earp was less lucky: While playing pool he took a bullet in the back and quickly died.

A Dangerous Love Triangle ———

Fueling the hatred between the Earps and Clantons was an 18-year-old named Josephine Marcus (*above, left*), who arrived in Tombstone in 1880 and was soon engaged to sheriff Johnny Behan (*above, right*). When the dashing Wyatt Earp (*top*) stole her away, Behan—who also was being challenged by Earp in his bid for reelection to sheriff—enlisted the Clantons' help, a move to serve vengeance as well as political expediency.

*"The grimly humorous phrase about our town was that Tombstone had a man for breakfast every morning, meaning someone was killed every night."*

◆

*Josie Earp*

Tombstone, Arizona———
The lure of silver from mines such as the one at far right quickly turned Tombstone into a mecca for fortune hunters, gamblers, merchants—and gunfighters.

A Fateful Encounter——

The night before the gunfight at the O.K. Corral, Ike Clanton confronted Doc Holliday *(above, left)*, Virgil Earp *(above, center)*, Morgan Earp *(above, right)*, and Wyatt Earp at a number of Tombstone saloons, including the Oriental *(top)*. The bar was a favorite of the Earp clan; Wyatt was part owner, and Morgan Earp and Doc Holliday occasionally worked there as faro dealers.

## The Aftermath

After the gunfight, the bodies of Billy Clanton (*top right*) and the McLaury brothers lay in state in the window of a Tombstone hardware store. Ike Clanton (*above, left*), the spark that ignited the violence, ran away once the shooting began. Frank McLaury (*above, center*) died from a shotgun blast delivered by Doc Holliday; his brother Tom (*above, right*) managed to shoot Holliday through the hip before being felled himself.

# Live by the Gun, Die by the Gun

For gunfighters, dying young came with the territory—and often without warning. Whether at the hands of law officers or revenge- or reward-seekers, death was a far cry from the face-to-face showdowns in dime novels. "Fair play is a jewel," said one outlaw, "but I don't care for jewelry." Even Wild Bill Hickok, who lived in constant fear of ambush, could not keep his guard up forever. While playing poker one afternoon in 1876—unwisely sitting with his back to the door—he was shot from behind. Six years later, Jesse James himself was shot in the back of the head in his own house, by a member of his own gang. The murder so scared Jesse's brother, Frank, that he turned himself in. Putting his life of crime behind him, Frank managed to achieve something few other outlaws did: old age.

The Death of Jesse James ————
A wanted man for nearly half his life, Jesse James *(shown in death at left)* died as he had lived—by the gun, shot in the back of the head in 1882 at the age of 35. The killer was Bob Ford *(above)*, an acquaintance who could not resist the $10,000 reward offered for the outlaw—dead or alive. Ten years later, Ford himself was murdered by James sympathizers.

Reflections of a Shootist ————
An aging Cole Younger *(left)*, who served his 25 years for the Northfield, Minnesota, robbery attempt, found religion and gave cautionary lectures about his "misspent life."

## The Violent End of the Dalton Gang ———

Cousins of the Younger brothers, Bob, Emmett, and Gratton Dalton tried to outdo their kin by robbing two banks at once in their hometown of Coffeyville, Kansas. But the town got wind of the plan and met the Daltons with gunfire as they left Condon & Company (*above*). Bob, Gratton, and two accomplices died instantly, their bodies unceremoniously piled in the street (*left*). Emmett survived and served 15 years.

## Wild Bill's Final Resting Place ———

At the time of his death in 1876, Wild Bill Hickok was so famous that souvenir hunters quickly chipped away his wooden tombstone. It was replaced by the board at right, and when that one met a similar fate, a stone marker.

# THE CODE OF THE WEST

## Courtly Kindness and Harsh Justice

Human relations in the Wild West consisted of a strange blend of courtesy and violence, governed by an unwritten set of sometimes contradictory rules known as the Code of the West. The code dictated that a person's word was sacred, property was inviolable, hospitality was a sacrosanct obligation, a horse was a man's most important possession. Those who broke the code met with contempt—or worse. A rancher who had the gall to demand payment for a meal from two out-of-work cowboys, for example, found the message "Meals—50 cts." branded on the side of one of his steers. So intolerable a crime was horse theft that anyone caught with a stolen mount could expect to be hanged from the nearest tree.

There were any number of twists in the code. A notorious gunman or gambler might be shot in full view of witnesses and the shooter never called to account. If a respectable citizen was the victim, however, the killer would most likely be hanged.

Citizens who thought the law weak or slow took it upon themselves to achieve order by the application of naked force. Paid gunfighters guarded cattle herds and stagecoach lines; impromptu posses hunted down bandits. Common all over the West were so-called vigilance committees—men organized to dispense unofficial justice. Acting swiftly and inexorably, these self-proclaimed law enforcers seldom tried to separate the innocent from the guilty when they encountered suspicious situations.

The High Price of Treachery——
Cards mix with blood and gun smoke in artist Frederic Remington's *Misdeal*. When an honest man playing against professional gamblers was determined not to be cheated, Remington wrote, he played for double stakes—"his life and his dollars."

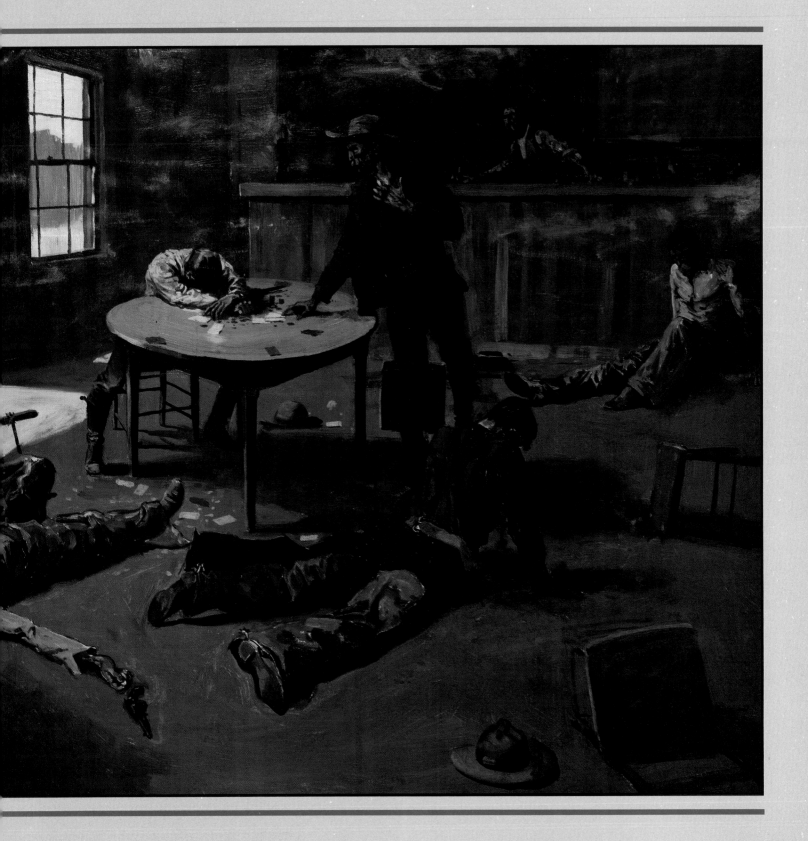

# Imposing a Cowman's Order on the Range

Cattle barons amassed herds worth millions of dollars on the open range. They tolerated a little rustling of unbranded calves among their peers, but strangers or small ranchers who picked up strays were burned out of their homes and sometimes killed.

The barons often hired professional gunmen to do their dirty work. Called cattle detectives or stock inspectors, these killers roamed the range, shooting anyone caught with unbranded stock—regardless of whose it was. One of the bloodiest "inspectors" was Tom Horn, a hulking Arizonan who charged a $500 bounty for every "rustler" he shot.

Campaigns against rustlers—or anyone else the big ranchers didn't like—sometimes escalated into near-military operations. Wyoming cattle barons launched one of these range wars to wipe out not only rustlers but small ranchers and homesteaders encroaching on what the barons considered their land. Forming a vigilance committee reinforced with hired guns imported from Texas, the men targeted a "dead list" of some 70 names. The plot ended up a fiasco, although several purported rustlers were brutally killed before the scheme collapsed.

### A Fiery Retribution

A team of vigilantes torches a ranch house suspected of being the hideout of rustlers. Artist Rufus Zogbaum sketched this scene in 1885 after a trip through Montana rangeland.

# Waging Wars for Land and Water

In the arid West, cattle lords vied with small ranchers and farmers over the possession or use of land—particularly if it contained water. During the 1870s, pressure on the land from rapidly multiplying cattle herds and waves of new settlers provoked growing hostility.

The cattle barons used subterfuge to grab large tracts of land. They staked out homesteading plots fronting on streams, for example, then ordered their ranch hands to file equally fraudulent claims next door.

As usual, when property was at issue the Code of the West endorsed the use of force. Disputes that festered for years might suddenly erupt in bloody shootouts like the one documented in the photograph at left.

With the arrival of barbed wire in the 1870s, cattle barons put up fences that blocked others from vital sources of water. Once again, the code was inconsistent. A rancher who strung a fence to protect a stream he claimed as his own would cut someone else's wire in a heartbeat if it kept his stock from water.

Gunfight at the Berry Spread——
Kansas farmers Daniel, Alpheus, and Burch Berry lie dead and Roy Berry (left, rear) wounded after a confrontation with a wealthy rancher, Chauncey Dewey, and his men. To the outrage of local farmers, everyone in the Dewey crew was exonerated of murder.

# Deadlines and Gunnysackers

Hard feeling also erupted between cattlemen and sheepmen. Sheepherders were looked down on, their stock accused of destroying range grass and leaving an odor intolerable to cattle. Even conservationist John Muir likened sheep to a plague of locusts. Merely ordering mutton at a restaurant in cattle country was considered a provocative act.

Cattle ranchers marked the range with arbitrary boundaries, or deadlines, that a sheepman crossed at his peril. A note left for one Montana herder read, "If you take your sheep to Powder River bring your coffin along. You will need it." A sheepherder who persisted might be visited by night riders known as gunnysackers for the masks they wore. Some gunnysackers put a fright into herders and scattered their flocks; others used violence. Valuable sheepdogs were shot. Sheep were clubbed, shot, dynamited, set afire, or stampeded over cliffs. In one incident near Rifle, Colorado, gunnysackers drowned nearly 4,000 sheep. The next day, townspeople found notes in the streets with the warning, "Mum's the word."

Making an Abattoir on the Range——
Masked cattlemen hold two sheepherders at gunpoint while destroying their flock. Though sheep and dogs were the usual targets, human blood was occasionally spilled as well.

# Law at the End of a Rope

**D**runkenness, banditry, and violence plagued the boom towns of the West, often provoking frightened citizens to take the law into their own hands. The result was sometimes ghastly.

But one Montana schoolmaster, after watching a gang of vigilantes gun down a cutthroat criminal, wrote, "Is it lawful for citizens to slay robbers and murderers when they catch them; or ought they to wait for policemen where there are none, or put them in penitentiaries not yet erected?"

Even in towns boasting sheriffs and marshalls, lynch law flourished—condoned, as often as not, by the authorities. In 1864, after desperados murdered more than two dozen settlers in Aurora, Nevada, vigilantes rounded up several of the killers and hastily erected a gallows at the doorstep of the town armory. As a U.S. marshal looked on, a "citizens' court" convicted and hanged the four men. Hangings were usually a last resort, even for vigilance committees, but by the end of the century, Western vigilantes had put some 700 alleged criminals to death.

**A** Judgment That Allows No Appeal——
Dragged from jail by a mob of angry citizens in Minneapolis in 1882, an accused rapist named Frank McManus meets his grisly end—hanged by the neck from a leafless tree.

The bustling main street of Nebraska City in 1865 attests to the town's growth from trading post to the picture of Western prosperity in only 10 years.

# EARLY IN 1867, GRENVILLE DODGE, CHIEF ENGINEER FOR THE UNION PACIFIC

Railroad, led a small surveying party into the foothills of the Rockies in the southeast corner of what would become the state of Wyoming. He was looking for a suitable site for a new town, to be called Cheyenne, that would serve as a repair center for rolling stock and a base camp for the construction crews who were rapidly extending the Union Pacific northwest from Julesburg, Colorado Territory, some 140 miles away. Dodge and his men spent long hours on horseback, but each night they had little more than saddle sores to show for their efforts. Finally, at the end of one arduous day, the engineer decided he had looked enough. He reined to a halt, dismounted, and took a hatchet from his saddlebag. Burying it in the ground, he said, "By God, Cheyenne will be right *here!*"

The capricious birth of the future state capital differed little from that of countless other towns conceived by railroads in the last half of the 19th century. Survey teams routinely struck out ahead of track-laying crews to choose townsites from the millions of acres the federal government had granted to the railroads. The locations were then plotted and sold to offset the huge costs of the transcontinental project. Speculators swarmed close behind the surveying parties, hoping to buy when the tracks were still far from town and land prices low, and to sell when the lines approached and prices shot sky-high.

Of course, railroaders and land sharks weren't the only ones creating towns after the Civil War. Even as the Union Pacific was stretching westward, merchants in Kansas, Nebraska, and the Dakota Territory were establishing villages where farmers could buy supplies, tend to occasional legal matters, and gossip. Gold- and silver-hungry prospectors were erecting rough-and-tumble towns in Colorado and Nevada, as were loggers in Oregon and buffalo hunters and cattle ranchers in Kansas. Immigrants from many countries, freed slaves, prohibitionists, vegetarians, religious colonists, and other groups were also founding towns. And cities were blossoming along numerous wagon trails and steamboat routes simply because the spots proved to be convenient stopping places for westering travelers.

The result was a network of communities as diverse as all of America.

Congress touched off the building boom by making the formation of such towns relatively easy—and profitable. Under the terms of the Townsite Act of 1867, a group of 100 or more settlers could form a so-called township company by obtaining a charter from a territorial or state legislature. Then for $400, or $1.25 an acre, they could withdraw 320 acres from the federal domain and take possession.

Once a few additional legal requirements were met, most companies wasted little time in commissioning a surveying team to make a town plat. They divided the land into salable units, creating a neat grid of streets and blocks that reproduced well in printed promotional materials. This was no small consideration for those entrepreneurs who began towns purely as speculative ventures. Their task was a stiff one: to persuade prospective settlers back East to buy lots in the frontier town, even though in almost every instance the municipality existed only on paper—and in the dreams of its founders.

To make a sale, the entrepreneurs—known as boomers after the building boom they hoped to set off—routinely larded their spiels with superlatives and dotted their placards with exclamation points. "Sale! Lots, Lots, Lots!!!" read one early handbill, advertising Pawnee, Kansas Territory. "The situation is such as scarcely to admit a doubt of its becoming in a short time a large and important place!" To be sure, many towns did exactly that, including Cheyenne. Soon after Grenville Dodge buried his hatchet there, a Union Pacific land agent began selling lots 66 feet by 132 feet for $150 each. A month later, the parcels were reselling for $1,000, and soon thereafter for $2,500. But not every town lived up to its optimistic sales pitch.

One underachiever was Sumner, Kansas, established three miles south of Atchison along the Missouri River by J. P. Wheeler, a freckle-faced real-estate speculator from Massachusetts. To publicize his town, Wheeler had his Eastern agents distribute a colorful sales brochure that described a thriving metropolis with wide avenues, fine residences, a machine shop, a hotel, schools, and churches. An illustration showed train tracks running through the town's center and steamboats landing at a riverfront business district. To readers back East, Sumner must have looked like a Western town with little wildness remaining to be tamed. But appearances could be deceiving.

As would-be Sumnerites soon discovered, there was little more to the city than a muddy street, a few general stores, and some ram-

shackle dwellings roofed with canvas or hay thatching. One outraged transplant cursed Wheeler's brochure as an "engraved romance" and a "chromatic triumph of lithographed mendacity." But mendacity did not defeat the hardy; in time, most swallowed their losses, packed up again, and moved on to another promising frontier town.

Such courage was a virtue born of necessity, because disappointments were many on the frontier. Fires, for instance, were a routine disaster, as the citizens of Alliance, Nebraska, came to know all too well. In the 11 months between August 1892 and July 1893, prairie fires savaged their tiny farming community three times.

Cholera, typhoid, diphtheria, and other scourges also beset the Westerners, partly because of a lack of qualified doctors, but also because of terrible sanitation. Drinking water was commonly drawn from sloughs and streams that did double duty as town dumps. Sewage ran in the streets and mingled with the droppings of horses and other animals to produce an unsavory curbside stew. Not everyone took the matter as a life-and-death issue. Patrons at a saloon in Dodge City, Kansas, are said to have looked on gleefully as one unlucky cowpoke stepped into a puddle and sank up to his belt buckle.

Despite such unpleasantness, even the most godforsaken frontier communities stood at least a fighting chance of making it, provided that they started out with certain essential characters. Next to the blacksmith, the most important of these was the newspaper editor, who was often one of the town's first citizens. The editor's job (at least in the beginning) was not so much to gather news as to attract new townspeople, and there was never a moment to lose: The first issue of many a paper was published even before a roof could be built over the press that printed it. A hotelier and a saloon keeper, partners in accommodating and entertaining wayfarers and prospective settlers, were also vital. More often than not, however, the proprietor of the general store became the town's most popular figure. He sold not only guns and chaps, bootjacks and baby carriages, but also Bibles for the devout and whiskey for the sinners. (*See pages 180-181.*)

The grandest of all such stores was probably Wright, Beverley and Company, which had something for everyone but specialized in catering to cowboys. "The jingling spur, the carved ivory-handled Colt, or the suit of velveteen, and the many, many other Texas necessaries, you here find by the gross or cord," reported Ford County, Kansas, *Globe* in 1877. The store's success transformed its principal

Settlers line up to conduct business amidst the tents and other makeshift shelters of five-day-old Guthrie in 1889. The town was formed literally overnight after Congress declared 3,000 square miles of Indian Territory, now part of Oklahoma, open to settlement.

owner, Robert M. Wright, into a wealthy and powerful man. But the establishment was only one of his many accomplishments. The most famous was the town he helped create—Dodge City.

Named after a nearby army fort, Dodge City became known as the wildest of all Western towns during its heyday from 1872 to 1885. Called the "Bibulous Babylon of the Plains" by the editor of the Kinsley, Kansas, *Graphic,* it was said to be a place where liquor ran like water, music played from dusk till dawn, and disputes were settled on the spot, in a hail of bullets. Most of this was reputation rather than reality. The saloons, for example, never numbered more than 14. Disputes were usually settled with fists, not six-shooters, and were rarely fatal: Dodge's homicide rate, about 1.5 deaths a year, was no higher than in other cow towns. And not one person was ever hanged in the city—legally or otherwise.

Wright and several others created Dodge in July 1872 to take advantage of the imminent arrival of the Atchison, Topeka, and Santa Fe Railroad, and of the multitudes of buffalo roaming the countryside. The year before, tanners in Germany had found a way to turn buffalo hide into a leather durable enough to be made into shoes, harnesses, and other items. Overnight, a bull hide was worth as much as $3.50, and droves of hunters set out to shoot their fortunes.

Traditionally, the hunters killed alone, with only a small party of hired hands to do the skinning. Yet a seasoned outdoorsman with a

# MERCHANTS OF COMFORT ON THE HARSH FRONTIER

Few frontier communities were lucky enough to start out with the full array of skills and talents that contributed to the convenience of life back East. Most made do with the bare minimum—a newspaper, a saloon, a general store, a smithy and livery, perhaps a hotel—and advertised for services that were missing.

"What we want now most is mechanics," pleaded the *Kansas Weekly Herald* in 1854, at a time when the word *mechanic* was used to describe any skilled artisan. "We have several kinds but not enough of them. We have not got a Sadler, Shoemaker, Tailor, Cabinet Maker, Hatter, nor Milliner in the place."

Until such specialists arrived, most towns relied on the resourcefulness and versatility of their citizens—something newspaperman Thomas A. McNeal learned when he set out to have a shave in Medicine Lodge, Kansas, in 1879. He was directed not to a barbershop but to a livery stable, where for 15¢ one of the hands set aside his horseshoeing implements, stropped a razor on his boot top, and scraped away McNeal's grime and whiskers.

Such improvisation usually proved temporary in thriving towns, however. In time, not only a barber but also a dry-goods merchant, a dressmaker, and other vendors opened for business, typically in false-fronted shops on Main Street (*right, top*). The shebang, or general store (*middle*), added such luxuries as frilly bonnets and chased gold watches to its inventory. And, if the town were truly fortunate, a doctor opened a drugstore (*bottom*), where he filled prescriptions and sold soap when he wasn't treating the infirm or injured.

—Main Street, Guthrie, Oklahoma—

—Fisher's General Store, Oakley, Kansas—

—McCarty's Drugstore, Dodge City, Kansas—

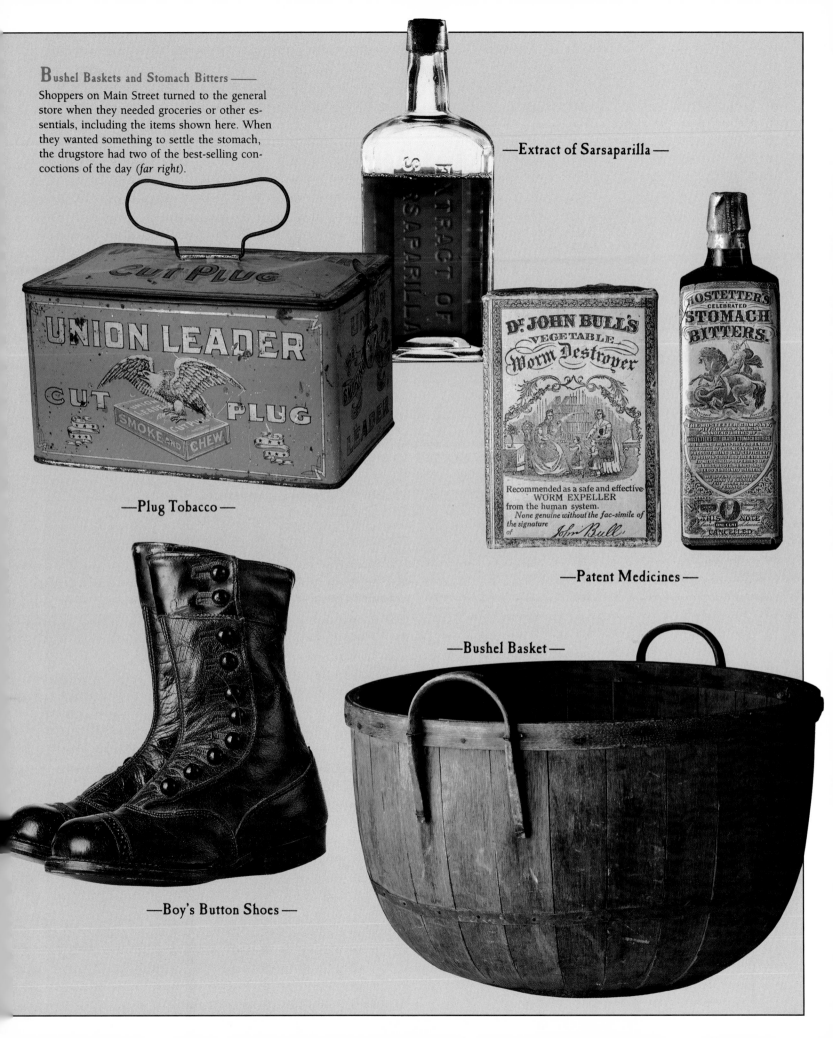

**B**ushel Baskets and Stomach Bitters —
Shoppers on Main Street turned to the general
store when they needed groceries or other essentials, including the items shown here. When
they wanted something to settle the stomach,
the drugstore had two of the best-selling con-
coctions of the day *(far right)*.

— Extract of Sarsaparilla —

— Plug Tobacco —

— Patent Medicines —

— Bushel Basket —

— Boy's Button Shoes —

Residents of Denver gather on May 20, 1864, on the banks of rain-swollen Cherry Creek, which the night before washed away a sawmill, a church, a newspaper, and several stores, as well as city hall and all its records. Some 20 Denverites lost their lives.

big, breechloading Sharps rifle could bring down dozens of buffalo a day—sometimes more. According to the *Dodge City Times,* one hunter killed 120 in just 40 minutes. A visiting Britisher marveled at the "continual line of putrescent carcasses" along the banks of the Arkansas River, not far from Dodge City. The stench of decay, he wrote, rendered the air "pestilential and offensive to the last degree."

The buffalo craze, combined with the arrival of the Santa Fe in September 1872, spurred rapid growth in Dodge. Hard on the heels of railroad workers and hunters came traders and land speculators. A harness shop opened, as did a hotel, a smithy, a restaurant, a dry-goods vendor, and a hardware store. Wright opened a supply shop and started shipping buffalo hides, meat, and bones back east. "Business began," he wrote, "and such a business! The streets of Dodge were lined with wagons, bringing in hides and meat and getting supplies from early morning to late at night."

But the early prosperity was short-lived. By 1875 the hides being shipped east far exceeded the demand. Prices tumbled. Though only three years old, Dodge needed a fresh source of income—a source cattle ranchers in the state of Texas were in the process of delivering.

For many years Texans had been driving their longhorns to rail-heads in central Kansas for shipment east. At each one—Abilene, Ellsworth, Wichita, and Ellis—the animals kicked up a storm of controversy. The cattle carried a microscopic tick, one that brought

no harm to its host but caused a deadly fever in milk cows raised by local farmers. To protect livestock, the Kansas legislature at first limited longhorns to the western, largely uninhabited part of the state. But as more grangers moved into Kansas, lawmakers extended the quarantine zone to the west and south. By 1876 only Dodge City and a few lesser towns along the Santa Fe were open to longhorns.

Seizing the opportunity, Wright quickly let the Texans know their cattle would be welcome in Dodge, ticks and all. He sent agents south to spread the word about "wholesome measures" recently adopted by its citizens. These included an increase in the number of hotels and restaurants and reductions in price on "liquor, cigars, tobacco, etc., for the especial trade of the cattle men." Wright's hustling paid immediate dividends: In 1877 almost 23,000 head of long-horn cattle thundered into Dodge—more than a quarter of the total carried east on the Santa Fe that year—and more would follow.

With them came the Texas cowboy. After months of tedious and boring work on the range, he typically arrived in town with money to burn and nothing to do but find a good time. For most, this meant cleaning up and then finding an eating house that offered "fancy groceries." Then he might watch a burlesque show at the Comique Theater, a combination bar, gambling hall, and stage that the cow-

### Westward Expansion's Ghostly Legacy

Sometimes abandoned towns vanished, as did Julesburg, Colorado Territory, in 1867, when workers for the Union Pacific threw everything—furniture, heavy equipment, even whole houses—onto an immense freight train and rolled it down the line. In contrast, when the mining town of Elkhorn, Montana, failed in the 1890s, its residents simply up and went, leaving bullet-hole-ridden buildings like this saloon and meeting hall to creak in the breeze. Still standing today, they serve as melancholy monuments to the high hopes and dashed dreams of Elkhorn's founders.

punchers referred to as the "Comikew," or pay 25¢ for a spin with a dance-hall girl. Many of these women were "as straight as a deaconess," remembered Eddie Foy, who performed at the Comique in 1878. "I knew some who were widows, some married ones with worthless or missing husbands, and not a few of them had children. Their job was to dance with the men, talk to them, perhaps flirt with them a little bit and induce them to buy drinks—and no more."

But for many cowboys, having fun meant "stepping up to the sinner's bench," as one Western townsman put it—drinking rotgut whiskey, gambling, and whoring. In Dodge, as Robert Wright remembered later, "All could be had for a price."

Yet during the daylight hours, according to one reporter, Dodge was "as quiet and orderly as a country village in Indiana." Photographers made portraits of families, barbers trimmed hair and waxed mustaches, and members of the Dodge City Cowboy Band tuned up for their next concert. Though they were a people of strong religious conviction—a nondenominational church was erected in Dodge as early as 1876—most were willing to adopt a live-and-let-live attitude as far as the cattle trade was concerned.

And with good reason. Property-tax revenues grew so quickly after the longhorns arrived, the city in 1879 was able to replace its small, wooden schoolhouse with a two-story brick structure with arched windows and a cupola. And voluntary donations from sinners—cowboys, gamblers, and "soiled doves"—helped pay for church buildings opened in 1880 and 1882.

However, Dodge's days as a cow town, like its days as a buffalo center, were numbered. In 1885, under mounting pressure from concerned farmers, the Kansas legislature again extended the longhorn quarantine line, this time all the way to the western border of the state. The end of the yearly cattle drives robbed Dodge of its economic and social lifeblood. "Dodge City, once famous for its extraordinary prosperity, its lavishness in prodigality and possession of wealth, at one fell swoop was reduced to extreme poverty," Wright noted. Businesses failed, grazing land and other property was sold at panic prices, and the cowboy vanished from the scene. Yet, Dodge City survived. And in surviving, the city became an icon of the Wild West and a symbol for the spirit of the people who tamed it. "Hurrah for little Dodge!" Wright would boast many years later. "She has a bigger heart, for her size, than any town in Kansas."

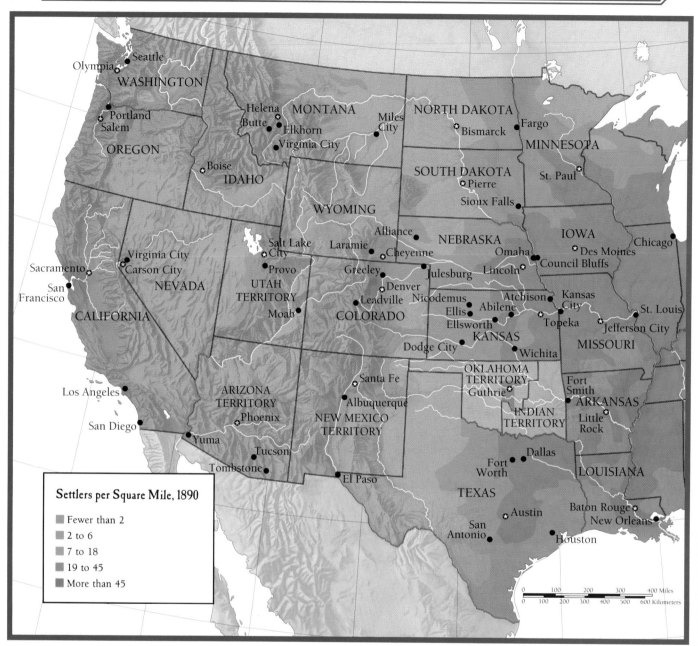

The Vanishing Frontier Line

In 1890, after almost 30 years of settlement abetted by the generous terms of the Homestead Act, steamboat travel, improved roads, and new rail lines, precious little of the West remained unclaimed. In fact, so many people were residing between the Mississippi River and the Pacific Ocean that the Bureau of the Census announced

that it could no longer draw a line to mark the frontier, which was defined as an area with fewer than two settlers per square mile.

Instead, as shown on this map, the region was mottled with isolated bodies of settlement, some populated by as many as 45 settlers per square mile, and dotted with

hundreds of towns, only a handful of which are represented here. Many of the new ones would die within a few years of their birth, the victims of poor planning, bad luck, or both. But others—Dodge City, Santa Fe, and Denver among them—would do more than survive; they would become icons of the Wild West.

# A WELCOME FOR ALL COMERS

In the second half of the 19th century, immigrants from every continent staked claims in the American West, a land of seemingly unlimited opportunity. Scandinavians came to Minnesota, the Irish to the Dakotas, the English to Utah. And they arrived in such numbers that some Western mining towns had a higher percentage of foreign-born residents than either Boston or New York City.

The immigrants were looking for places where they could get a fresh start on life, strike it rich, or like the Mormons, worship as they chose. Driven from previous settlements in Ohio, Missouri, and Illinois, the Saints wandered westward until they came upon a sun-scorched, seemingly inhospitable valley in northern Utah in 1847. There they founded Salt Lake City and, finally far removed from religious persecution, set to work erecting the kingdom of God in granite and mortar *(far right, bottom)*.

Thousands of other Americans—former slaves—joined the westward march following the Civil War. Led by Benjamin Singleton *(right)* and other visionaries, the so-called Exodusters established a handful of small communities on the prairies of Kansas, Colorado, and Oklahoma and tried to make a living working the soil. But with meager skills and little capital and discriminated against by other settlers, they would enjoy little success as farmers. Most would be forced to move again, this time to cities in the North and West, where they became cooks and took other jobs.

---

*"There is abundant room for all good citizens, and no room for loafers or bummers. We want all good people there, who are willing to live by the sweat of their own brow!"*

◆

*Benjamin Singleton*

---

The BLACK MOSES——
"Old Pap" Singleton led as many as 8,000 former slaves to the state of Kansas.

## A Time of Joy ——

A Chinese family gathers to celebrate a wedding in their new hometown—Idaho City, Idaho. They were a small part of a large wave of settlers who reached the American heartland by traveling west to east, rather than east to west.

## A House of Worship ——

Tens of thousands of Mormons watch the emplacement of their Temple's capstone on April 6, 1892, after almost 40 years of back-breaking labor. Together with the Tabernacle, whose huge, arching roof is partially visible at far left, the Temple forms the spiritual core of Salt Lake City.

# A Bargain Struck with the Devil

One of the hard truths of Western economics was that sin paid. Drinking, whoring, and gambling may have brought more than one man to ruin, but they were the economic life's blood of many frontier communities, even those with God-fearing townspeople, such as El Paso, Texas. "The town's Christians who peddled groceries, hardware, mowers, plows, coffins, and mining machinery," said one sharp-penciled merchant, "they knew the thing that brought customers from afar into their stores was El Paso's invitation to step up to the sinner's bench. And they took advantage of it. They even encouraged it!"

Although most saloon owners failed and many prostitutes, in desperation, became alcohol or drug addicts, town business leaders were prepared to look the other way so long as their town grew—provided that establishments like those at right stayed clustered on the edge of the town, in so-called red-light, or tenderloin, districts.

*"There were good and bad saloonkeepers and good and bad saloons. Q.T. ran a high-class place. . . . Across the street was Uncle Sam's place, and quite different in every way. Once when I saw it I wondered, what drew the men to a dirty place like this?"*

◆

*Anne Ellis*

**A Gambler's Paradise——**
Above, miners in a well-appointed Leadville, Colorado, saloon gamble their hard-won earnings on roulette and other games of chance while a waiter brings refreshments.

**Through the Eyes of a Child——**
Raised in poverty in a Colorado mining camp, Anne Ellis, like the prostitutes and saloon keepers she met as a young girl, hoped for a better life. "I have known in my life only the most ordinary people," she wrote, "and always like to read of them, so I can and will write of just such folks as myself." Her memoirs would earn her an honorary degree from the University of Colorado.

### Soiled Doves
Prostitutes share the laps and drinks of a pair
of ham-handed patrons in a saloon in Denver's
red-light district.

# A Hot Time in the Old Town Tonight

For most of the hopeful emigrants who came west, overnight success and riches proved as elusive as they had been in the East. Faced with failure and frustration, they eagerly escaped to the entertainment offered by touring performers such as the trio pictured here and by a series of speakers that included the feminist Amelia Bloomer and preacher Henry Ward Beecher. British playwright Oscar Wilde, wearing a costume hailed as the most ridiculous ever seen in America, lectured on aestheticism in Leadville, Salt Lake City, and other cities in 1882. When not in the lecture hall or theater, young, active frontier folks made their own fun racing horses, playing baseball, holding quilting and spelling bees, and enjoying other pursuits, some of which are shown on the following pages.

A Shapely Prince——
Actress Adah Isaacs Menken titillated Westerners in the 1860s with her portrayal of Ivan Mazeppa, a Tartar prince who is stripped naked and bound to a wild stallion in punishment for falling in love with an already-betrothed woman. Only the horse actually appeared on stage nude.

A Wisecracking Irishman——
Song-and-dance man Eddie Foy loved to poke fun at his audiences, a practice that endeared him to most Westerners but irked some, including a killer named Ben Thompson, who once aimed his gun at Foy. The entertainer remained calm: "A man accustomed to killing tigers," Foy quipped, "would feel himself belittled if he were asked to go on a squirrel hunt."

A Wealthy Thespian——
Edwin Booth was one of the first actors to tour widely throughout the West. His performances of Shakespeare's tragedies were so popular among the forty-niners he earned as much as $25,000 a month.

The Variety Theater——

Advertisements for local merchants frame a bucolic view of Glacier Park in this Helena, Montana, theater. In such halls, a wide range of entertainers—singers, comedians, acrobats, and other crowd pleasers—performed acts calculated to satisfy every taste, from the maudlin to the bawdy.

## A Band of Cowboys ——

Decked out in chaps, boots, and hats, members of the Dodge City Cowboy Band assemble for a concert in Silverton, Colorado. The band's director—already acting out the cowboy myth—used a six-shooter instead of a baton so he could, as he put it, "kill the first man who strikes a false note."

## Christmas Revels ——

Dressed-up residents of Virginia City, Nevada, celebrate Christmas in 1865 by dancing well into the morning. Social dancing was one of the most cherished, and most common, diversions in the West, even in towns with so few women the men had to dance with each other.

Up to Their Ankles ——
Women in Douglas County, Kansas, practice
their marksmanship and wade in the shallow
waters of a cool pond during an outing in
the 1890s.

# Early Attempts at Urban Renewal

The first citizens of Dodge City and other towns discovered that law and order was something they had to enforce for themselves. So they loaded their guns, banded together in so-called vigilance committees, and took to the streets. These shadow lawmen put a good scare into the criminal element but also frightened striking laborers and law-abiding minority citizens as well. Townspeople banned the vigilantes and established the justice system we know today—with court trials, judges, and elected lawmen. The marshall kept the peace in Dodge by ordering every cowboy to check his gun with city founder and store owner Robert Wright *(below)*.

*"When a certain party or parties got too obnoxious to the decent part of the community, they would be notified to leave town, and if they did not go, the vigilantes or respectable citizens would raise up in their might and shoot them to death."*

◆

*Robert M. Wright*

G̲uarantor of the Peace ———

Thirty years after the conclusion of the Civil War, the streets of Lawrence, Kansas, were patrolled by African-American policeman Sam Jeans. Abolitionists founded the city in 1854 in an effort to ensure that Kansas entered the Union as a free state.

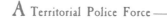

A̲ Territorial Police Force ———

After years of public pressure to rid the territory of bandits and cattle rustlers, the Arizona Rangers were created in 1901. The group poses here in front of a copper mining camp at Morenci, where they had been called to suppress a labor strike.

Gunplay's Sad Outcome ——

Two women and a boy gaze at a pair of dead men sprawled across a wooden sidewalk in Hays City, Kansas. Occasional fatal shootings and other acts of violence among cowboys encouraged a successful movement among Kansas townspeople to ban Texas longhorns.

A New Jail ——

The citizens of Marfa, Texas, erected this isolated but imposing courthouse and jail (below) in 1886, one year after Presidio County residents voted 391 to 302 to make the two-year-old city their county seat.

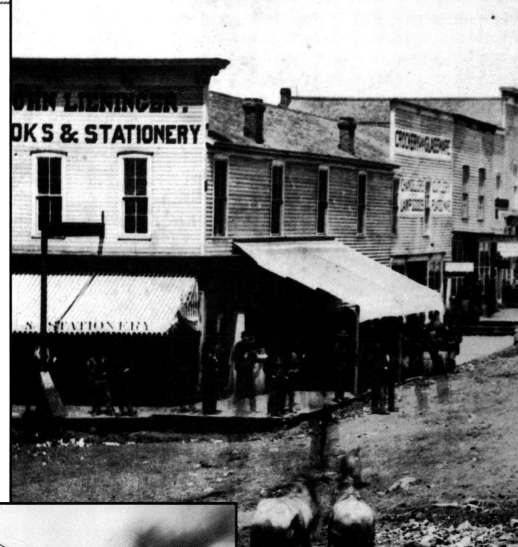

**A Dirty Downtown** ———
Residents in Leadville, Colorado, in 1879 carefully pick their way down Harrison Avenue, the mining town's debris-cluttered main street. Its unkempt appearance was typical of many frontier towns.

**A Fire out of Control** ———
Fire consumes a building in Sterling, Nebraska, as citizens stand by helplessly. In many towns, the fire departments were little more than volunteer bucket brigades furnished with ladders at public expense.

An All-Too Familiar Aftermath——
Townspeople poke through the charred
remains of Creede, Colorado, half of
which was destroyed by a blaze on
June 5, 1892. The silver-mining town
would never fully recover.

THE JUNCTION 105

# The Long Reach of Victorian Civility

Most townspeople fretted about continuing the Victorian customs that they had known back East and talked about "civilizing" or "modernizing" their settlements. One frontier woman admitted that even though she had set down roots in the West, she still wanted to "live East."

For such a person, a wedding like the one at far right was an important indication of a community's stability and permanence. It usually heralded not only the imminent arrival of children—considered the best indicators of a town's future—but also the opening of schools and churches *(following pages),* the enactment of inheritance laws that would provide for the orderly transfer of land and businesses from one owner to another, and the attraction of like-minded families.

Bundles of Joy———

Recent settlers in a frontier town, a husband and wife pose for a portrait with their children, cherished signs of hope for the future.

Well-Schooled Youngsters———

Children link hands during a patriotic pageant at the public school in Scofield, Utah, in the 1890s. Westerners spent more money building schools, reckoned per person, than citizens anywhere else in the nation.

In a show of optimism and camaraderie characteristic of all settlers in the West, an entire band turned out to help the newlyweds at center celebrate their marriage.

## A Picture of a Darkroom Trailblazer

Before 1890, any woman who worked on her own in the field of photography was considered eccentric, to say the least. But as women strived for increased social and economic rights toward the end of the century, the idea of women photographers became more acceptable, and practitioners such as M. E. Tyler, pictured on the cabinet card at left, went into business for themselves. Tyler specialized in portraiture in Ashland, Oregon, in the late 1880s and 1890s. Examples of her work are affixed to her skirt, a common advertising practice of the era, and a portrait of herself adorns the banner.

The Church ——

Though not always this grand, places of worship were typically among the first structures erected in frontier towns. In Dodge City, a church predated the arrival of the Texas longhorns by more than a year.

Promoting the Hometown ——

Members of a Farmersville, Texas, booster club prepare banners bearing the names of city institutions. The women met trains and gave speeches urging wayfarers to consider doing business and settling in Farmersville.

**Learning the Three Rs**

Students work on a reading lesson in a single-room schoolhouse near Horton, Kansas, in the late 1890s. Hanging behind the teacher's desk is an American flag with 45 stars, one for every state but Oklahoma, New Mexico, Arizona, Alaska, and Hawaii, which had yet to join the Union.

# SOLDIERS

Wielding sabers and firing revolvers, a detachment of U.S. cavalrymen blast their way through an Indian war party.

# WHEN AMERICANS SPOKE OF FULFILLING THEIR MANIFEST DESTINY TO

extend U.S. territory from the Atlantic to the Pacific, they ignored a crucial reality: That territory, though a blank space on U.S. maps, was inhabited by hundreds of thousands of Native Americans. The first whites who moved west got along well enough with the people of the land, but in the 1840s, as the trickle of settlers turned into a flood, the Indians took up arms to hold onto their ancestral lands. When the government sent federal troops to subdue them, all-out war ignited. By 1865, in spite of concentrating its strength against the South in the Civil War, the army had forced the Indians to give up most of their territory. Once the Confederacy had surrendered, the federal army could again turn its full attention to the "Indian question." With railroads to be constructed, homesteads to be claimed, and gold to be mined, the country's soldiers were charged with safeguarding any whites who ventured west.

The task was formidable—made more so when Washington shrank the army from a wartime high of 1.5 million soldiers to just 25,000. Men who had earned field promotions to major general were reduced to colonels, while colonels and majors were reduced to captains, and occasionally even sergeants. Still, despite low pay—$16 a month in 1866, cut to $13 in 1869—bad food, and spartan living conditions, the army had no problem filling its ranks.

Men enlisted for many reasons, chief among them the prospect of a secure job. For those who were newly arrived in the country—and nearly half the volunteers fit that description—a job was the first priority. "I was about the greenest thing that ever hit New York," recalled German-born Charles Windolph many years later. An old, German-speaking man, Windolph added, "told me to join the army to learn English so I could amount to something." Still others joined—or rejoined—because they took to army life. At 16, John Ryan ran away from home and lied about his age to fight in the Civil War. When the war ended, a few months of civilian life made him realize where he belonged: "The army fever struck me once more and Nov. 23, 1866, I re-enlisted for five years at Boston." Both Ryan and

Political cartoonist Thomas Nast decried congressional cutbacks in military spending in his caricature of an understrength "skeleton" army, feet entangled in red tape, attempting to guard frontier settlers from the threat of Indian depredations.

Windolph ended up in the Seventh Cavalry, serving under Lieutenant Colonel George Armstrong Custer.

These two, and the thousands of other recruits posted to the West, soon discovered the harsh realities of life at a frontier fort. The days were made up of drills and hard labor, such as chopping down trees for firewood, and the cold, lonely nights offered little relief. Many men turned to gambling, prostitutes, and especially drink. By the 1880s some 4 percent of all American soldiers were hospitalized for alcoholism.

With a government tired of spending money on war, forts suffered from chronic shortages of everything, including ammunition. Soldiers unable to take target practice for lack of bullets were hardly prepared for battle. Worse yet, when government rifles issued to friendly Indians as a gesture of goodwill fell into the wrong hands, soldiers could find themselves on the wrong end of their own weap-

ons—as happened in the years following the Medicine Lodge peace conference of October 1867, when the Cheyenne, Comanche, Kiowa, and Arapaho turned government rifles on the army.

The Medicine Lodge gifts were ill considered to begin with: Less than a year earlier, warriors from some of the same tribes had handed the army one of its worst defeats ever. On December 21, 1866, Colonel Henry Carrington, the commander of Fort Phil Kearny, Wyoming Territory, sent Captain William J. Fetterman and 80 men to pursue a band of Indians that had attacked a woodchopping detachment. Wary of ambushes and aware that Fetterman's departure left the fort vulnerable, the colonel told Fetterman not to pursue the Indians beyond a hill known as Lodge Trail Ridge. But the captain, hungry for glory, ignored his instructions and marched his men past the ridge and into a hail of arrows launched by a combined force of 2,000 Sioux, Cheyenne, and Arapaho warriors. Within just 40 minutes, every soldier was dead. Private William Murphy, a member of the rescue party dispatched by Carrington, recalled the carnage: "All of the bodies were stripped, scalped and mutilated with the exception of two, who were not scalped."

The Fetterman Massacre, as it came to be called, stunned the army and the country at large. Retribution, justified or not, was swift. General William Tecumseh Sherman, whose conduct during the Civil War had earned him a reputation for ruthlessness, sent a message to his superior, Ulysses S. Grant. Sherman urged Grant to "act with vindictive earnestness against the Sioux, even to their extermination, men, women and children." At the same time, General Philip H. Sheridan, commander of all Plains forces, was devising a brutal plan designed to hit the enemy at its weakest.

Sheridan's plan addressed the army's two major problems. First, the Indians' guerrilla tactics were difficult to combat. And second, they moved camp as often as every few days, making them difficult even to find. Sheridan realized that only when the tribes hunkered in their semipermanent winter camps did they present a massed target the army could fight on its own terms. The "winter strategy," as it was known, called for regiments to find these camps and destroy them.

To spearhead the first major campaign, Sheridan picked one of his favorite officers: George Armstrong Custer. A Civil War hero whose daring exploits had earned him a field promotion to major

## Tools for Treating the Wounded Soldier

Although great advances had been made in military surgery during the Civil War, most notably in the widespread use of anesthetics, the survival rate for seriously wounded soldiers on the Western frontier was less than 50 percent. The majority of the instruments in the surgeon's medical kit (*below, left*) were intended for amputations—the only recourse Indian-war doctors had for saving the victims of bone-smashing bullet wounds. Injuries to the head and abdomen were usually fatal.

As much as anything else, the wounded soldier owed his grim prognosis to the vastness of the country in which he had the misfortune to be injured. Being carried for hundreds of miles in mule-borne litters like this one was such agony that it drove one wounded man to beg, "Make this easier for me or kill me."

general at the age of 25, Custer was a lieutenant colonel in the post-war army. But the reduction in rank did little to reduce his ego. He longed to win as much fame fighting Indians as he had fighting Confederates—no matter what the cost. In November of 1868 he led his Seventh Cavalry to a Cheyenne winter camp near the Washita River in what is now Oklahoma.

As Custer prepared to attack at dawn on November 27, a shot rang out from the Indian village and the charge was sounded. John Ryan later described one moment in the savage battle. An Indian woman was trying to escape with a white child when she was overtaken by some troopers. "She seized a butcher's knife," Ryan wrote, "and plunging it into the child's body, killed it instantly. No sooner had she committed this crime than the whole side of her head was blown off by our man."

The Seventh Cavalry killed 103 Indians, slaughtered 800 of their horses, and burned the village. Although most of the Indian dead were women and children, the battle was hailed in military circles as a great victory. But then Custer committed an act of such gross misjudgment that it would haunt him for the rest of his life.

Because he had not bothered to reconnoiter the Cheyenne vil-

—Spencer Model 1865 Carbine —

lage, Custer did not realize that it was one in a long string of encampments. When Major Joel Elliott took off with a small party to pursue survivors, warriors from one of the camps ambushed them. Despite reports of gunfire in Elliott's direction, Custer, anxious to avoid confrontations that might lead to more losses, made only a perfunctory search and then left. The frozen bodies of Elliott and his men were retrieved weeks later.

Abandonment of his own troops did not endear Custer to his men. Many of them already despised him, for he drove them without mercy; setting a blistering pace on one march two years earlier, he had allowed stragglers to be killed by Indians and had ruthlessly executed deserters. But such issues were unimportant; what truly mattered to Custer was his public image: to "link my name not only to present but future generations."

Custer was not above lying to his own superiors to enhance his reputation. In 1874 the Seventh Cavalry was sent to the Black Hills of South Dakota to investigate rumors that the area contained gold. Marching into sacred—and legally protected—Sioux territory, the expedition found little of the precious element. But Custer sent word to Washington that gold could be found "among the roots of the grass." Charles Windolph, who had himself found a few tiny gold specks, believed the strike to be extensive and reflected on how it would affect the Sioux: "All the soldiers in the United States couldn't hold back the tide then. You could sign all the Indian treaties you could pack on a mule, but they wouldn't do any good."

Windolph was right. Waves of trespassing prospectors soon descended on the area. The Sioux, many of whom had been conciliatory toward the whites, ultimately despaired of a peaceful solution and prepared for battle.

Custer's foray into the Black Hills was but one of numerous treaty violations, acts that sowed widespread mistrust and cynicism. One soldier whose behavior was an exception was Lieutenant Colonel George Crook, respected by the fierce mountain-dwelling Indians of Arizona and New Mexico territories.

Crook earned this respect by fighting the Indians in their own style, using guerrilla-type raids and man-to-man combat. This approach was actually a matter of necessity, for Crook enjoyed few of the tactical advantages available to other commanders. Not only did

—Colt Model 1873 Revolver —

In 1873 the U.S. Army began replacing Civil War vintage weapons such as the Spencer carbine with .45-caliber single-shot breechloading rifles and carbines manufactured at the Springfield, Massachusetts, Armory. Frontier cavalry soldiers carried the Springfield carbine and single-action Colt revolvers. Their Indian foes used the traditional bow and arrows and war club along with firearms such as the muzzleloading Leman rifle, issued as part of treaty agreements, and rapid-fire Henry and Winchester rifles, obtained from civilian traders.

—U.S. Model 1873 Carbine —

—Winchester Model 1866 Rifle—

the Southwest's warm weather preclude winter campaigns but its terrain was too treacherous for massed assaults.

The key to Crook's success lay in an old Southwestern proverb: It takes an Apache to catch an Apache. Using Apache scouts—easily found among the group's often warring factions—the colonel located hideouts that the white troops would never have found on their own. One of the most formidable was Skeleton Cave, a natural cavern in the side of a cliff overlooking the Salt River. The Yavapai Indians were using the cave as a base for launching attacks on settlers, and in December of 1872, about 220 of Crook's men, led by Captain William Brown, set out to capture it. Brown mounted a direct attack on the cave with half his men and sent the other half, under Captain James Burns, to guard the rear against ambush.

The siege quickly turned into a standoff, with approximately 110 Indians sheltered deep within the cave and as many soldiers on a ridge some 40 yards away. Brown finally broke the impasse by ordering his men to fire at the cave's sloping roof. The bullets shattered against the hard surface and ricocheted deep inside, forcing the Indians to the mouth of the cave. At that point, Captain Burns unexpectedly joined the battle. Burns had led his men to the cliff above the entrance to the cave, where they began rolling large boulders over the edge. When the dust cleared, nearly 100 Yavapai were dead—shot, crushed, or both. The victory was a strategic turning point: Federal troops had proved they could defeat these formidable warriors in their deepest strongholds.

With the demoralized Southwestern Indians on the run, General Sheridan called on Crook to play a role in his plan to defeat the Northern Plains Indians once and for all—and to secure the gold fields in the Dakotas. Harassed by prospectors in the Black Hills, large numbers of Sioux and Cheyenne had gathered near the Yellowstone River in Montana Territory and were preparing for battle. Sheridan proposed to force them back onto their reservations with a three-pronged offensive: Crook would come north from Fort Fetterman, Wyoming; Colonel John Gibbon would lead a column east from Fort Ellis, Montana; and General Alfred Terry would command a force that included Custer and the Seventh Cavalry heading west from Fort Abraham Lincoln, Dakota Territory. As it happened, Crook was checked by a Sioux attack, and the force that Sheridan had planned on was substantially reduced.

—Apache War Club—

—Leman Indian Treaty Rifle, circa 1855 —

Meanwhile, General Terry had decided on a strategy. Learning from his scouts that the Indians had camped near the Little Bighorn River, he ordered Custer and the Seventh to march south along Rosebud Creek to the eastern side of the camp, while Terry himself would lead Gibbon's men south up the Bighorn River. Custer would drive the Indians north into the arms of Terry and Gibbon.

Custer reached his mark first and, fearing that he had been spotted, prepared to attack at once. All signs indicated an enormous Indian presence, but, using tactics that had worked before, he chose to split his regiment into four parts. Major Marcus Reno would take 175 men south of the Indian encampment, while Captain Frederick Benteen would move with a force of 115 from the west, leaving Custer with 210 men. These three assault battalions would form a miniature version of Sheridan's original attack force, while the pack train would follow with a 135-man escort.

According to John Ryan, the plan began well enough: "Reno's battalion started down the valley, first on a trot, and then at a gallop, marching in columns of twos. A very brave young officer in command of the scouts, rode ahead. He swung his hat around in the air, and sung out to them, 'Thirty days furlough to the man who gets the first scalp!' " But the Indians counterattacked and routed Reno's companies, and when Benteen came to the major's aid, Custer's battalion was left to face as many as 1,000 warriors on its own. Although Custer and his men fought courageously—Indians later spoke of the bravery shown by "Long Hair" and his soldiers—in less than an hour, they were all dead. Reno and Benteen were besieged for two days but were rescued by Terry's belated arrival.

Custer's Last Stand was the watershed of the Indian wars. Never again could the Native Americans fight with the strength they had amassed at the Little Bighorn. Moreover, the U.S. Army was now more determined than ever to force the Indians to stay on their reservations. Over the next 15 years, expanded regiments of cavalry and infantry—filled with recruits dubbed Custer Avengers—slashed through the Plains.

The last great campaign of the Indian wars was the pursuit of the Chiricahua Apache warrior known as Geronimo. Starting in the 1870s, Geronimo surrendered to federal authority on several occasions, only to escape his reservation to make a living raiding settlers.

Measuring five square feet, the regimental flag of the Second Cavalry was carried by all mounted troops of the U.S. Army. Infantry units staggered under a much larger banner, 36 feet square. Unlike Civil War troops, who charged into the fray with sabers rattling and flags flying, Indian-war soldiers rarely carried the colors into battle.

But in 1886, pursued by General Nelson Miles and 5,000 soldiers, the aging, battle-weary renegade turned himself in for the last time, bringing with him his band of 38 men, women, and children.

Although the pitched battles had ended, relations between whites and Indians did not improve. The federal government had forced the various tribes onto reservations and compelled them to abandon their nomadic ways. But reservation farmland was generally poor, and government rations were meager. By the late 1880s many people were starving and without hope. In their desperation, the Sioux embraced a new religion.

The Ghost Dance, which had originated in the Southwest, involved ritualistic dancing that was supposed to offer its adherents glimpses of their honored dead. In adopting the religion, the Sioux added their own touch: ornamented shirts, called ghost shirts, which they claimed made them impervious to the white man's bullets.

The army attempted to quash the movement, ordering its hired Sioux reservation police to arrest the venerable Hunkpapa Sioux

# THE DISCIPLINE AND PRIDE OF THE BUFFALO SOLDIERS

When the post-Civil War army was reorganized in 1866, four of the newly created regiments—the 24th and 25th infantries and 9th and 10th cavalries—were made up of African-American enlistees. All four regiments would see extensive service on the Western frontier. The Plains Indians dubbed them "buffalo soldiers," perhaps because of the heavy overcoats they wore or the texture of their hair, or because the troops were often as hard to bring down in a fight as the revered, hard-charging buffalo. In any case, the troopers bore the sobriquet with pride.

The military offered African-Americans a rare opportunity for achievement in a bigoted society, and as a result, their regiments had the lowest desertion and the highest reenlistment rates in the frontier army. At a time when most soldiers were scorned as misfits, the deportment of the buffalo soldiers set them apart as paragons of military discipline. "The prejudice against the colored soldiers seems to be without foundation," one Montana newspaper reported; "there are no better troops in the service." But racism was still a huge obstacle—a point brought home when Lieutenant Henry O. Flipper *(right)*, quartermaster at a small Texas outpost, was cashiered on trumped-up charges in 1882.

Henry O. Flipper, who had been born a slave, was the first African-American to graduate from West Point. Unjustly dismissed for embezzlement, he went on to become an engineer, editor, and high-ranking official in the Interior Department. His name was finally cleared in 1976.

Three months after the clash at Wounded Knee in 1890, an unidentified Ninth Cavalry corporal was photographed at Pine Ridge, the South Dakota reservation that saw the last fighting of the Indian wars. The buffalo soldiers played a major role in the grueling winter campaign.

Clad in full-dress uniforms, African-American soldiers of Company B, 25th U.S. Infantry, stand at attention outside their barracks at Fort Randall, Dakota Territory. Before coming to the Northern Plains in 1880, these soldiers had battled Apaches along the Texas-Mexico border.

chief Sitting Bull, alleged to be a Ghost Dance leader. On December 15, 1890, when the guards tried to take Sitting Bull into custody, he resisted. In the ensuing scuffle, he was shot in the back of the head.

Afraid the army had come to kill them all, a number of Sitting Bull's followers fled the reservation. But two weeks later, they found themselves surrounded by soldiers of the Seventh Cavalry—Custer's old command—at Wounded Knee Creek, South Dakota. Captain Edward Godfrey recorded what happened on December 29, as Colonel James Forsyth attempted to disarm the Indians: "The medicine man was exhorting the warriors that the ghost shirt would protect them from the bullets of the soldiers," Godfrey wrote. "Major Forsyth forbid him from exhorting, and the medicine man threw a handful of dust into the air. A warrior fired a pistol shot, which was followed by other shots, and then the firing became general."

Withering fire killed nearly half of the 350 Sioux men, women, and children at Wounded Knee. For three days, while a blizzard raged, the bodies were left where they had fallen. Hastening to the field from Chicago, Forsyth's superior, General Miles, surveyed the scene and proclaimed the incident "a most abominable, criminal military blunder and a horrible massacre of women and children."

For the Plains Indians, Wounded Knee was the last act of defiance. There would be no more battles. But the veterans of the frontier army would take their memories of battle well into the 20th century. Sergeant John Ryan was discharged in 1876 and became a police captain in Newton, Massachusetts, where he lived until 1926. German immigrant Charles Windolph, whose bravery at the Little Bighorn won him the Medal of Honor and a promotion to sergeant, retired from the army in 1883. He married and went to work in the gold mines of South Dakota. Windolph, the last white survivor of Custer's Last Stand, died in 1950.

The memory of George Armstrong Custer was kept alive by his adoring wife, Elizabeth. In numerous writings over the next 57 years, the widow sought to immortalize her husband as a brilliant warrior. A different sort of memoir came from Indian-war veteran Lieutenant Willam Roe. "The stories of Washita, Wounded Knee, Little Big Horn and the Yellowstone will be told in coming centuries," he wrote, "when perhaps a new civilization shall have banished forever injustice, brutality and organized murder."

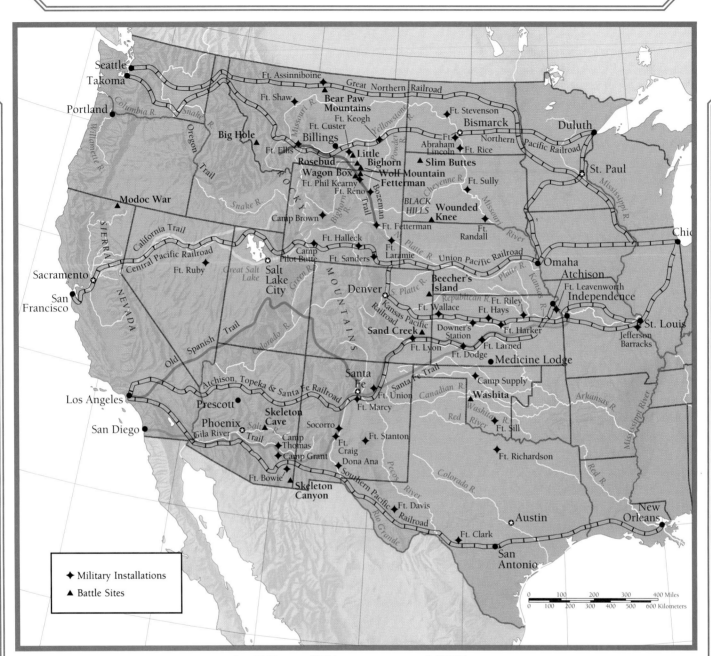

# A Vast Theater of War

From the end of the Civil War in 1865 to the last decade of the 19th century, a woefully understrength U.S. Army was charged with safeguarding the settlement of nearly 2.5 million square miles of Western territory. Overland wagon routes such as the Bozeman and Oregon trails and five new transcontinental rail lines carried an inexorable tide of emigrants into Indian homelands, in flagrant violation of treaties intended to protect the territories from white incursion. The resulting violent confrontations brought the military into action.

Most frontier soldiers operated from widely scattered camps and forts strategically established near railroads and trails. These outposts were staging areas for military offensives that tried to force the Indians onto government reservations.

Over the course of three decades, the Indian wars were fought in countless skirmishes and dozens of pitched battles throughout the Great Plains from Dakota Territory to New Mexico. Although it was understrength, the U.S. Army ultimately won—a victory that cost the Plains Indians their ancestral way of life.

# THE MEN
# IN THE RANKS

**W**hen Lieutenant Colonel George Armstrong Custer decided to dispatch a last messenger before launching his doomed attack at Little Bighorn, the courier he selected was Giovanni Martini—a young Italian whose command of English was decidedly shaky. That a man who had arrived in the United States barely three years earlier would be entrusted with so fateful a duty was not at all unusual; nearly half of the men serving with the ill-fated Seventh Cavalry that day were not Americans by birth.

Census records, enlistment forms, and studies made by the adjutant general of the army reveal that 45 percent of the personnel serving in a typical American regiment of the 1870s were foreign born. Slightly more than 20 percent of these immigrants-in-arms were Irish, 12 percent German, and 7 percent English—figures that are remarkably consistent with period percentages of foreign immigration to the United States. In a comment reflective of the ethnic bias of the time, the editor of the *Army and Navy Journal* noted that foreign-born enlistees were "patient and plodding," thus embodying "the instinct of military subordination."

The large number of newly arrived immigrants who were willing to accept the spartan conditions and harsh discipline of the Regular Army for a scant $13 a month reflected the period's economic uncertainty. America during the 1870s was rocked by a series of financial panics that cost many workers their jobs. Whether foreign or native born, those whose lack of education barred them from other opportunities had little choice but the requisite five-year term of enlistment. One colonel conceded that of the troops assigned to his command "the large majority are driven to enlistment by absolute want."

On the Western frontier, these reluctant warriors confronted not only hardship and boredom but the always looming prospect of a violent and brutal death. Nonetheless, when the survivors looked back on their army days, many romanticized their experience with an aura of adventure. "With my leg over the saddle, pocket full of ammunition and my trusty Spencer in my hand," one old sergeant recalled, "the world was a good place to live, and life held no cares."

**C**harles Windolph, Seventh Cavalry——
Unable to find work in New York, German-born Charles Windolph joined the army to learn English but wound up serving 11 years. He attained the rank of first sergeant, won the Medal of Honor for his bravery at the Little Bighorn, and at his death in 1950 was the last white survivor of that famous battle.

*"You felt like you were somebody. . . . You were a part of a proud outfit that had a fighting reputation, and you were ready for a fight or a frolic."*

◆

*Charles Windolph*

## The Fetterman Massacre

On December 21, 1866, Captain William J. Fetterman and his 80-man detachment were annihilated by Sioux, Cheyenne, and Arapaho warriors near Fort Phil Kearny, Wyoming. A highly imaginative engraving of the vainglorious captain's last stand that appeared in *Harper's Weekly* played to exaggerated notions of the danger awaiting soldiers on the frontier.

## John Ryan, Seventh Cavalry

Despite three Civil War battle wounds, 21-year-old John Ryan succumbed to adventure's call—what he termed "army fever"—and signed on with the Seventh Cavalry. The son of Irish immigrants, Ryan was described by his commander as "brave, capable and trustworthy."

# Garrisoning the Frontier

The life of a soldier in the West revolved around his post. Each isolated fort was a self-contained community that adhered to the daily rituals and obligations of military duty in strict accordance with army regulations. The largely ceremonial functions of guard mount and dress parade *(right)* were augmented by arduous fatigue duties—felling and hauling timber for lumber and fuel, tending to horses and livestock, or harvesting vegetables from the post garden.

The effort involved in simply keeping a post functioning, particularly in the winter months, worked to the detriment of drill and combat readiness. This dangerous state was heightened by the fact that the army continued to fight as it had during the Civil War, despite the completely different nature of Indian warfare. In the end, though, alcoholism and desertion, prompted by the sterility of life on post, caused more casualties than did bullets.

Parade Ground Rituals ——

Arrayed in column of companies, an infantry regiment undergoes the daily inspection of arms at Fort Yates, North Dakota—named for an officer slain with Custer at Little Bighorn.

Training for the Field ——

A group of cavalry soldiers gather at their carbine range amid sandy scrub. In order to conserve ammunition and reduce military spending, an 1872 directive allotted each soldier a scant 90 rounds a year for target practice. In the wake of Custer's defeat the army finally instituted a course of instruction that rewarded sharpshooters with prizes and furloughs.

**B**attling the Elements ———
Troopers of the First Cavalry assemble for fatigue duty at wintry Fort Keogh, Montana. Soldiers stationed on the Northern Plains endured sub-zero temperatures for weeks on end, braving the elements in bulky buffalo coats and overshoes. General Nelson A. Miles, who launched a series of winter campaigns from Fort Keogh, recalled, "I equipped my command as if I were organizing an expedition for the Arctic regions."

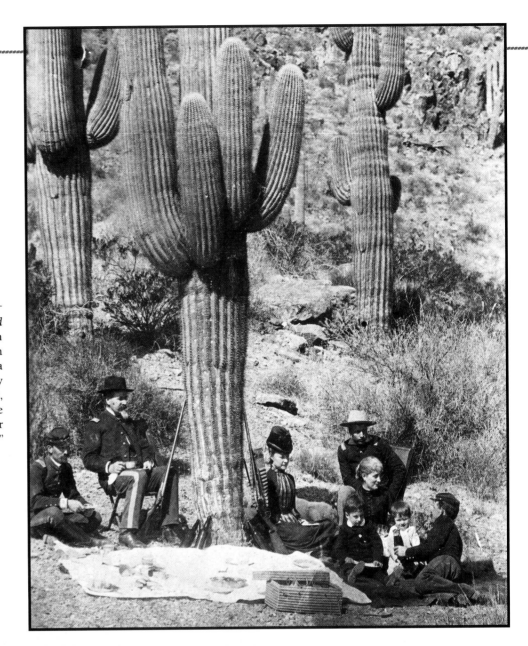

**P**icnic near Fort Grant, Arizona——
Rifle close at hand, Major Anson Mills *(seated at left)* joins officers and ladies of the 10th Cavalry, including his wife and two children *(right),* for a picnic near their post on the Gila River. Despite the rare opportunity for family outings, Major Mills considered Fort Thomas, where he was stationed in the mid-1880s, "one of the most desolate posts in which we ever served—the hottest and the most sickly."

**T**he Custers Entertaining, 1875——
George Custer offers a musical score to a piano-playing guest during a gathering in the commanding officer's quarters at Fort Abraham Lincoln, Dakota Territory. Custer's wife, Libbie, *(seated, center)* recalled that her husband "had a very keen sense of his social responsibilities as post commander, and believed that our house should be open at all hours."

**Cavalry Barracks, Fort Keogh, Montana** — Originally a squalid encampment of log huts on the banks of the Tongue River, Fort Keogh had assumed a more substantial and orderly appearance by 1880. The barracks that housed enlisted men stood on two sides of a diamond-shaped parade ground, across from the more homelike quarters of their officers.

**Barracks at Fort Robinson, Nebraska** — Spartan but spacious, the interior of a mid-1890s cavalry barracks at Fort Robinson reflects a military insistence on cleanliness and order. Unmarried enlisted men slept in the bunks at left, their personal belongings neatly arranged in footlockers, and their carbines aligned in circular gun racks.

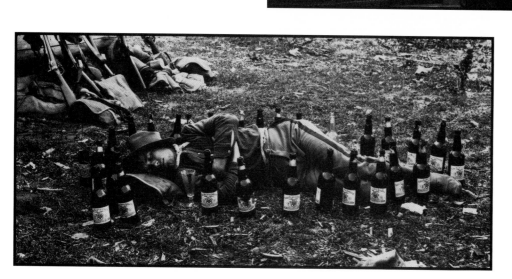

**The Problem of Drink** — This prankish photograph of a sleeping soldier surrounded by empty bottles belies the severity of a problem army authorities considered no laughing matter. An 1881 decree banned liquor sales on military posts, but some soldiers could not resist the temptations of saloons and gambling dens in the rough towns that sprang up near many Western forts. During the 1880s one out of 25 soldiers would be hospitalized for alcoholism.

# A Brutal Clash of Cultures

In the decades following the Civil War, the army's assignment to maintain the sanctity of land vouchsafed by government treaty to Native American peoples proved all but impossible to carry out. From Montana to Arizona, the relentless tide of westward emigration was accelerated by the completion of a half-dozen major railroad lines, even as news of mineral wealth drew thousands of prospectors to Indian Territory. As Senator John Sherman noted, "If the whole Army of the United States stood in the way, the wave of emigration would pass over it to seek the valley where gold was to be found." Caught between the mutually exclusive obligations of enforcing the treaties and safeguarding white civilians, the small frontier garrisons found themselves at war with a proud and desperate people who realized all too well that the spread of white civilization meant nothing less than the destruction of their own.

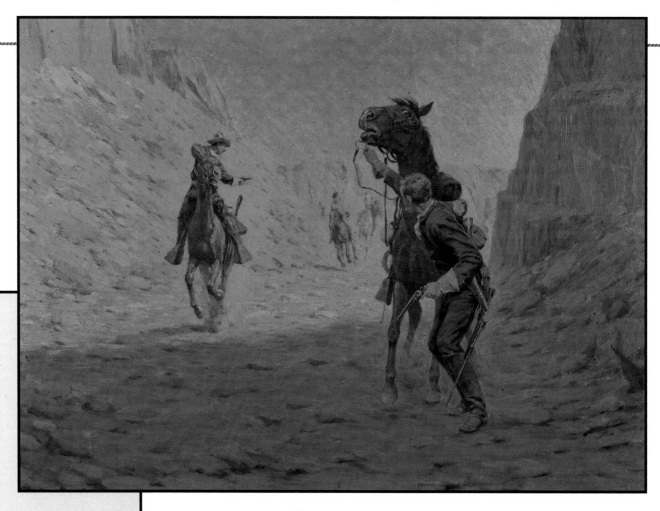

**B**attling a Fearsome Enemy —————
Covering the retreat of their comrades, two cavalry troopers prepare to make a stand against pursuing warriors. The Indians defended their territory so ferociously that frontier soldiers, terrified of capture and torture, advised one another to "keep the last bullet for yourself."

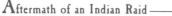

**A**ftermath of an Indian Raid —————
A U.S. officer and an army scout examine the scalped remains of a hunter waylaid by a Cheyenne war party. Such atrocities, though sporadic, led fearful settlers who were taking over Indian lands to demand military protection against angry Native American groups.

"The village rang with unearthly war whoops, the quick discharge of firearms . . . the cries of infants and the wailing of women."

◆

*Captain Albert Barnitz, Seventh Cavalry*

### Attack at the Washita

On the cold dawn of November 27, 1868, the 800 troopers of Custer's Seventh Cavalry thundered into the sleeping village of the Cheyenne chief Black Kettle. Striking from four sides, the soldiers quickly overran the camp, killing more than 100 Indian men, women, and children. A white hostage and her two-year-old son also died in the fighting, while army losses totaled 22 dead and 15 wounded.

### Opening the Black Hills ——

A winding train of more than 100 supply wagons marks Custer's 1874 reconnaissance through the Black Hills of South Dakota—a verdant land, rich with game, that held both practical and religious significance for the Sioux people. The discovery of gold by expedition members sparked a frenzied rush of prospectors and speculators, initiating the bloodiest chapter in the Indian wars.

## Custer's Last Stand

The greatest debacle suffered by military forces during the Indian wars occurred on June 25, 1876, on the banks of the Little Bighorn River in southeastern Montana. The utter defeat of Lieutenant Colonel George Armstrong Custer's vaunted Seventh Cavalry came at the hands of a large but tenuous coalition of tribes—principally Sioux and Cheyenne—that had gathered around the charismatic leader Sitting Bull. Unaware that the other elements of his attack had been stalemated, Custer *(seen below in an 1873 photograph)* rode north with five companies to cut off the flight of the women and children. Instead, the soldiers were encircled by hundreds of warriors, who rained arrows and fired bullets into the disintegrating company formations.

In this painting of Custer's demise by Edgar Paxson, who devoted 20 years of research to the work, the buckskin-clad commander *(center)* is shown with his usually long hair cut short, a precaution he took prior to the expedition. Standing just below his personal battle flag—an embroidered yellow silk gained when Lee surrendered at Appomattox—Custer clutches a fatal wound in his left side. Other characters include his brother, Captain Tom Custer, shown to the left of the yellow flag in a white hat, firing one revolver and cocking another over his left shoulder. A mounted Sioux named Rain-in-the-Face is about to strike Tom Custer from behind.

# Unorthodox War in the Southwest

While soldiers on the Northern Plains moved out in large-scale expeditions against the Sioux and the Cheyenne, troops stationed in Arizona and New Mexico faced a more elusive adversary. The loosely organized Apache bands were masters of guerrilla warfare who used the hostile, largely unexplored terrain to advantage. That the soldiers ultimately prevailed was due to the unorthodox tactics of their commander, Lieutenant Colonel George Crook.

"An Indian in his mode of warfare is more than the equal of the white man," Crook once wrote. "The only hope of success lies in using their own methods, and their own people." Dogged and often ruthless in war, Crook nonetheless treated his adversaries with respect—a trait that led many Apaches to ally themselves with their former enemy. These scouts guided Crook's forces to the obscure campsites and rendezvous of his wily opponents.

An Innovative Commander ——

George Crook, shown here with one of his Apache scouts, was a man of few words who ignored regulations, shunned military finery, and preferred to lead his troops from the saddle of a pack mule rather than a cavalry horse. One admirer noted, "Crook, in his quiet, steady way, did more to settle the Indian difficulty than Custer and all the other dashing cavaliers put together."

## Seminole Scouts on the Texas Border

Soldiers in the Southwest also relied on the scouting prowess of a unique cadre of so-called Seminole-Negroes, the descendants of runaway slaves who had fled to Mexico in about 1850 after fighting alongside the Seminoles in earlier battles against the U.S. Army. Led by John L. Bullis, a white officer of the African-American 24th Infantry, these hardy scouts, who never numbered more than 50, played a major part in ending Indian warfare on the Texas-Mexico border. Three of them received the Medal of Honor.

> *"We are not afraid of the Americans
> alone . . . but we can not fight you and our
> own people together."*
>
> ◆
>
> *Chautlipan, Apache*

**D**eath at Skeleton Cave ——

Cavalry troopers and Apache scouts blaze away at a band of Indians called the Yavapai, who were trapped in a cavern in Frederic Remington's painting of the battle of Skeleton Cave. Crook's scouts led the soldiers to the site, deep in the recesses of Salt River Canyon, Arizona. Of more than 100 Yavapais, only 25 survived the one-sided fight.

## A Leader of Warriors

No Indians proved more difficult to subdue than the Chiricahua Apache band led by Geronimo (*shown in the studio portrait at left, and at the center of his rifle-toting warriors, above*). Settlers and soldiers would have readily agreed with the journalist who described Geronimo's followers as "hereditary slayers," with "the eye of a hawk, the stealth of a coyote, and the courage of a tiger." Only after some 5,000 troops were deployed against him did the warrior finally lay down his arms.

## Indignity on the Reservation

While Geronimo and many of his followers were exiled to Florida, thousands of other Apaches struggled to survive the degradation of life on Arizona's San Carlos Reservation. Forced to adopt the white man's ways, families lined up once a week to receive a paltry ration of flour and beef (*right*).

# "Blind Stupidity or Criminal Indifference"

At 51, General Nelson A. Miles was the most famous Indian-fighting general in the U.S. Army; but he was well aware of the misery that precipitated the last great Indian outbreak. "We have taken away their land," Miles wrote. "They say, and very justly, that they are tired of broken promises."

On December 29, 1890, the simmering tensions exploded in violence at Wounded Knee Creek, South Dakota, when Colonel James Forsyth's Seventh Cavalry tried to disarm a group of Ghost Dancers, followers of a messianic religion that had begun in the Southwest. Although the Sioux had surrendered, a pistol was fired, and full-scale shooting broke out. The clash left 25 soldiers and at least 150 Indians dead, including many women and children.

Miles accused Forsyth of "blind stupidity or criminal indifference" and relieved him of command. But the War Department, determined to portray this final confrontation of the Indian wars in a heroic light, stopped any further investigation of the incident.

A Frozen Field of Carnage ——
Three days after the slaughter at Wounded Knee, Lieutenant Sydney A. Cloman (*left*) of the First Infantry accompanied a burial party to the corpse-strewn battlefield. His military demeanor belies the shame and anger some officers felt in the wake of the indiscriminate killing of noncombatants.

## An Irate Commander

General Nelson A. Miles (*center*) took personal charge of military forces at Pine Ridge two days after Wounded Knee and initiated an investigation of what he called "a useless slaughter of Indian women and children." Surveying the field of operations with Miles are the scout Buffalo Bill Cody (*left*) and staff officers Frank Baldwin and Marion Maus. All four men were recipients of the Medal of Honor.

# INDIANS

The tipis of a Plains Indian encampment pierce the sunset sky in a romantic view of the cultures encountered by the white man

# ON AN EVENTFUL DAY IN 1519, TEN STALLIONS AND SIX MARES WERE BROUGHT

ashore from a Spanish galleon anchored off the coast of Mexico. So awesome and mysterious did the horse appear to the Native Americans seeing it for the first time that they assumed it was some spirit incarnate. Drawing from the nearest animal analogy they could think of, they called it god dog or medicine dog. Over the next century and a half, the horse would spread among the Indians of the West, through trade and horse-stealing raids, and would gradually modify the way the Indians traveled, hunted, and made war. By the time the first white fur traders began showing up on the Great Plains in the 18th century, some of the Indians who greeted them had become among the finest horsemen in the world.

Western Indians were by no means of a uniform type. They belonged to distinct communities, each with its unique customs. They spoke many different languages and hundreds of dialects, though they could communicate with one another through an almost universally recognized sign language. By the mid-19th century, the nomadic Indian peoples of the Great Plains, who migrated with the seasons like the buffalo they hunted, had mastered horsemanship to become efficient hunters and fearsome mounted warriors. Bravery in warfare and skill at hunting were the foundation stones of a good life for the men of such tribes—the most powerful of them being the Sioux, Cheyenne, and Arapaho in the north, the Comanche and Kiowa in the south. By contrast, the agricultural Pueblo Indians of the Southwest—the Hopi, Zuni, Acoma, Taos—though they had been among the earliest Indians to encounter horses, used the animal more for trade than for travel. They dwelt in easily defended apartment complexes of adobe and stone, near which they grew corn and beans.

Regardless of their many differences in lifestyle, however, the Indians were uniform in one respect—their concept of land. They held territory, of course, and cherished it as their birthright. But it was land possessed in common for the use of the entire community. No individual Indian would dream of claiming personal ownership of a plot of ground. The land was a source of identity, and the people

were part of the natural order that lived on it and took sustenance from it. The contrast between their way of looking at the land and the European concept of land as property like any other material object—to be bought and sold, owned and exploited, used by its owner to the exclusion of all others—foreordained the tragic and devastating conflict to come between the Western Indians and the expanding American nation.

By 1860 the U.S. government had executed more than 350 treaties with various Indian peoples. Most acknowledged the sovereignty of the Indian nations and their title to their land. But most were drawn up by U.S. authorities for the purpose of taking land in the eastern part of the country, promising in exchange other land in the West, along with money and annual deliveries of food and supplies. Most treaties promised that the new land out West would belong to the Indians forever. Most of those promises were broken.

The earliest encounters between Western Indians and American explorers and traders were not wholly unfriendly. Indeed, the Indians soon learned to prize highly the metal knives, axes, and arrowheads; the cloth; the rifles; and—to their woe—the rum and whiskey that they could obtain from the whites in exchange for beaver pelts. They were also fairly tolerant of the first trickle of emigrant wagon trains that traversed their hunting grounds in the early 1840s.

Later in the decade, however, the Indians' tolerance began to give way to the first stirrings of anger. The discovery of gold in California produced a flood tide of forty-niners streaming across prime hunting grounds, killing or driving away the buffalo that were the very life-blood of the Plains Indians. Indian attacks on the invading wagon trains were met with military retaliation.

The point of view of the Native Americans was captured in the eloquent language of Satank, a Kiowa chief: "The white man once came to trade, he now comes as a soldier. He once put his trust in our friendship and wanted no shield but our fidelity. He now covers his face with the cloud of jealousy and anger and tells us to be gone as an offended master speaks to his dog."

With tensions stretched to the breaking point among the more militant chiefs and warriors, it was inevitable that some incident would spark open conflict. In the summer of 1854, a dispute erupted at Fort Laramie, Wyoming, over a settler's stray cow that had been

killed and butchered by a hungry Brulé Sioux. The young lieutenant who set out to punish the offending Indian would not accept Sioux offers of restitution; instead, his soldiers fired a volley that mortally wounded the chief who was trying to mediate. Outraged, the Indians fought back and killed the lieutenant and every man in his command.

Despite efforts toward peace by chiefs such as the Brulé Sioux Spotted Tail—who at one point gave himself up as hostage to the army to spare his people from punishment—the following years would see relations between the Plains Indians and the Americans poisoned by a tragic spiral of mutual distrust and small-scale raids and murders. Badly outgunned and poorly organized for sustained warfare, the Indians would suffer progressive encroachments on their land. Confined to reservations, they would lose not only their freedom but their very hold on the means of staying alive.

In the winter of 1862, conditions grew intolerable for the Santee, an eastern branch of the Sioux nation living on a reservation in Minnesota. Left to freeze and starve when their annual shipment of government supplies failed to arrive on time, they went off their reservation and launched a campaign of terror and killing that took the lives of 450 white settlers. Henry Whipple, then the Episcopal bishop of Minnesota, described it as "the most fearful Indian massacre in history." The incident convinced many whites that only relentless force would work against the Indians.

In the Southwest, Americans were also learning hard lessons about the fighting qualities of another community of Native Americans—the Apache—who occupied a large area of Mexican Territory in what is now western Texas, New Mexico, eastern Arizona, and northern Mexico. The Apache had been making deadly raids against the Mexicans for 200 years, spreading terror and taking booty in the form of cattle, sheep, and horses.

When their homeland came under American jurisdiction by way of the Mexican War in 1848 and the Gadsden Purchase in 1853, the Americans inherited the implacable enmity of the Apache Indians—though not at first. The U.S. government seemed in no rush to establish a presence in the new territory, and the few American prospectors who showed up in the mid-1850s were held by the Apache to be of no concern.

In 1860, however, a shiftless white settler wrongly claimed that

warriors of the Chiricahua band of Apache had kidnapped his son, a charge the army decided to act upon. The result was tragically like the incident at Fort Laramie six years earlier, except that in Cochise, chief of the Chiricahua, the Americans had made an enemy even more hostile and dangerous than the Sioux. Cochise's men killed 150 Americans in the first two months after the outbreak of fighting and proceeded to wage a fierce guerrilla war against the U.S. Army and American settlers that persisted for more than 10 years. In 1870 army commander General William Tecumseh Sherman remarked, "We had one war with Mexico to take Arizona, and we should have another to make her take it back."

Finally, in 1872 President Ulysses S. Grant sent a peace envoy to Cochise, who agreed to end the war on the condition that his people be allowed to keep their weapons, return to a reservation on their own land that would be closed to white encroachment, and live their lives in their traditional way without interference. Cochise's victory was total—but short-lived. The great chief died two years later, and the peace he had won did not long survive him.

Within a few years after Cochise's death, groups of Chiricahuas began leaving the reservation to resume raiding in Mexico. Their leader was Geronimo, a once-friendly man who had become permanently embittered when his family was wiped out in an act of treachery by the Mexicans. Geronimo and his men—their number never exceeded 100—confined their depredations to Mexico for several years. But then, in 1885, he and his band left the reservation and killed an American rancher and his family.

This time the U.S. cavalry came after him. Led by General George Crook and aided by more than 200 Indian scouts, the soldiers finally ran Geronimo to ground in Mexico's Sierra Madre in 1886. Geronimo sent word that he was ready to surrender but instead stole away with 20 men and 18 women and children. Crook was replaced by General Nelson A. Miles, whose first act was to deport the entire Chiricahua band to Florida, including the new family Geronimo had acquired after joining Cochise's people. Miles then went after Geronimo with no fewer than 5,000 troops.

Geronimo and his 38 followers continued to evade capture for several months, killing more white Americans. Finally, during a parley with a cavalry officer, he was told that if he surrendered he would be sent to Florida. Angrily, Geronimo swore that he would continue

# THE GREAT BUFFALO: A SOURCE OF FOOD, CLOTHING, AND SHELTER

The mighty herds of buffalo that darkened the Great Plains were the mainstay of many Indian peoples. A buffalo had almost everything within its enormous body that the people needed for life on the prairie. Its skin provided clothing, bedding, and shelter; the thickest part of the hide from the neck became a shield. Buffalo meat was central to the diet—roasted when fresh or dried to make jerky or pounded with fat and berries to make pemmican, a concentrated food easily carried on the trail. From the animal's coarse hair the Indians made rope, pillow stuffing, and balls for games; its bones became tools and toys.

But the buffalo was far more than merely a grazing cornucopia. Its strength inspired warriors to take names associated with the buffalo, believing that its qualities would serve them in the hunt and at war. And every tribe had important religious ceremonies of celebration and thanksgiving for the fellow creatures that bestowed the gift of life.

The Buffalo Dance ———
Mandan warriors imitate the milling movements of their quarry in the Buffalo Dance, performed to lure the spirits of the beasts back to the tribal hunting grounds. Full buffalo heads adorn the leaders of the dance, two of the tribe's most esteemed warriors.

**A High-Speed Hunt**

Guiding his mount with his knees, a hunter draws a bead on a fleeing buffalo bull. Even a well-placed arrow would likely only wound the beast, which might rumble on for another mile before collapsing.

**A Symbolic Skull**

Painted with a symbol representing the four winds and adorned with sagebrush for use in an Oglala Teton Sioux Sun Dance ceremony, this buffalo skull served as an altar representing the essence of life.

the war, but after the officer informed him that his family was already gone from the reservation, all the fight went out of him and the once-indomitable warrior gave up.

During the years the Apache were waging their guerrilla war in the Southwest, the hostilities on the Plains grew increasingly complex. Factions and individuals on both sides of the conflict sought peace but were overruled or ignored by those bent on war. After the Sioux outbreak in Minnesota in 1862, attacks on isolated white settlements and emigrant wagon trains throughout the High Plains increased. Then, in November of 1864, Colonel John M. Chivington, commander of the Third Colorado Volunteers, and a would-be delegate to the U.S. Congress, announced that he had attacked a camp of 1,000 Cheyenne warriors and had slain more than 500, at a spot in Colorado called Sand Creek. Of his militia he said, "They all did nobly."

But a congressional investigation soon revealed the ugly truth of the event. The Indians at Sand Creek had been a peaceful band of about 500 Cheyenne, two-thirds of them women and children. Their chief, Black Kettle, was a steadfast advocate of cooperation with the whites and had led his group to Sand Creek on specific instructions from the army, whose protection he believed he enjoyed.

When Black Kettle heard the bugle calls of the approaching troops, he raised an American flag, with a white flag beneath it, atop his tipi and counseled his frightened people to stay calm. The soldiers opened fire and then charged through the camp, shooting and slashing the screaming, running Indians, killing babies in their mothers' arms, and dismounting to mutilate the victims. Of the 123 killed, 98 were women or children.

The reaction back East to the atrocity was horror. General Grant reportedly described it as nothing less than murder. The army's judge advocate general, Joseph Holt, called it a "cowardly and cold-blooded slaughter, sufficient to cover its perpetrators with indelible infamy, and the face of every American with shame and indignation."

The Plains Indians, had they been listening, would no doubt have agreed. But the warriors among them were not inclined to listen to any pronouncements by white people. At a large gathering of Cheyenne, Northern Arapaho, and Sioux warriors on the Republican River, one chief declared, "We have now raised the battle-ax until death."

Death came swiftly for 45 men of a cavalry unit lured out of Fort

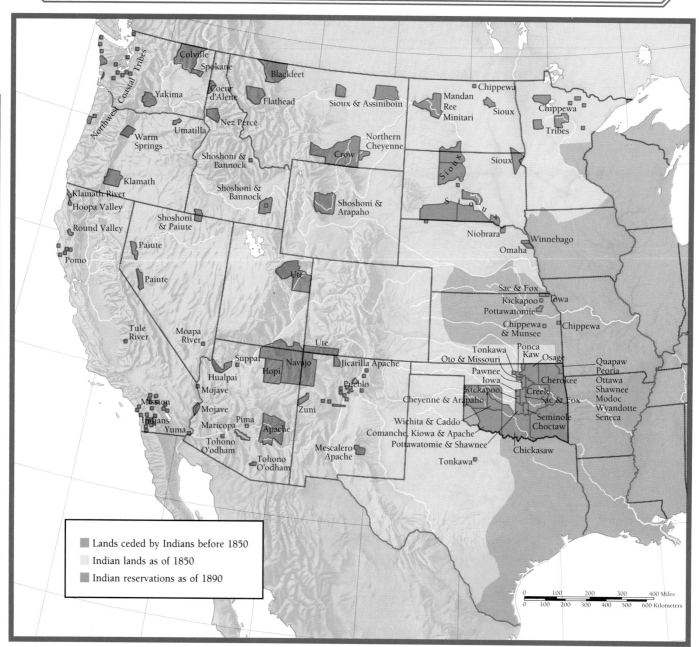

Lands ceded by Indians before 1850

Indian lands as of 1850

Indian reservations as of 1890

# Dwindling Dominion

The concept of individual rights to land came to the West with the white man; although they were territorial, Native Americans had never considered their domain something they owned. The earth was jointly occupied but not possessed by any one person.

Whites, on the other hand, were accustomed to treating the occupants of any land as the owners of that land. Early treaties routinely enticed or coerced the Indians into granting the right to fish or hunt, or merely to pass through the areas. Later treaties of acquisition were more far reaching, and occupation by white people—agreed to or not—soon followed.

In the end it mattered little what the Indians thought they were giving up. During the peak period of land transfer, between 1853 and 1857, 174 million acres changed hands—more than the area of Texas. The federal government vigorously enforced these treaties—except when it was more advantageous to break them—and by 1890, the broad domain of the Native Americans had shrunk to a few landholdings and a scattering of reservations.

Rankin and ambushed. The warriors then sacked every ranch for a distance of 80 miles west of the fort, killed eight people, took 1,500 head of cattle, and pillaged the town of Julesburg.

The Sand Creek affair and the Indian retaliations that followed touched off a long-overdue debate among Americans about the "Indian question." From the beginning, whites had avoided coming to grips with the problem by the simple, if harsh, expedient known as removal—literally removing the Native Americans from their homelands to lands farther and farther west. But after the Civil War, Americans began settling all over the once-wild West. There was no longer open country left to serve as an exile for the Indians.

Proposed solutions to the problem ranged from extermination to assimilation. A war of extermination against the Plains Indians, however, was not only morally reprehensible to most Americans but also expensive; it cost as much as two million dollars a year to maintain a cavalry regiment. The opposite extreme was to try to transform the Indians into settled, self-supporting, middle-class Americans. At various times after the Civil War both methods were attempted without notable success, for the Indians, too, were faced with two extremes—either wage war to the death against the whites or cooperate to the unpalatable extent of settling down in reservations and learning how to farm.

During the period of raids and retaliatory attacks following the Sand Creek massacre, one chief who refused to condone violence was Black Kettle, who had survived Sand Creek. In late November 1868, he was camped on the Washita River in western Oklahoma when a party of raiding warriors joined his group. Early the next morning, he heard a gunshot and the sound of a bugle. Incredibly, his peaceful camp was being attacked again, this time by the Seventh Cavalry, under Lieutenant Colonel George Armstrong Custer. This time Black Kettle grabbed his rifle, and this time he was killed, along with his wife and about 100 other women and children. There was no public outcry over the Washita massacre. The army was now apparently free to attack any band of Indians who were not totally subjugated.

Ironically, earlier that same year, the fierce resistance of the Oglala Sioux chief Red Cloud had forced the government to abandon the Bozeman Trail and all its forts. When the Americans gave up the forts, the Sioux burned them to the ground. Then, in a treaty negotiated at Medicine Lodge, the victorious Sioux, Northern Cheyenne,

Chanting for a glorious future, a man and woman take part in the Ghost Dance ceremony that swept across the Plains around 1890. Highly decorated ghost shirts offered certain kinds of protection: The crows painted on the Arapaho garment at far left represent the belief that dancers would be flown out of danger when nonbelievers were destroyed. Many also believed the shirts made the wearers impervious to bullets.

and Arapaho bands agreed to accept a large reservation encompassing all of western South Dakota—including the Black Hills, which held great spiritual significance for the Sioux. Not all agreed, however; the formidable Hunkpapa Sioux chief and medicine man Sitting Bull refused to accept any limitations on his movements.

There matters uneasily stood until 1874, when Custer, whom the Indians called Long Hair, led a surveying expedition into the Black Hills. Custer reported finding gold in the mountains, and white prospectors began pouring into this sacred Sioux territory. The army was either unable or unwilling to stop them, so the government offered to buy the land from the Sioux.

Although Red Cloud advocated peace, his influence had waned. Among those who angrily refused the offer were the Sioux war chief Gall, Sitting Bull, and a rising young chief named Crazy Horse. The government responded in late 1875 by threatening punishment to any Indians caught off the reservation. This warning was met with scorn by a force of free-ranging Sioux, Arapaho, and Cheyenne warriors that had grown to about 2,000 men. It was the only time in the history of the Plains wars that the Indians had been able to assemble so great a force of men agreed on a single course of action.

Slumped in death with a trooper's bullet in his head, the frozen body of Chief Big Foot lies on the snow-covered battlefield at Wounded Knee Creek in South Dakota. About 150 Sioux, many women and children, died with Big Foot in the massacre that closed the Indian wars in 1890.

No such possibility occurred to an arrogant, ambitious Custer as he approached their camp on a river bearing the Indian name Greasy Grass, but which the whites called the Little Bighorn, on June 25, 1876. Eager to mete out the government's punishment to the recalcitrant Indians, he disregarded orders to wait for reinforcements, divided his 210 men into three columns, and rode heedlessly against the full fury of the enemy. In a short, frenzied battle led by Crazy Horse and Gall, Custer and his entire force were wiped out.

Despite their great victory, the Plains Indians were no better suited to fight the army's type of war than they had ever been, and now more troops than ever swept into the field against them. Crazy Horse and 1,500 followers were forced onto the reservation within a year after Little Bighorn, and a few months later the chief himself was killed—stabbed with a bayonet when he resisted soldiers who had come to arrest him on suspicion of fomenting new trouble.

Sitting Bull held out against the increased army pressure, eventually leading his band across the border into Canada, where it remained for four years. He finally returned with 150 people and surrendered. After becoming close friends with Buffalo Bill Cody and touring for a season with his Wild West show, Sitting Bull returned to the reservation in 1889.

About that time the Indian peoples of the West were caught up by a new religious idea, one that had originated with a medicine man in

Nevada. If they would perform a special new ceremony, said this creed, their dead ancestors would return to life, and the buffalo would once again cover the Plains. The ceremony aroused concern among white authorities, who called it the Ghost Dance and feared it would incite the Indians to go back on the warpath. Their fears increased when they learned that members of Sitting Bull's band were making special shirts for the Ghost Dance that were supposed to protect the wearers from deadly bullets. The authorities blamed Sitting Bull for the perceived unrest and on December 15, 1890, sent a party of Indian police to arrest him. A shootout erupted, and Sitting Bull was killed, along with eight of his followers and six police.

Still ill at ease about the Indians' intentions, officials next cast suspicious eyes on a Minniconjou Sioux chief named Big Foot, despite his having long been a member of the peace faction among the Sioux. A force of 450 cavalry troopers was sent to round up Big Foot and his band of about 350 followers and bring them to Fort Cheyenne. On the way to the fort, the Indians and their escort stopped for the night of December 28, and Big Foot's people made camp beside a creek called Wounded Knee.

The next morning, soldiers entered Big Foot's camp to search for guns. One Indian panicked, drew a pistol from under his robe, and fired a wild shot. The cavalrymen cut loose a fusillade against the helpless Indians, killing Big Foot and about 150 men, women, and children. The bodies lay unattended in the snow of the camp for three days before an army burial detail came to collect them. Frozen into their grotesque death poses, the corpses were picked up, thrown into wagons, and hauled off to a mass grave.

The massacre, which history books would call the Battle of Wounded Knee, was the last violent incident of the long and bloody Indian wars. In its one-sidedness and injustice, it fairly reflected the nature and outcome of the Native Americans' entire experience with the United States. It also made true prophecy of something spoken much earlier by a Lakota Sioux named Black Elk. "A long time ago," he said, "my father told me what his father told him, that there was once a Lakota holy man called Drinks Water who dreamed what was to be. . . . He dreamed that a strange race had woven a spider's web all around the Lakotas, and he said, when this happens you shall live in square gray houses and you shall starve." For the Indians, a Wild West that was wild no more was a square gray house.

# LIVING LIGHTLY ON THE LAND

No matter how widely they roamed across the plains, mountains, and deserts of the West, the Indians retained a deep spiritual connection with the earth and its fruits. Always striving for harmony with their environment, they fashioned a material culture and social organization that allowed them to live lightly on the land.

Perhaps the most representative part of that culture was the tipi, the conical buffalo-hide tent used by many Plains communities. Easy to erect and take down, a tipi allowed its users to move with the herds and the weather, leaving scarcely a trace of their passage. There was no sacrifice of comfort, however; the tipi was cool in summer, warm in winter, and proof against snow, rain, and even the gale-force winds that sometimes swept the prairie.

Setting up the tipis was a job that fell to the women. Responsible for tanning and stitching the hides—sometimes a dozen or more—that made up a tipi's cover, the women were generally considered the owners of the structure. Most of the group's other domestic affairs were also conducted by women, who gathered vegetables, fruits, and nuts; carried firewood and water; and made clothing, baskets, and other objects essential to the well-being of the family and the community as a whole. Women often took particular pride in their artisanry, and their efforts were honored by their people: The most skillful craftswomen won prestige as high as that accorded to the bravest warriors.

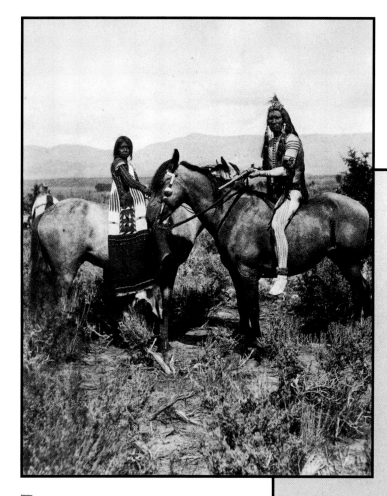

Traveling Companions ———
A Uinta Ute warrior and boy pause at the start of their summer migration into the Utah mountains; the horses would carry them back to the Great Basin Valley in winter.

A Village of Tipis ———
An Arapaho man stands before his tipi at a camp in southwestern Oklahoma. Two external poles control the flaps flanking the tipi's smoke hole, allowing adjustments of the draft to carry smoke away.

A Weaver of Baskets ———

A Paiute woman in the Great Basin weaves a grass basket outside her house of twigs and brush. Baskets were used for grain storage and for carrying household possessions; coated with pine resin, they even served as water bottles.

Moving On ——
A visionary leader takes his people to a new location for their camp, their possessions on tipi-pole travois dragged by horses. Every Western Indian group acknowledged individuals with special powers, which often included foretelling the future, controlling the weather, and healing battle wounds.

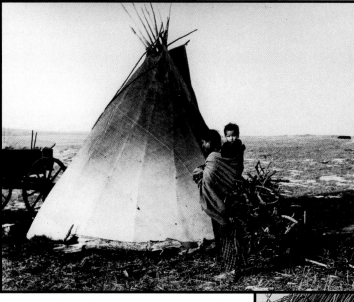

Tending the Home Fires ——

A Sioux woman, baby secured to her back, carries firewood to her family's tipi. Although often ignored by white observers, women occupied a distinctive place in Indian cultures and wielded substantial influence.

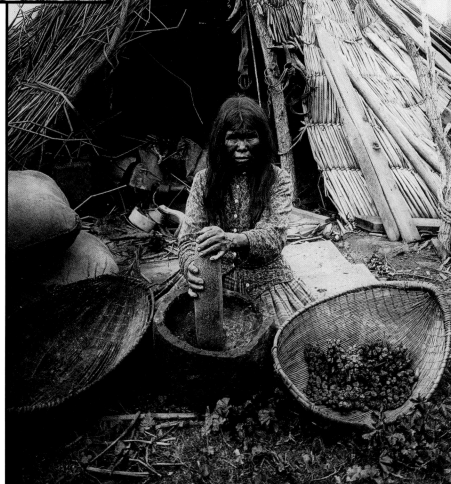

The Daily Bread ——

With her rough wooden mortar and pestle, this Paiute woman grinds nuts or grain for part of the day's meals. Women were the sole preparers of food, whether it was what they gathered themselves or meat provided by the community's hunters.

## Masters of the Horse, Masters of the Plains

The capture and training of horses *(right)* was essential to life on the Great Plains in the 19th century. The swift-running animals made buffalo hunting so efficient that many Indian groups accumulated surpluses of meat and hides. Horses also allowed the nomadic Plains Indians the luxury of more material comfort; a single horse could carry 200 pounds of possessions on its back or drag 300 on a travois. The finest animals, however, were reserved for battle or hunting, led to the scene of action by a warrior on an ordinary mount.

# The Way of the Warrior

Because the skills of the hunt were crucial to success in battle as well, boys began their training early. Games revolved around hunting activities, and youths were encouraged to seek dreams and visions that would guide their martial endeavors—always subject to supernatural influences.

Among many Indian peoples, boys entered the ranks of men by joining military societies, whose actions went beyond defending camps and leading war parties. The societies played a strong role in the group's life, organizing hunts and sponsoring feasts and dances of celebration and supplication.

Satanta (White Bear) ——
This Kiowa war leader never yielded to the encroaching whites. Captured when he continued to raid settlements despite signing a peace treaty, Satanta killed himself in 1878 rather than submit to imprisonment.

Preparing for Battle ——
Sioux warriors dance in a circle near their tipis, seeking spiritual guidance before departing to fight. Failure to observe the strict rituals and taboos of warfare, they believed, could lead to dishonor in combat.

# Apache Devil Dancers

Elaborately costumed Apache dancers wield swords and bows as they seek the support of mountain spirits in hunting and war. The dance required strict attention to every detail. According to tribal tradition, certain madness awaited any dancer who failed to put on his headdress exactly as he was told.

**I**ntertribal Warfare ——
Two bands of mounted warriors clash on the western Plains. Such conflict between groups arose from disputes over hunting rights, the desire for revenge, or simply the desire to steal the enemy's property, particularly horses.

**S**itting Bull's First Coup ——
Sitting Bull wins his first battle honors at the age of 14 by riding down a Crow warrior to count coup. This copy of Sitting Bull's sketch, made later by his uncle, also contains Sitting Bull's signature—a seated buffalo at top right.

— Coup Stick —

## Supernatural Tools of the Warrior's Trade

Men whose lives revolved around warfare looked for every advantage in combat, including magical assistance. Before battle, each warrior painted his face and body with designs that would protect him; most also wore or carried some article imbued with mystical powers, such as those shown here. War masks, for example, played a part in ritual dances meant to guarantee success in an impending battle or raid.

Once combat was joined, other objects came to the fore. The coup stick held a central place in the Indians' concept of war, which placed a higher value on bravery than on killing the enemy. Any warrior who could approach a live foe close enough to touch him with a coup stick won greater honor than he could by slaying him from afar with an arrow. Often war bonnets displayed honors in symbolic form, with past coups indicated by feathers of a particular type or shape. The bravest warriors thus sought combat with those among the enemy who wore the greatest honor on their heads.

The shields that many warriors carried with them into battle were adorned with images of personal protectors, often taken from visions or dreams. The shields also offered practical protection, their stout layers of buffalo hide deflecting enemy arrows and lances.

—Cherokee War Mask—

—Crow Shield—

— Comanche War Bonnet —

# A Paper Trail to the Reservation

The U.S. government took over much of the Native Americans' Western domain through peace treaties, often accompanied by colorful signing ceremonies. But the treaties were sometimes little more than legal pretexts for seizure of the land. The government interpreted any chiefs' signatures as binding their entire community, but some leaders, not part of the negotiations by choice or happenstance, refused to acquiesce. Such recalcitrance was doomed to failure, for the balance of military power lay with the more numerous and better-armed whites.

*"The white man, who possesses this whole vast country from sea to sea, who roams over it at pleasure, and lives where he likes, cannot know the cramp we feel in this little spot, with the undying remembrance of the fact, which you know as well as we, that every foot of what you proudly call America, not very long ago belonged to the red man."*

◆

*Chief Washakie, Shoshoni*

**Sitting Bear** —
The implacable Kiowa warrior Sitting Bear was still riding on raids at age 69, when this picture was taken. Arrested a year later in 1871, he provoked soldiers to kill him.

**Washakie** —
A steadfast friend of whites, Washakie and his Shoshoni warriors fought beside the U.S. Army against the Cheyenne and Sioux. Even enemies called Washakie a great warrior; the allied leader, President Grant, thanked him with a handsome silver-trimmed saddle.

**A Temporary Agreement** —
Under the watchful eyes of their people at Medicine Lodge Creek, Kansas, in 1867, Kiowa representatives *(right)* reluctantly negotiate a plan to move onto a reservation in Indian Territory. Many later resumed raiding after the government cut back Kiowa hunting rights.

**Red Cloud** —
The only Western chief to win an extended war against the United States, Red Cloud of the Oglala Sioux *(above)* attacked travelers and forts along the Bozeman Trail so fiercely that the government was forced to seek peace under the Treaty of Laramie *(right)*.

**Renouncing a Way of Life** —
Sioux leaders and U.S. military officials work on a treaty at Fort Laramie, Wyoming, in 1868. To promote farming, the government pledged land, supplies, and one cow per family. Many warriors, such as the absent Sitting Bull, vowed to keep fighting rather than follow a plow.

257

# Visits Meant to Impress the Visitors

Incredulous at the stubborn resistance of an enemy clearly inferior in numbers and equipment, the federal government attempted to impress Indian leaders with the power and scope of the white man's culture. Summoned to the East on various pretexts, the chiefs toured military installations and art galleries, visited legislators and bureaucrats, and sometimes received audiences with the Great Father himself, the president of the United States. Such a visit in early 1870 proved sobering for the militant Sioux chief Red Cloud. Though he continued to press for the right of his people to roam their lands freely, he also admitted that they were but a handful compared with the populations of the bustling cities. Over the next 40 years, he was a strong advocate for peace.

*"God Almighty has made us all, and He is here to bless what I have to say to you today. I am a representative of the original American race, the first people of this continent. We have given you nearly all of our lands, and if we had any more land to give we would be very glad to give it. We have nothing more."*

◆

*Red Cloud, Sioux*

Red Cloud as Supplicant——
Only a few years after victoriously signing the Treaty of Laramie, Red Cloud prepares to plead for the interests of his Sioux people at the Carlisle School in Pennsylvania.

**A** Long Way from the Plains ———
In the unlikely setting of a Washington art gallery, a large group of visiting Sioux (*above*) take a break from 1877 talks with President Rutherford B. Hayes.

**At** the Great Father's Mansion ———
As early as 1857, a diverse delegation of visiting chiefs poses on the steps of the White House, some in traditional garb and others dressed like their hosts. The group included Pawnee, Potawatomi, Ponca, Sioux, and Winnebago leaders.

# From Wide-Open Country to Confined Camps

Peace treaties left conquered Native Americans with only a fraction of their former lands. They were told to settle into a new life on the reservations, where soldiers and government agents kept a close watch. But the victors often showed small concern for the welfare of the Indian people, and supplies and services sometimes vanished in an inefficient bureaucracy with too many unethical agents.

*"It is cold, and we have no blankets. The little children are freezing to death. . . . Hear me, my chiefs. . . . I am tired. My heart is sick and sad. From where the sun now stands, I will fight no more forever."*

◆

*Chief Joseph, Nez Percé*

An End to Nomadism ——
The smoke of many fires obscures Sioux tipis crowded inside a winter compound near the Minnesota River. The enclosing walls simplified the army's job of keeping the Indians from straying off the reservation.

A Handout for Former Hunters ——
No longer able to supply their own needs by hunting, reservation Indians in the Dakota Territory wait for meager rations distributed by a government agent, standing near a pile of food sacks.

Their domestic duties unchanged on the reservation, Apache women gather firewood from a pile provided by the government.

Sarah Winnemucca ——

A Paiute fluent in English after a childhood among whites, Sarah Winnemucca spoke and wrote passionately about injustices in the reservation system. She evoked tears, but not relief. Disillusioned by government betrayals, she retired from public life.

# The Two Lives of a Comanche Chief

For 15 years the Comanche warrior Quanah, later known as Quanah Parker, fought against the advancing whites, winning respect as a clever and tenacious fighter. Though never vanquished, Quanah saw the shape of the future; to preserve his people, he led them onto a reservation in Indian Territory on June 2, 1875.

For the next 35 years, until his death at 65, Quanah enjoyed success in business and politics. The son of a white woman (below), he never renounced the warrior heritage of his Comanche father, fiercely defending the group's interests and serving so well that the Comanche Indians ruled that no man after him would be called chief.

But his best efforts only slowed the Comanche's decline. By the time of Quanah's death in 1911, the reservation was broken up, and his people were as few and as scattered as the buffalo they had once hunted.

## The Story of a Twice-Captured Mother

Quanah's mother, Cynthia Ann Parker, was nine years old in 1836 when abducted by raiders who killed her father. She adjusted well to her new life, marrying a rising young chief at age 18 and bearing two sons and a daughter. She refused an offer of ransom in the 1850s, citing her love for her Comanche family. Recaptured with her young daughter in 1860, Cynthia Ann lived unhappily with an uncle in Texas for four years. When a fever claimed her child, the grieving Cynthia Ann starved herself to death.

### New Home for an Off-Duty Judge ———

The Comanche White House (left), as locals called Quanah's home, was built by a cattle baron who paid the tribe for grazing rights. Between sessions of the Court of Indian Offenses, where Quanah presided, he relaxed in a comfortable office (below). The large painting behind the retired warrior depicts Custer's Last Stand.

### Keeping the Old Ways ———

Already a successful businessman, Quanah proudly donned his traditional regalia for Comanche ceremonies in the 1890s. With his braids wrapped in beaver fur, he stands before a tipi holding a fan made of eagle feathers.

# THE SCOUTS

## Wise Men of a Wild Land

The eventual settlement of the territory between the Missouri River and the Pacific owes much to a rough fraternity of colorful scouts—former hunters and fur trappers who had mastered the art of survival in that unmapped terrain. Knowing the land and its perils, the scouts were invaluable guides for explorers and missionaries, surveying expeditions, and emigrant wagon trains. Their trail wisdom also proved vital to the army in its efforts to pacify the Indians and to railroaders pushing the iron track across searing deserts and formidable mountain ranges.

The best scouts brought a kind of genius to their dangerous trade. They knew the West's waterways and water holes as well as the passes that could be navigated and those so rugged they would destroy any expedition trying to cross them. The scouts knew the best campsites and how and where to hunt game to fend off starvation. Many knew the rudiments of Indian languages and could act as interpreters and peacemakers. Increasing numbers were themselves Indians—or part Indian—schooled since childhood in the ways of the wilderness.

Those who earned their living as scouts were instinctive loners, but they shared an independent spirit and a mighty thirst for adventure. While the names and deeds of most have faded from memory, a few of the pathfinders who opened the way to the West live on as larger-than-life legends from an unforgettable past.

The Challenge Ahead——
Intently studying the contours of a wide valley at sunset, three scouts search out potential obstacles for the next day's journey in an 1851 painting by artist William Ranney.

# Reading the Land between the Lines

The most basic skill needed by a scout was "reading sign"—seeing and interpreting the often minute and subtle traces left behind by passing animals and people. Lodgepole furrows scratched through pony tracks suggested Indians traveling with women and children—not a war party. A veteran scout could deduce from a patch of flattened grass not only that a horse had gone by but also how long ago, whether it carried a rider, and whether the rider was white or Indian. From a paw print they could tell whether a bear was long gone or only 10 minutes away. These could be life and death matters—the difference between walking into an Indian ambush or avoiding it, between becoming a meal for a bear or having a bear for a meal.

Skilled and brave as some of them were, the scouts seldom lived up to their knight-errant popular image, spread by the dime novels of the time. Real-life scouts, such as those shown in the gallery here and on the following pages, were generally unkempt, with beards and long, greasy hair, and they usually wore a bizarre mixture of Indian buckskins and ill-fitting white men's clothes. Most were prickly characters and some were downright ornery, especially when drunk. Gentleman or knave, each took his place among the hardy souls who rode out ahead.

**J**im Beckwourth——

Born in 1798 to a Southern planter and one of his slaves, Beckwourth lived much of his life among the Crow Indians. He was such a ferocious fighter that his original tribal name, Morning Star, was changed to Bloody Arm. The pass he found through the Sierra Nevada, near today's Reno, became part of a major emigrant route to California.

**J**im Baker——

The bottle brought out the devil in the usually gentle Baker. On one binge, he tried to slice off his wife's ear for suspected infidelity. In 1841, Baker and 22 fellow trappers held off 500 Cheyenne, Arapaho, and Sioux at the Little Snake River. Chief scout at Fort Laramie and guide to many a wagon train, he died a Wyoming farmer in 1898.

**S**tephen Hall Meek——

This patriarch of the Plains gained notoriety by once taking an Oregon-bound wagon train on a supposed shortcut—and then getting lost. Meek, who learned his trade through many years as a trapper, tried several times to quit scouting, only to discover he was unsuited for anything else. He made a good living at it well into his eighties.

## Message Underfoot ——

A dismounted scout intently examines tufts of prairie grass for evidence of Indians or game in an 1852 painting by Arthur Fitzwilliam Tait. His companions are equally intent, scanning for signs of enemies and getting the lay of the land. All carry the scout's most essential equipment: a rifle, a canteen, and a blanket.

# Getting the Wagon Trains Through

In 1841, a veteran Western trapper named Thomas "Broken Hand" Fitzpatrick guided the first emigrant wagon train from its jumping-off point in Missouri to California. For decades after that epochal trip, virtually every wagon train that set out on the great trek west had its own shepherd to lead the greenhorns across the Plains, over the great wall of the Rockies, through the wastelands of what are today Nevada and Utah, and finally up and over the Sierras to the West Coast. In the process, the scouts transformed the uncharted land into one whose rivers, valleys, and mountains were mapped and traversed by proven routes.

Leading clumsy wagons full of neophytes required more than just a good sense of direction. Many of the men who spearheaded the Great Emigration were not only skilled at woodcraft but also masters of medicine and statecraft. They served as paramedics for the sick and injured, having long since learned about medicinal herbs and how to set broken bones. They had to be cheerleaders, encouraging the faint of heart to keep going. And if a wagon train was wracked by dissention, they often had to be both judge and jury. Finally, they were the main source of entertainment, telling stories of their own adventures around the campfire.

Counselor and strategist——
Seated at left, a veteran scout outlines the next day's route to members of his wagon train in an 1853 William Ranney painting. Many scouts added humor to their nightly talks by telling outrageous tall tales. Jim Bridger (*below, left*), for example, was famous for his deadpan accounts of a stream that ran so fast it became hot, and of an invisible glass mountain.

Jim Bridger——
Founder of Fort Bridger, a vital trading post on the Oregon Trail, this walking atlas of the West was the first white man to encounter the Great Salt Lake and to explore the Yellowstone area. A legendary raconteur, he once held a party of Sioux and Cheyenne spellbound for an hour—using only silent sign language.

Two Moon——
One year after fighting at the Little Bighorn, the Cheyenne chief helped negotiate a treaty with the government. Later, as a valued scout for the army, he puzzled at the ways of whites. "The white man eats and drinks all the time," he noted. "The Indian drinks when he finds water and eats when he kills game."

### Mickey Free

Born in Arizona to a Mexican mother and a part-Indian, part-Irish father, Free was kidnapped and raised by Apaches. Later he reveled in helping the army outwit the Indians he had grown to hate. They despised him in turn—as did his army comrades, one of whom once described him as "half Mexican, half Irish and whole son of a bitch."

### Tom Tobin

This masterful tracker once stalked a pair of murderers for five days, then showed up at Fort Garland, Colorado, with their heads in a sack. Tobin loved the life of a scout and clung to his frontier buckskins long after more civilized garb was commonly available. Here he wears a colorful mélange of Eastern and Western clothing.

### Pah-nayo-tishn ("Coyote Saw Him")

Nicknamed "Peaches" because of his light rosy complexion, this Cibecue Apache led General George Crook's command into the Sierra Madre to breach the mountain sanctuary of a band of Chiricahua Apaches—including Geronimo himself. The venture proved the wisdom of the old Southwest proverb: It takes an Apache to catch an Apache.

# Eyes and Ears of the Army

After the Civil War, what had been a trickle of white settlers heading west became a flood. Inevitably, the onslaught provoked an eruption of hostility from the Native Americans whose lands and very way of life were in jeopardy. The army—untrained to fight this swift-striking and elusive enemy—turned to civilian scouts. The guides who once had carefully steered their charges clear of danger were now asked to lead them, along with their creaky gun carriages and supply wagons, into the heart of it. The army also exploited longstanding intertribal feuds among the Indians. Along with hiring individual warriors to act as scouts, the government sometimes engaged several hundred at a time as auxiliary troops.

Whatever their origin, the scouts quickly became the indispensable eyes and ears of the army. On the march, they chose the route, selecting safe campsites and fords, as well as tracking Indian bands and estimating their strength. They frequently acted as couriers, carrying vital dispatches across hundreds of miles of dangerous territory. Ultimately, they proved so effective that one of them was deemed worth a regiment of soldiers. But the work was perilous. As General Custer once mordantly noted, being a scout was "congenial employment, most often leading to a terrible death."

## Comrades in Arms

Trapped on an open plain, a detachment of U.S. Cavalry fights for its life against a band of fast-riding Sioux in a painting by Frederic Remington. The troopers are aided by a buckskin-clad white scout, who confers with an officer, and a pair of Indian scouts who wear warriors' eagle feathers in their hair.

## California Joe

Moses "California Joe" Milner, who scouted at age 17 during the Mexican War, boozed himself out of a job when in 1868 Custer made him chief scout of the Seventh Cavalry. Milner celebrated by getting so drunk he had to be hogtied and returned to camp lashed to a mule. Custer sacked him—but continued to rely on the scout's experience and expertise.

## Will Comstock

Custer's favorite scout, Comstock had lived among the Cheyenne and other Indians, who knew him as Medicine Bill and told how once he bit off a squaw's poisoned finger to save her from a rattlesnake bite. He carefully hid his real identity: grandnephew to James Fenimore Cooper, whose romantic tales of the "noble savage" were derided on the Plains.

### Texas Jack Crawford

Chief scout for the Fifth Cavalry, Crawford learned to read and write at 17, while recovering from a Civil War wound. Later, the self-named poet-scout penned books, plays, short stories—and dozens of saccharine verses about the West. Himself a teetotaler, he once rode 300 miles to deliver a bottle of whiskey, unsampled, to Buffalo Bill Cody.

### The Apache Kid

En route to prison in 1887 for killing an Indian who had had a hand in his father's death, the Apache Kid—once a respected army scout—vanished into the sagebrush. For years he eluded all pursuers, littering his trail with fresh corpses. Despite rumors of his death in 1894, the fugitive reportedly turned up later in Mexico. His body was never found.

### Christopher "Kit" Carson

As chief scout for explorer John C. Fremont, Carson and a lone companion once took on—and defeated—30 outlaw Indians. Carson's exploits inspired dozens of dime novels. Given a book cover that showed him clobbering Indians with one hand and rescuing a damsel with the other, he remarked, "That thar may be true but I hain't got no recollection of it."

ONICLERS

The sun rises over the still waters of an Edenic West in Albert Bierstadt's majestic 1870 painting *Sierra Nevada Morning*.

# WHEN MISSOURIAN ORION CLEMENS LANDED THE JOB OF SECRETARY TO

the governor of Nevada Territory in 1861, his 27-year-old younger brother Samuel tagged along, gainfully employed as the secretary's secretary but with high hopes of making his fortune out West. The journey from St. Louis to Carson City, the territorial capital, was something of a rude awakening. After a six-day steamboat ride along the Missouri to St. Joseph, during which the vessel repeatedly ran aground, the Clemens brothers boarded a stagecoach for the 21-day-long trek to Nevada. Overloaded with both people and mail, the coach suffered a severe breakdown, and for the duration of the journey the put-upon passengers survived on food that was nearly inedible—rock-hard bread and a would-be tea called slumgullion that, in Sam Clemens's words, had "too much dish rag and sand and old bacon rind in it to deceive the intelligent traveler."

With the resilience of youth, however, Clemens remained optimistic, his head filled with visions of the riches that were surely awaiting him at his destination. Fantasy soon yielded to reality. Leaving his brother's employ to try his hand at silver mining proved a mistake when the hoped-for riches failed to materialize. Unexpectedly, a new job came along instead. Impressed by his many letters to the editor, the *Virginia City Territorial Enterprise* offered young Clemens the position of city editor. Impressed by the $25-a-week salary, Clemens accepted the job.

Initial efforts were discouraging: "I wandered about town questioning everybody, boring everybody, and finding out that nobody knew anything." But once he read the copy he had written—often embellished with factual fudgings, half-truths, and an occasional outright lie—he filled with pride: "I felt that I had found my legitimate occupation at last."

Sam Clemens had found himself in his writing. And America soon found in him a national treasure, when the reporter gave up the newspaper business to spend his time writing fiction—a pursuit that freed him from having to stick, however loosely, to the facts. He even wrote a novelized account of his Western exploits, called *Roughing It,*

under the pen name by which he is universally known: Mark Twain.

Mark Twain would be in good company as a chronicler of the West. As the frontier population grew, news accounts, photographs, and paintings of all things Western were increasingly in demand on both sides of the Mississippi. Sometimes the chroniclers were visitors, drawn by the same romantic visions that had lured Sam Clemens. The West they portrayed, whether in words or images, often entwined reality and romanticism in a way that was difficult to disentangle. But just as often, the artists and writers wanted only to preserve, in some form, the West that was fast disappearing. Their illustrations and written accounts of the frontier era are now our only link to a land and a way of life that no longer exist.

The most diverse legacy of the old West can be found in its newspapers. Though the majority quickly folded, some 10,000 of them sprang up in the latter half of the 19th century. As one Nevada editor remarked, "American pioneers carry with them the press and the type, and wherever they pitch their tent, be it in the wilderness of the interior, among the snow covered peaks of the Sierra or on the sunny sea beach of the Pacific, there too must the newspaper appear."

Newspapers arose not only from the public's desire to be enlightened and entertained. They also gave a town a sense of legitimacy, binding its citizens together and providing them an official voice. Newspapers aided settled regions in their quests to be designated territories, and aided territories in their pursuit of statehood; they were imperative for any town hoping to be named a county seat. In remote frontier and mining towns the newspaper was a de facto government, allowing for a frank exchange of ideas and keeping a watchful eye over local officials who were otherwise subject to little regulation.

A Western paper's sense of civic responsibility took rather a different form from that of its Eastern counterparts. If dailies like the esteemed *New-York Tribune* prided themselves on honesty and even-handedness, many Western editors believed in neither. "Independence in All Things, Neutrality in Nothing," proclaimed the masthead of the *Frontier Index,* a paper that was published by an ex-Confederate named Legh Freeman, whose venomous articles result-

Missouri native Samuel Clemens wrote a lively chronicle of his initiation to the West in his book *Roughing It*—under the now-famous pseudonym Mark Twain.

ed in the destruction of his print shop by an angry mob in 1868.

Violent words and deeds were also exchanged between rival papers. Lacking the diplomatic skill to settle their differences peaceably, many Western editors felt compelled to vent their spleen in print. The editor of the *San Francisco Star,* for example, referred to the nearby *California* as a "dim, dirty little paper," with a "lying sycophant" for an editor and an "overgrown lickspittle" for a publisher. And in Oklahoma, the head of the *Watonga Republican* called his counterpart at the *Watonga Rustler* an "ignorant, egotistical, scrawny, miserable, contemptible, disgusting, measly, mangy, depraved, lying, hypocritical, blear-eyed, doughfaced, idiotic, dwarfed, pinched-up, quaking old numbskull."

For all their vigor, these attacks remained strictly verbal, which was not always the case in the days when gentlemen still fought duels to the death, and less gentlemanly types resorted to other means. A notable case was that of Daniel Anthony, who during his publishing career in Kansas shot and killed one rival publisher, caned another, and seriously wounded a disagreeable reader. Anthony was not immune to retaliation: He was shot twice, beaten, and—at the ripe age of 67—horsewhipped.

When they were not marveling at (or being appalled by) the shenanigans of their local news purveyors, Western citizens had the option of turning to a variety of national publications, such as *Harper's Weekly* and *Scribner's Monthly,* for whom news from the frontier was always a surefire circulation booster. The national newspapers also offered illustrations, an attraction that most regional newspapers were not able to match.

At first these images were in the form of woodcuts or lithographs *(page 294),* but by the mid-1880s, the halftone process had made these methods obsolete. The technique, which divided an image into a collection of finely spaced dots that could be engraved on a printing plate, made it possible to transfer photographs directly to newsprint. The innovation was long overdue, given that photography had been around since the late 1830s and had, in fact, played a significant role in shaping the public's perception of the West.

The photographic process used at the time called for even amateurs to be equal parts artist, chemist, and weightlifter *(pages 278-279).* Before the invention of flexible, synthetic film, heavy, fragile

glass plates for each photograph had to be prepared on the spot, requiring photographers to take along hundreds of pounds of equipment. Making just one exposure took approximately half an hour, and there was no guarantee that it would turn out. Frontier photographer William Henry Jackson once claimed that he "prayed every time the lens was uncapped."

One of the most accomplished photographers of his day, the New York-born Jackson started at an early age, working in photography studios as a young man until he enlisted in the Union army. After his tour of duty, he headed out West, eventually setting up a studio in Omaha, Nebraska, in partnership with his brother Edward. In time, Jackson's skills attracted the attention of Ferdinand Vandeveer Hayden, who was the chief geologist for the U.S. Geological and Geographical Survey of the Territories; in 1871, Hayden offered Jackson a position as photographer on an upcoming expedition to the Yellowstone region in Wyoming.

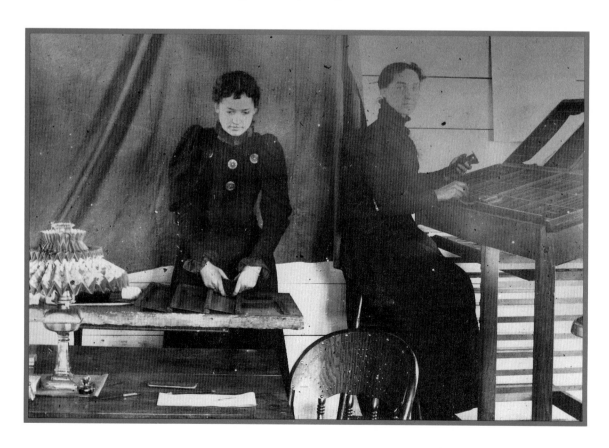

Women like the ones shown here setting type for the *Kansas Workman* in the 1880s often found work with newspapers throughout the West, some as editors and even publishers—a virtually unthinkable role for a woman in the 19th-century East.

# THE TRIALS OF FRONTIER PHOTOGRAPHY

The photographers who took part in 19th-century government surveying expeditions faced a logistical nightmare. The bulky, fragile photographic equipment of the day was ill suited for use outdoors, much less the remote regions being surveyed. Hundreds of pounds of gear including cameras, glass plates, and developing solutions had to be unpacked to shoot a single picture—which had to be developed on the spot—then repacked to move to another site. Getting a camera to the best vantage point sometimes required herculean effort. For his shot of the Mountain of the Holy Cross, for example *(pages 290-291)*, William Henry Jackson had to haul his gear up to the 1,320-foot summit of Notch Mountain. Despite these hardships, photographers such as Jackson, whose picture-taking adventures are shown here, managed to bring back images of stunning detail and beauty.

**M**aking Do——
In the field, Jackson lacked a proper darkroom, but with the resourcefulness typical of frontier photographers, he made one from a tent *(above)*.

**C**arrying the Load——
Survey members carefully load a mule with unwieldy crates, the kind used to carry photographic gear, as Jackson takes their picture.

**A** Tool of the Trade——
The 1873 camera at right used 17-by-19-inch glass plates and was standard issue for the frontier photographer. Although it folded up for traveling, it still weighed a hefty 70 pounds.

Getting the Picture ⎯⎯⎯
Jackson braves Overhanging Rock at 3,254-foot-high Glacier Point to photograph the Yosemite Valley.

German-born painter Albert Bierstadt *(left)* amassed a fortune through the sale of his works, including the huge canvases whose $25,000 price tags made him the highest-paid artist of the era.

Over the next eight years, while Hayden charted vast regions of the West, Jackson made images of the land that would stir the souls of all who saw them. Without his pictures of Yellowstone, no one, including the government sponsors of the expeditions, would have believed written accounts of the area's extraordinary beauty.

Although Jackson shot thousands of breathtaking photographs in the course of his long career—he died in 1942 at the age of 99— much of his fame rests on one image. On Hayden's 1873 expedition through Colorado, Jackson sought to confirm legends he had heard of a large cross formed by snow on the face of a mountain. "No man we talked with had ever seen the Mountain of the Holy Cross," the photographer wrote later. "But everyone knew that somewhere in the far reaches of the western highlands such a wonder might exist." After months of searching, the quest came to an end: "Suddenly, as I clambered over a vast mass of jagged rocks, I discovered the great shining cross dead before me, tilted against the mountainside. It was worth the labor of the past three months just to see it for a moment." Jackson's pictures of the mountain *(page 291)* added to the myth of the West as heavenly country.

While Jackson captured the majestic landscape of the West, an-

other photographer used his skills on a personal level. Soon after Solomon D. Butcher moved with his family from their Illinois home to Custer County, Nebraska, in 1880, the 24-year-old decided that while he liked the frontier, he hated homesteading. Over the next few years he tried his hand variously as a medical student, teacher, and postmaster, and then, in 1882, he set up a photography studio. The studio failed after only a few years, but his experiences inspired a new plan: He would produce a photographic history of Custer County, documenting the lives of his pioneer neighbors.

On and off for the next sixteen years Butcher rode from farm to farm, taking pictures of the doughty men, women, and children who made the frontier their home. The self-appointed task did not make the photographer rich; Butcher's subjects could usually offer little more than a hot meal and a cot to spend the night. But his persistence resulted in nearly 3,000 images and notes—a priceless and unflinching record of the homesteading era.

While cameras were unrivaled in their mechanical ability to render precise details—be the subject a spectacular mountain range or a sod house alone on the prairie—they were as yet unable to reproduce the colors of the West. And for many people, a skillful artist, translating his impressions through paint on canvas, remained a more desirable medium for capturing the region's essence.

One of the first painters to find fame depicting the West was Albert Bierstadt, who moved with his family from Germany to New England as a one-year-old infant in 1831. When he was in his twenties, he returned to Germany to study painting at Düsseldorf's Royal Academy for several years before settling in Massachusetts. Perhaps inspired by earlier trips through the Alps and the Apennines, Bierstadt decided to seek out the most magnificent vistas the New World had to offer and in 1859 joined a government surveying expedition along the Oregon Trail.

The paintings he made on his return—on oversize canvases to do justice to the mountains that were his subjects—were an instant success. One, of Wyoming's Lander's Peak, fetched $25,000, a sum believed at the time to be the largest ever paid for an American landscape. Bierstadts eventually found their way into museums from Washington, D.C., to St. Petersburg and earned their creator the nickname "prince of the mountain regions."

For all his acclaim as a painter of American themes, Bierstadt's style betrayed his European training. He consistently described the American landscape in terms of European geography. In one letter, for instance, he referred to the West as "the Italy of America in primitive condition."

One painter who vowed to paint "as an American, on an American basis, and American only" was Thomas Moran, although, like Bierstadt, he was born in Europe and emigrated to the United States at a young age. Moran learned art mainly from his family, which counted among its ranks many noteworthy artists. In fact, a dozen members of the talented clan, including Thomas, his brother Peter, and his son Edward, came to be known as the "twelve apostles of art."

In 1871, at the age of 34, Moran was working as an illustrator for *Scribner's Monthly* and was asked to create some images for a travelogue called "The Wonders of the Yellowstone." Enthralled by the sights that he was painting from someone else's sketches, he resolved to go and see them for himself and signed up for a Hayden expedition to the area.

The sketches he made on the trip became paintings upon his return, illustrations that he sold to *Scribner's* as well as a Bierstadt-size 7-by-12-foot panorama of Yellowstone canyon. As one *Scribner's* editor remarked, "watching the picture grow was like keeping one's eyes open during the successive ages of world creation."

Moran's *Grand Canyon of the Yellowstone,* coupled with Jackson's photographs, helped persuade Congress in 1872 to designate Yellowstone the country's first national park. The painting played such a large role in this decision that the National Park Service later referred to Moran as father of the park system. Congress bought the painting for $10,000 and hung it in the Capitol.

Despite his claim to the contrary, Moran was, like Bierstadt, essentially a European-style painter of American subjects. It fell to two other men, both born in America, to portray the West in a way as fresh as the land itself.

Frederic Remington was a 19-year-old football star and art student at Yale in 1880 when his father died, leaving him a small inheritance. With some money in his pocket but little direction in his life, the young man left school and worked a string of jobs, none of which amounted to much. A turning point came when the father of the woman he wanted to marry forbade the union. Like other young men

Artist and avid fisherman Thomas Moran rests streamside with a fine catch during one of his many sojourns to the West.

before him, he went west to get away, ultimately buying a sheep ranch near Kansas City. Although ranching suited him, it proved unprofitable and he sold the spread after a year.

Remington stayed out West, however, wandering farther afield and encountering—and endlessly drawing—the Apache in Arizona and the Comanche in what is now Oklahoma. Eventually, he won his sweetheart's hand and set to work turning his hundreds of sketches into paintings. The couple moved to New York to be near the magazines that Remington hoped would buy his art. His break came in 1886, when the struggling artist ran into an old friend from Yale, who

was now an art editor at *Outing Magazine*. The friend bought Remington's entire portfolio, commissioned further illustrations, and set the artist on the path to fame. By the time of his death in 1909, he had completed almost 3,000 paintings and illustrations as well as 25 meticulously detailed sculptures.

In all his depictions of cowboys and Indians, Remington is most famous for the way he showed their horses. Indeed, in scene after scene of cattle drives, solitary riders, and imagined Indian battles, he endeavored to live up to the words he suggested as his own epitaph: He Knew the Horse. One of the most notable triumphs of his equestrian insight can be seen in an early painting that shows a horse at full gallop with all four hoofs off the ground. He was ridiculed for this depiction at the time, but sophisticated photography later proved the astuteness of his vision.

Remington, like Bierstadt and Moran, found inspiration in the West, making frequent trips and returning each time to his New York

In his New Rochelle studio Frederic Remington works on a sculpture called *The Buffalo Horse,* depicting the collision of a horse and buffalo. Remington took great pride in representing animals—especially horses—with painstaking anatomical accuracy.

"Tower Falls" ———

In this 1872 painting, Thomas Moran captures the geologic energy that created the vaulting stone pinnacles surrounding Yellowstone's Tower Creek falls. Moran called this view "the most weird and impressive scene in the park."

"Indian Encampment, Shoshone Village"

In this 1860 depiction of a people living in harmony with nature, Albert Bierstadt harkens back to a time before the invasion of the whites, when Native Americans were free to make camp anywhere in this wide land.

"Grand Canyon of the Yellowstone" ——

In Thomas Moran's 1872 masterpiece, covering more than 84 square feet of canvas, the scale of nature's grandeur overwhelms the tiny human figures in the foreground.

**"The Great Hot Springs, Gardiner's River"**

Among the natural wonders Moran witnessed at Yellowstone were numerous hot springs, such as the steaming vents and bubbling waters of the springs at Gardiner's River, which he painted in 1871.

# Photographs of
# Western Wonders

Had photographers not accompanied government surveying expeditions to the West, Eastern officials might have thought the surveyors deranged. Their reports of titanic waterfalls, geysers that spewed searing mud, and trees that had turned to stone defied belief, yet the photos they brought back offered proof that such marvels did exist. Along with the paintings of Thomas Moran, Albert Bierstadt, and others, these pictures convinced the country that the West was a land of unique wonder.

But while government photographers such as William Henry Jackson fired the public's imagination with bold landscapes like the images shown here, another photographer kept his camera fixed on the homely realities of ordinary people. Between 1886 and 1901, Solomon D. Butcher combed the countryside around Custer County, Nebraska, photographing his pioneering neighbors (*pages 292-293*). His legacy is a remarkable pictorial history of America's homesteading era.

Teapot Rock——
Jackson shot this unusual rock formation during an 1870 U.S. Geological Survey expedition through southern Wyoming.

### Mountain of the Holy Cross ———

Taken in 1873, this image of the fabled cross of snow is Jackson's best-known photograph.

### Cliff Dwellings ———

In 1874 a survey team in Colorado came upon the remains of an ancient Pueblo Indian civilization at Mesa Verde. Jackson photographed reporter Ernest Ingersoll of the *New-York Tribune (seated)* and an assistant at the site.

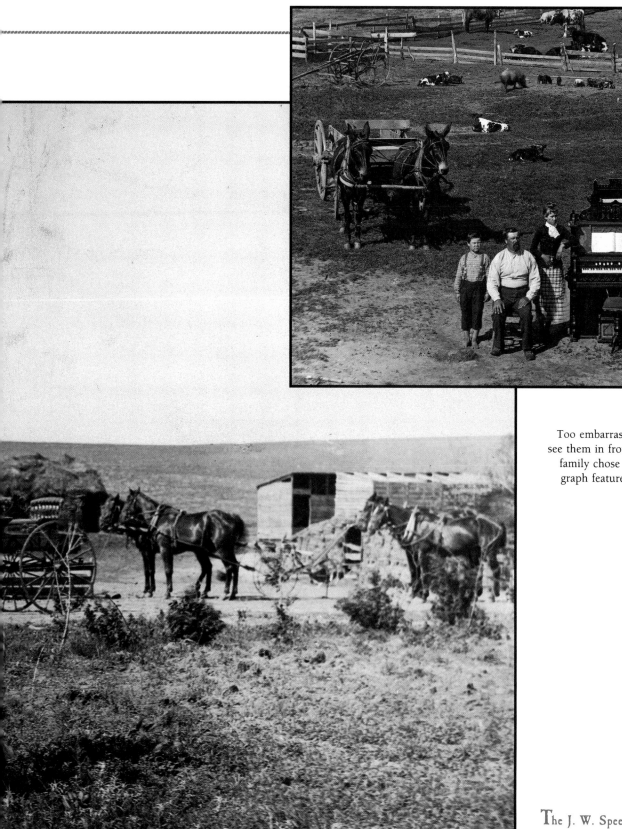

**Poor but Proud** ——
Too embarrassed to let their Eastern friends see them in front of a sod house, this pioneer family chose instead to let Butcher's photograph feature one of their few links to East Coast civilization—an organ.

**The J. W. Speese Family** ——
Eight members of the Speese family, released from slavery after the Civil War, pose for Solomon Butcher's camera outside their sod house in Westerville, Nebraska. Butcher remarked that the Speeses were "very highly respected citizens."

# The West in Words and Pictures

The public's demand to experience the West vicariously was tailor-made for the illustrated newspaper. Combining sometimes fanciful reports of events with detailed engravings, these publications gave readers a taste of everything from gold strikes to Indian raids and bank robberies.

Reproducing the images was a painstaking process. One common method was to create a printing plate from a woodcut. The woodcut began with a drawing of an event, which then had to be copied in reverse onto a wooden block. Skilled artisans then carved out, or engraved, the areas on the block that would appear white in the printed picture. To save time on large illustrations, a picture was often divided into several blocks that were engraved separately and then bolted together.

The woodcut process created work for a large number of artists, from those who roamed the country sketching newsworthy events to those who redrew the images onto the wood, and the master engravers who carved the highlights and shadows. In fact, even after printers invented methods of reproducing photographs on newsprint in the 1880s, many artists, including such luminaries as Thomas Moran and Frederic Remington, continued to see their work in the illustrated papers.

"Harper's Weekly"——
This self-styled *Journal of Civilization* was the most popular illustrated paper of its day. The September 7, 1867, issue featured a pictorial account of a relatively rare event—an Indian attack on a railroad crew.

CHEYENNE INDIANS ATTACKING A WORKING PARTY ON THE UNION PACIFIC

FRANK LESLIE'S ILLUSTRATED NEWSPAPER

Entered according to Act of Congress, in the year 1887, by Mrs. Frank Leslie, in the Office of the Librarian of Congress at Washington—Entered at the Post Office, New York, N.Y., as Second-class Matter.

No. 1,636.—Vol. LXIII.]        NEW YORK—FOR THE WEEK ENDING JANUARY 22, 1887.        [PRICE, 10 CENTS.

DAKOTA—A CURIOUS INDIAN CEREMONY AT STANDING ROCK AGENCY—THE SIOUX CHIEF "FIRE CLOUD" DEDICATING THE SACRED STANDING ROCK TO PEACE AND PLENTY.

FROM A PHOTO. BY BARRY.—SEE PAGE 397.

[September 7, 1867.

August 4, 1867.—[Sketched by T. R. Davis.]

"Frank Leslie's Illustrated Newspaper"
This issue of a popular paper, started in 1855 by an English-born engraver who had immigrated to America in 1848, depicts a Sioux Indian ritual in Dakota Territory.

# Creating a Myth on Canvas

Frederic Remington and Charles Russell helped create an enduring myth of the American West. Their works portray a bygone era of wild cowboys, intrepid soldiers, and wide-open spaces. But despite their similar themes, the two men took very different approaches to their subjects.

Remington, an Easterner through and through, composed his paintings from independent pieces, like jigsaw puzzles. He never actually witnessed an Indian battle, for example, although he did see soldiers and he did see Indians during the time he spent in the West. To depict a battle, he simply painted the two groups together, firing at each other. As a result of this technique, Remington's action-packed works were only faintly grounded in reality.

Charlie Russell also knew the importance of romance, but since he actually lived in the West and spent many years as a cowboy, most of his paintings of cowpunchers sprang directly from his life on the range. The same firsthand experience infuses his depictions of Native Americans, whom he portrayed with a rare realism and dignity.

**"Dash for the Timber"** ——

This 1889 Remington of an Indian fight showcases the action, attention to detail—and vivid imagination—for which the painter is famous.

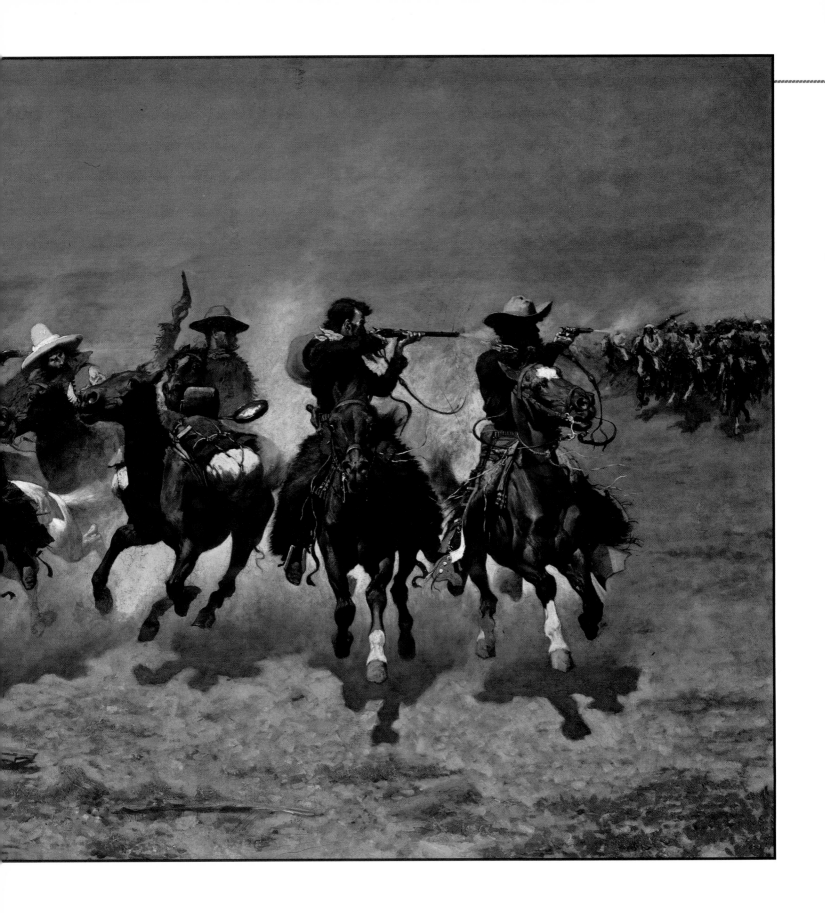

"Three Generations" ——

Russell, who spent six months with the Cree Indians in Canada during 1888 and 1889, captured the warmth of a family gathered around a campfire in a painting finished 10 years later.

"Chief Crowfoot" ——
Painted sometime in the early 1880s, this somber image of a Blackfeet chief is believed to be Charlie Russell's first Indian portrait.

"Self-Portrait" ——
Standing next to his trusted horse and wearing his trademark southwestern sash, Charlie Russell regards the Montana countryside in this 1899 self-portrait.

# SEARCHERS

A spectacular thunderstorm sweeps through the Grand Canyon in this painting by Thomas Moran, who accompanied surveyors to the area in 1873.

# Out West, it seemed, a fortune was waiting for anyone hale enough to

work a vein of ore or to saw down trees and muscle them out of the forest. Stands of yellow, sugar, and white pine, spruce, Douglas fir, and other species—many of them bigger around and taller than any found in the East—blanketed the countryside from the Rockies to the Pacific. And gold, silver, copper, and other precious minerals lay buried in the earth as far north as Coeur d'Alene, Utah, and as far south as Tombstone, Arizona.

But the West offered other types of wealth as well. To conservationists, it presented natural wonders so unusual and beautiful that they merited government protection forever. To ethnologists, scientists who specialize in the study of the world's cultures, it provided a living laboratory in which Native American traditions and lifestyles could be documented in all their diversity and splendor.

Clearly, if America was to exploit the West intelligently, a comprehensive inventory of all its resources—natural as well as human— would be required, along with a reliable assessment of the dangers and rewards to be expected in harvesting them. To obtain this information, the government chose to finance a series of surveys, one of the first of which was conceived by a 25-year-old Yale graduate and man of science named Clarence King.

The idea occurred to King while he stood at the summit of a peak near Yosemite in the summer of 1866. For the past three years, he had been exploring the Sierra Nevada and the desert regions of southern California and Arizona with the California Geological Survey. But as he peered eastward toward the deserts and ranges of Nevada, King realized that the geology of the West could be mastered only by studying "the whole mountain system of western America from the Plains to the Pacific."

Early the next year, King traveled to Washington, D.C., armed with several letters of recommendation, including one from the renowned scientist James D. Dana and another from Josiah D. Whitney, director of the California survey. King asked the federal government to fund a massive scientific undertaking: a survey of all the area lying

between the Sierra Nevada and the western slope of the Rockies.

In the years before the Civil War, only the army's elite Corps of Topographical Engineers would have been entrusted with such an expedition. In the 1840s and 1850s corps members such as John C. Fremont and William H. Emory had conducted more than two dozen surveys of the West. They had mapped the Oregon Trail, established the country's southwestern border with Mexico, scouted possible routes for the transcontinental railroad, and taken on other huge and important challenges. But after Robert E. Lee surrendered to Ulysses S. Grant in 1865 at Appomattox Courthouse, Virginia, thereby ending the war between the states, the military demobilized rapidly. As a result, not only was King's idea approved, he was given a mandate even more comprehensive than his original notion.

In orders signed by General Andrew A. Humphreys, the army officer charged with overseeing the expedition, King was directed "to examine and describe the geological structure, geographical condition and natural resources" of an 800-mile-wide belt of country extending from Nevada's western boundary to the 105th meridian, a north-south line that passes just east of Denver, Colorado, and Cheyenne, Wyoming. He was to start in California and make his way eastward along the 40th parallel, "with sufficient expansion north and south to include the line of the 'Central' and 'Union Pacific' railroads." The 40th parallel runs about 30 miles north of Reno, Nevada, skirts the city limits of Boulder, Colorado, and far to the east, forms the border between Nebraska and Kansas.

That such an immense expedition would be led by a youthful civilian was practically revolutionary, a point stressed by Secretary of War Edwin Stanton when he handed King his commission. "The sooner you get out of Washington, the better," Stanton said. "You are too young a man to be seen about town with this appointment in your pocket—there are four major generals who want your place."

Taking these words to heart, King lost little time getting underway. By midsummer, he had established base camp at Sacramento, California, and assembled his team. With him were a number of civilian scientists—geologists, topographers, a botanist, and an ornithologist—an escort of cavalry troopers, some hired hands, and a photographer, Timothy O'Sullivan, who had cut his teeth while traveling with the Army of the Potomac during the Civil War.

The survey began its first season on July 3. Riding on horseback

On the cold, rocky summit of Colorado's Sultan Mountain in 1874, two surveyors take the bearings of neighboring peaks with a theodolite. The two were members of the Hayden expedition, sent by the U.S. government to survey the Rocky Mountains and nearby plains.

and in mule-drawn wagons, the explorers pushed through the snow-mantled Donner Pass and descended onto the Great Basin, the parched and alkaline wasteland stretching between the Sierra Nevada in California and the Wasatch Range in Utah. Like Mark Twain, who had crossed the region by stagecoach six years earlier and pronounced it "one prodigious graveyard," King and his men found searing heat, choking dust, and many signs of earlier travelers' battles with nature—wayward wagon wheels, discarded household possessions, and occasional grave markers.

The civilians progressed much as a military expedition would—in a stop-and-go fashion. After marching a distance, the men selected a campsite and pitched their tents. Sometimes they ran the Stars and Stripes up a flagpole along with the survey's own banner. The camp served as a base of operations from which the botanist and ornithologist made short-distance forays to classify the local flora and fauna while the topographers and geologists ranged more widely, collecting rock samples and plotting the lay of the land. When their work was completed, the scientists struck camp and resumed the march.

In this way, the expedition was able to finish a large volume of work in a relatively short period of time. By December, the team had collected thousands of rock specimens, taken 300 barometric read-

ings, made more than 2,000 meteorological observations, and surveyed a huge block of country reaching from the boundary of California to the center of Nevada. A successful first season had been achieved, but not, King reported, without "tremendous effort." In August, in the mosquito-infested Humboldt Sink region, almost every member of the expedition had contracted malaria—then known as mountain ail—and King himself had been struck by lightning on a peak in central Nevada in late September. "I was staggered and my brain and nerves severely shocked," he wrote in his account of the incident. "My right side and arm turned brown." The effects of the stroke, he noted stoically, "wore off in the course of a week."

Expedition members wintered in the mining towns of Carson City and Virginia City, Nevada, where King and fellow geologists Samuel Emmons and James and Arnold Hague conducted an exhaustive investigation of the famous silver and gold deposit the Comstock Lode. Their analysis, along with work completed in subsequent seasons, would ultimately be the subject of the survey's first publication, *The Mining Industry*. A detailed inventory of all mines in operation from Nevada's Washoe Mountains to the Rockies, it contained virtually everything there was to know at the time about unearthing and refining silver and gold in the West. Enthusiastically received by the mining industry, the report also delighted the legislators who controlled the survey's purse strings. They gladly authorized funding for additional fieldwork in 1870.

Geologist Ferdinand Vandeveer Hayden, a contemporary of Clarence King's, was another explorer who understood the necessity of pleasing his sponsors. Hayden routinely peppered his reports with overly optimistic statements designed to appeal to entrepreneurial readers. While in charge of the Geological Survey of Nebraska in 1867, for example, Hayden predicted that coal and iron-ore deposits uncovered near the new state's western border would "exert the same kind of influence over the progress of the great west that Pennsylvania exerts over all the contiguous states."

Few in Washington seemed to mind that no thorough research supported the pronouncement. Congress in 1869 doubled Hayden's money, rechristened his undertaking the U.S. Geological and Geographic Survey of the Territories, and sent him west once again, this time to explore the territories of Colorado and New Mexico.

That year, Cyrus Thomas, Hayden's entomologist and botanist,

observed that the Cache la Poudre River in northern Colorado, Cherry Creek in Denver, and the Arkansas River were all swollen with more water than ever before, the result of seven years of gradually increasing rainfall. Because the string of rainy seasons coincided roughly with the settlement of the Plains, Thomas concluded the facts were somehow connected and forecast that as the population multiplied, the amount of moisture would also increase.

"This is the plan which nature herself has pointed out," Thomas wrote. "The perpetual snows of the great central axis are the sources of the various streams which rush down upon the margin of these plains, but chiefly sink in their effort to cross it. Let the population gather around the points where these burst from the mountains, and as it increases, pushing out on the plains eastward, I believe the supply of water will accompany it."

Though many Westerners at the time subscribed to the so-called rain-follows-the-plow hypothesis, subsequent dry seasons proved the theory to be malarkey. Its inclusion in Hayden's third report, however, harmed neither his reputation nor his survey, both of which grew by leaps and bounds, thanks to the explorer's infectious enthusiasm for the West and tireless lobbying. In 1870 Congress appropriated $25,000 for a campaign into Wyoming and the following year set aside $40,000 for an expedition into the Yellowstone River country—the only area within the continental boundaries of the United States that the government still considered terra incognita.

In July 1871 Hayden ventured into Yellowstone and was soon bowled over by its extraordinary sites, including Mammoth Hot Springs. "The beholder stands amazed at nature's handiwork," he wrote in his journal, "a snowy white ground, with every variety of shade, of scarlet, green and yellow, as brilliant as the brightness of our aniline dyes." The hot pools of the springs, he noted, "were so perfectly transparent that one could look down into the beautiful ultramarine depth to the bottom of the basin."

Photographer William Henry Jackson and landscape painter Thomas Moran accompanied Hayden on that expedition. The artists kept practically constant company, often making trips independent of the main group; Moran helped the photographer solve composition problems, and Jackson included the painter in his images. Together they successfully recorded the hot springs, Tower Falls, the Grand Canyon of the Yellowstone, and the geysers of Firehole

Basin—natural wonders that previously had been only the stuff of rumor and speculation around the campfire.

Widely reproduced throughout the country, Jackson's photographs and Moran's watercolors and sketches sent a wave of excitement through both houses of Congress. Inundated by the pictorial evidence, and by the writings and personal urgings of Hayden and other explorers, the lawmakers unanimously passed a bill making the Yellowstone region the country's first national park—a measure President Ulysses S. Grant signed into law on March 1, 1872. Then the legislators appropriated $75,000 for the survey to return to the field.

In the following years, Hayden's team explored the Teton Mountains and commenced an ambitious effort to map the rugged central Rockies. During this foray, Jackson made first-ever photographs of the Mountain of the Holy Cross, a towering peak in central Colorado whose snowy crags had long been the subject of mystery and legend, and of the prehistoric Indian cliff dwellings at Mesa Verde in the territory's extreme southwestern corner.

These were high points for Hayden and his men; the low point came on July 9, 1873, when one of his teams climbed a mountain in South Park, Colorado, and discovered another government-funded party—an army survey led by Lieutenant George M. Wheeler— already at work on the summit. Wheeler was two years into a projected 15-year effort to map all the territory lying west of the 100th meridian, a north-south line that bisects present-day North and South Dakota, passes just east of Dodge City, Kansas, and farther south, defines part of the Texas-Oklahoma border.

Though the long-term benefits of such an undertaking were judged to be great, in Hayden's eyes the lieutenant was nothing more than a trespasser in the arena of civilian surveying. "You can tell Wheeler," he threatened, "that if he stirs a finger or attempts to interfere with me or my survey in any way I will utterly crush him."

At congressional hearings held the next year to investigate the apparent duplication of activities, Wheeler did little to blunt charges that the army was trying to regain its prewar mapmaking role at the expense of the civilian surveys, but he was allowed to continue work—at least for five years. Then, in 1879, Congress ordered all government-sponsored expeditions combined into one, the U.S. Geological Survey, and Wheeler's organization was dismantled.

Clarence King served for one year as the first director of the new

survey. Then another well-known civilian geologist and explorer, John Wesley Powell, took his place. Powell had achieved nationwide celebrity for an expedition in Utah and Arizona in 1869, when he led a four-boat flotilla on a privately financed 14-week trip down the Green and Colorado rivers—a feat of extraordinary peril.

Boulder-strewn rapids claimed one of his boats early on, and key pieces of Powell's scientific gear and 2,000 pounds of provisions, including most of the explorers' spare clothing, were lost to the swift-running waters. Morale declined steadily in the days that followed as the men—tired, constantly wet, and faced with starvation—fought to keep the remaining vessels afloat.

Finally, in the Grand Canyon, three of Powell's companions decided they had had enough. Figuring their chances of staying alive were better on foot than in a boat, they abandoned the expedition and struck out overland for a nearby Mormon settlement. "We had to let them take to the mountains," wrote George Bradley, one of those who stayed behind. "They left us with good feelings though we deeply regret their loss for they are as fine of fellows as I ever had the good fortune to meet."

Had the three been able to endure the voyage for only two more days, they would have been with Powell when he reached his destination, the placid waters at the confluence of the Virgin and Colorado rivers along the Nevada-Arizona border. Instead, not far from the rim of the canyon, the men were attacked and killed by local Indians who mistook them for miners who had earlier murdered a member of their community.

Despite the deaths, Powell received government funding for a second trip down the Colorado in 1871 and later explored the plateau country of southern Utah and Arizona north and west of the Colorado River, a task he completed in 1873. After that, his interest in topography and geology was eclipsed by mounting concerns about the federal government's land-use policies and fears for the West's vanishing Native American populations.

"The people are divided into two great parties," he wrote, "one crying for blood, and demanding the destruction of the Indians, the other begging that he may be left in his aboriginal condition, and that the progress of civilization may be stayed. Vain is the clamor of either party. The march of humanity cannot be stayed. Whether we desire it or not, the ancient inhabitants of the country must be lost."

—Falling
Ax—

Indeed, the Indians had already been ravaged by disease, destroyed by arms, or forcibly removed from their original homelands. Only in the desert Southwest were Native American societies to be found that were still intact and at home. Before they disappeared, Powell and a host of other researchers—John Gregory Bourke, Alice C. Fletcher, and Francis La Flesche among them *(pages 318-319)*—hurried to learn their languages, customs, and traditions.

Powell was assisted in this by James C. Pilling, a skilled stenographer whose training in shorthand enabled him to record Indian words as quickly as they were spoken, and by the photographer John K. Hillers. Hired originally as an all-purpose crewman, Hillers learned the ins and outs of producing negatives during the second river trip and became photographer-in-chief in time to document the Marble and Grand canyons in Arizona and what is now Zion National Park in southern Utah.

From Zion, Powell traveled to the Mormon community of Kanab, near the Arizona border, where Hillers photographed the Southern Paiute. These images, along with other portraits taken the following year, were displayed at the Centennial Exhibition in Philadelphia, which opened on May 10, 1876. They included shots of Southern Paiutes dressed up either in clothing that Powell had collected years earlier from Utes living in northwestern Colorado, or in fringed buckskin shirts and fake headdresses that had been manufactured under the direction of Powell's sister. Some of the Indian women were photographed with one or both of their breasts exposed. Despite their many inaccuracies, the portraits remain a valuable cultural record of one of the last Indian groups in the West to come into sustained contact with whites and other settlers.

In 1878 Powell aired his other great concern—the government's wasteful land-use policies—in his *Report on the Lands of the Arid Regions of the United States*. While conceding that the West was blessed with bountiful riches, such as the gold and silver mines of Colorado and Nevada *(pages 320-323)* and the timberlands of the Northwest *(pages 324-327)*, he also argued that the large arid regions could not support a dense population. Powell predicted that trying to impose an Eastern-style small-farm pattern would lead to disaster for the settlers, disruption of a fragile environment, and even spoilation of the land itself.

What was needed, Powell wrote, was an approach to public

Loggers felling huge Western trees developed special tools for the job. The falling ax at right, for instance, has an extralong haft—up to 4 feet—to reach into the heart of an 8-foot-thick tree. Similarly, though Eastern falling saws were rarely more than 7 feet long, the one above is 10 feet—and saws for felling sequoias reached 18 feet. Metal boot spikes called calks gave secure footing on oversize logs and at great heights.

—Calked Boots—

309

# RECORDER OF SCENIC GLORIES AND A VANISHING WAY OF LIFE

In May of 1871 Jack Hillers, a sandy-haired 28-year-old newly discharged from the U.S. Army, was in Salt Lake City looking for a job as a teamster when he met John Wesley Powell. A famous surveyor setting off to explore the Green and Colorado rivers, Powell offered Hillers work as a boatman. The young man quickly accepted, thereby making a decision that would change his whole life. Because of it, he would become one of the preeminent photographers of the West, a recorder of timeless images that would be widely admired in his own day and still revered a century later.

Hillers began by voluntarily assisting the photographer on Powell's expedition. Hillers toted the bulky gear, set up the lightproof tent, mixed chemicals for developing, and prepared the large glass plates with emulsion. Soon Powell made Hillers his chief photographer and kept him taking pictures for almost three decades. Although tormented by a Civil War back injury, Hillers wrestled some 300 pounds of equipment up and down mountains and gorges. He worked in and with river water so cold that it could not be used unheated for photo processing, and often turned his skin blue by the end of the day.

Hillers's magnificent scenic pictures were widely published and immensely popular for home 3-D viewing on stereopticons. But his most important work was probably the thousands of photographs he made of Native Americans, like the ones seen here. Even such portraits were not easily achieved; he faced, among other problems, the possibility of being attacked by Apaches. Nonetheless, Hillers gave America what is probably its most complete and still cherished visual record of that era's fast-disappearing Indian life.

Sallie, Hopi Woman——

Jack Hillers photographed these pueblo dwellers in 1879 for the Bureau of Ethnology. He was a poor speller, but his written observations at times were as acute as his visual images. He noted that married women like the one above "wear their hair long and done up in a long role hanging down each side," whereas maidens like those at top right wear their hair "done up on the side in the shape of a ram's horn, and are as a general thing pretty." He also noted they prechewed food for the cook pot "to arouse the animal passion" of young warriors and so "hasten marriage."

Unmarried Hopi Women ———

Pedro Pino, Zuni Governor ———

Hopi Man with Spindle ———

land policies guided by the nature of the land, not the nature of man. To this end, he advocated the abolition of water monopolies, the classification of the arid regions according to their future use—as mineral, coal, irrigable, timber, or ranch land—and the development of an overall plan for their exploitation. As it turned out, few immediate results came from Powell's report, but it did start people thinking, and it won him the respect of conservationists such as John Muir.

Like Powell, Muir had devoted most of his adult life to exploring. In 1867, after studying at the University of Wisconsin, Muir walked from the Middle West to the Gulf of Mexico. Later, he took passage for the Isthmus of Panama and California, where he continued roaming—traveling on foot through the mountains of Nevada, Utah, Oregon, Washington, and Alaska—and started writing.

Muir's articles, more than 60 of them in all, lured a succession of famous and powerful figures to the Yosemite Valley, including the essayist and poet Ralph Waldo Emerson, whom Muir described as "the most serene, majestic, sequoia-like soul I ever met." The naturalist implored each visitor to join his struggle to have Yosemite designated the country's second national park. "God has cared for these trees," Muir said, "saved them from drought, disease, avalanches and floods, but he cannot save them from fools—only Uncle Sam can do that!" The fools, in his estimation, were sheepherders and loggers who were steadily denuding the Yosemite Valley watershed of its trees and brush. Without such vegetation, which normally trapped the spring rains and melting snow, the water flooded the lower areas and left the uplands parched, with disastrous consequences. Only by stopping the grazing and tree cutting, he argued, could this national treasure be preserved.

Swayed by Muir's lobbying, Congress in September 1890 voted to create Yosemite National Park. Two years later, Muir founded the Sierra Club to publish information about the mountain regions of the Pacific Coast and to preserve the forests of the Sierra Nevada. About 160 friends of nature, most of them prominent business people and academics, signed on as members. They were joined by several well-regarded honorary members, including the editor of *Century* magazine, which published Muir's most influential writings, the secretary of the Department of the Interior, the head of one of England's most respected scientific institutions, and a famed explorer, geologist, ethnologist, and conservationist—John Wesley Powell.

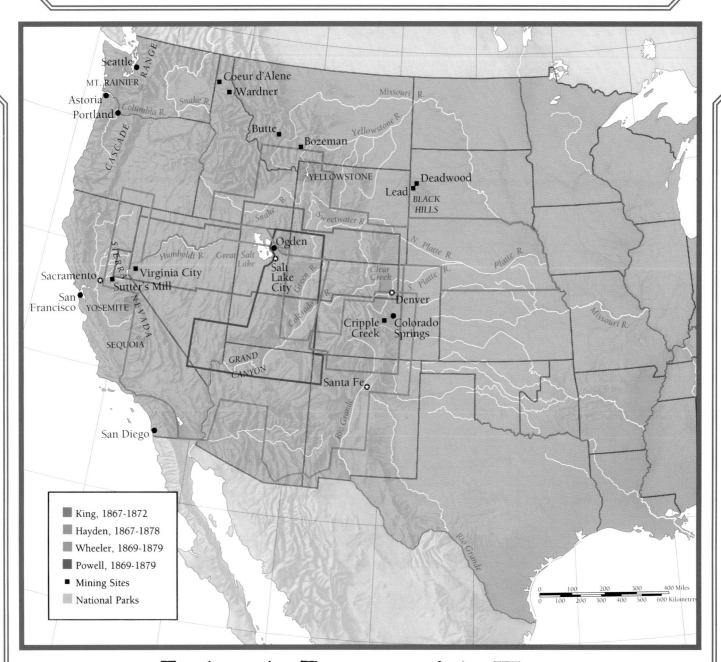

King, 1867-1872
Hayden, 1867-1878
Wheeler, 1869-1879
Powell, 1869-1879
■ Mining Sites
National Parks

Map labels: Seattle, MT. RAINIER, CASCADE RANGE, Astoria, Portland, Columbia R., Snake R., Coeur d'Alene, Wardner, Missouri R., Butte, Yellowstone R., Bozeman, YELLOWSTONE, Deadwood, Lead, BLACK HILLS, Snake R., Sweetwater R., Ogden, Great Salt Lake, Humboldt R., Salt Lake City, N. Platte R., Clear Creek, Platte R., Sacramento, SIERRA NEVADA, Virginia City, Sutter's Mill, Green R., S. Platte R., Denver, San Francisco, YOSEMITE, Colorado R., Cripple Creek, Colorado Springs, SEQUOIA, Missouri R., GRAND CANYON, Santa Fe, San Diego, Rio Grande, Rio Grande

# Finding the Treasures of the West

People went west in search of different kinds of riches—material wealth, of course, but also adventure, knowledge, and beauty that could lift the heart or bring peace to the soul. The four Great Surveys managed to discover some of each kind: evidence of extensive mineral deposits, valuable scientific information, and inspiring views. Prospectors found wealth at places such as Clear Creek, Colorado, where George Jackson started a big rush in 1859; Butte, Montana, site of the Anaconda copper mine; Wardner, Idaho, where Noah Kellogg's donkey discovered silver; Virginia City, Nevada, with its Comstock Lode; and Cripple Creek, Colorado, whose mines yielded $18 million in gold in one year alone. Loggers single-mindedly seized their green treasure wherever there were forests. Fearing they would leave none of the wilderness unscarred, conservationists induced the government to create four national parks by 1900. The Grand Canyon did not become a national park until 1919.

# THE GREAT SURVEYS

"The rushing waters break into great waves on the rocks and lash themselves into a mad white foam," wrote John Wesley Powell of his 1869 voyage through the Grand Canyon. A thousand feet down in a gorge, he had no choice but to go on: "There is no hesitation!!!" Such was the thrill and the danger of probing the last place marked *unknown* on maps of the West. But in fact, there were other large areas about which little was known, and with the Civil War ended, America resumed exploration, launching four major expeditions known collectively as the Great Surveys.

One of them, starting in 1867, was led by Ferdinand Vandeveer Hayden, a scientist who documented the wonders of Yellowstone and got a national park created there within eight months of first seeing the site. Another expedition, beginning the same year, was placed in the tender hands of Clarence King, a 25-year-old Yale graduate whose daredevil feats eclipsed a solid body of scientific accomplishment. A third was led by Lieutenant George M. Wheeler. Given the job mainly as a sop to the army, he achieved less than his civilian counterparts. John Powell, who had raised his own financing for his 1869 Grand Canyon trip, received government funds for the fourth Great Survey—further exploration of the Colorado and other rivers in 1871. All four leaders were confident of finding rich resources. "The deserts are not all desert," wrote Clarence King. "All that is needed is to explore and declare the nature of the national domain!"

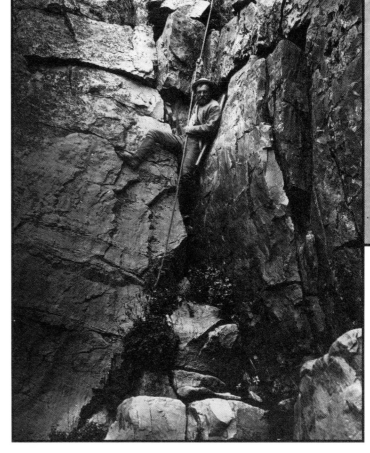

A World of Natural Splendors ———
Idaho's Snake River cascades into the mist at Shoshone Falls in this picture by photographer Timothy O'Sullivan. Photos such as this one—in which the falls' thunderous roar seems almost audible—stirred interest in the West and public support for the surveys.

R isking Life and Limb ———
Showing off his bravery and flamboyant style, Clarence King nonchalantly perches high on a mountainside. Once, when he ignored clear signs of imminent lightning, he was struck by a bolt but survived with burns. His work did not suffer from his antics; the survey he led along the 40th parallel found evidence of coal in Wyoming and silver in Nevada.

**A** Rest by the River———
George Wheeler (*foreground*) relaxes by the lower Colorado before starting an arduous upstream journey into the Grand Canyon. Wheeler's rambling route often duplicated the work of other explorers—in this instance, Powell. And yet, said one rival, Wheeler bypassed unexplored regions "as large as Connecticut and Rhode Island put together."

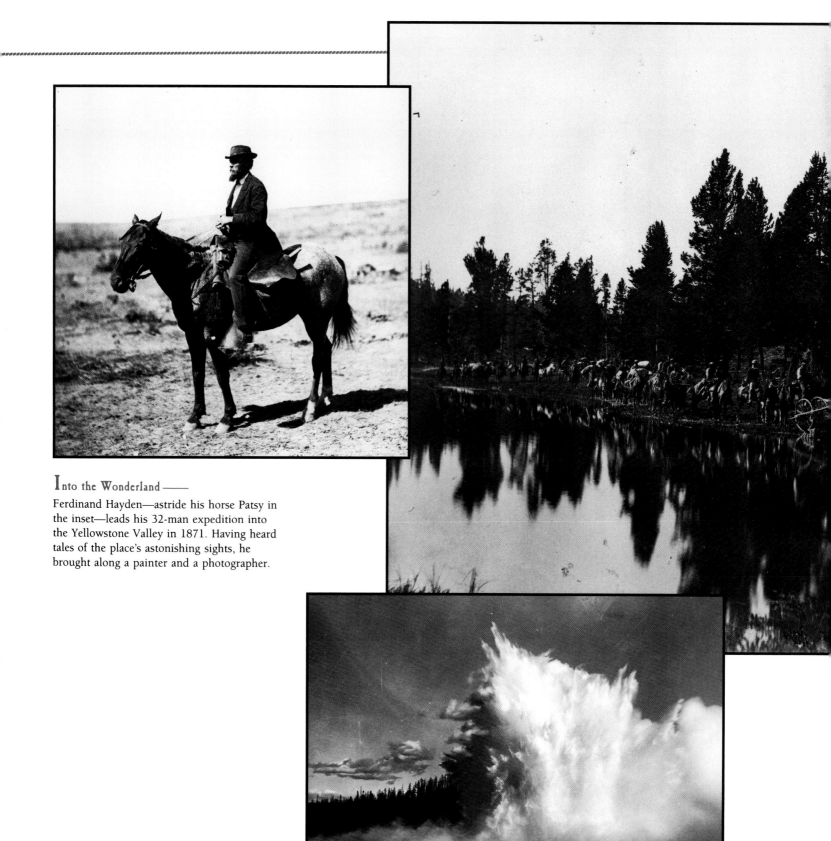

**I**nto the **W**onderland——

Ferdinand Hayden—astride his horse Patsy in
the inset—leads his 32-man expedition into
the Yellowstone Valley in 1871. Having heard
tales of the place's astonishing sights, he
brought along a painter and a photographer.

**A** **W**atery **E**xplosion——

In a powerful display of natural subterranean
forces, Excelsior Geyser spews to a towering
height. At the time of Hayden's visit, the geyser regularly erupted to some 300 feet. It
became dormant in 1888.

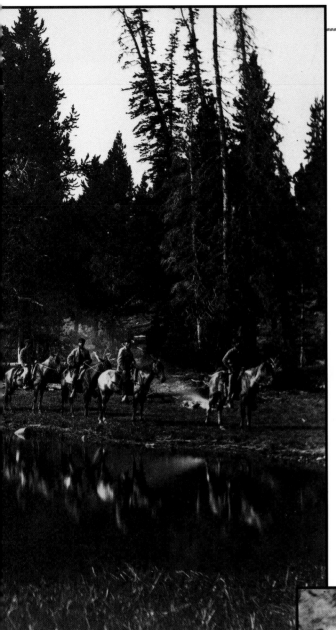

No photos from the surveys were more eagerly snapped up by the public than those of the Grand Canyon taken during John Wesley Powell's explorations. Most, like this one, were shot by photographer Jack Hillers.

*"Down these grand, gloomy depths we glide, ever listening, for the mad waters keep up their roar. . . . We listen for falls, and watch for rocks, or stop now and then in the bay of a recess to admire the gigantic scenery."*

◆

*John Wesley Powell*

Indian and Explorer ——

Near the Arizona border, Powell poses with a Paiute leader named Tau-gu in 1873. Powell's survey led him to study Native American cultures and eventually to his appointment as director of the Bureau of Ethnology.

# Dedicated Students of Indian Life

"I can tell you that lying on the ground, in a tee pee full of Indians sound asleep and looking up through the opening in the center to see the stars that come and go with the hours stimulates ethnographic reflections," wrote Alice Fletcher *(right)*. Passing a night in a crowded tipi may seem a strange thing for a proper Victorian lady to do, but Fletcher would go to any lengths to further her study of Indian cultures. She even watched a Lakota Sun Dance to its grisly, flesh-tearing finale, although she required a dose of brandy "to keep from fainting."

Fletcher was not alone in her devotion to learning, writing, and lecturing about Indians. Kindred spirits included explorer John Wesley Powell, who became the first director of the Bureau of Ethnology; a former Apache fighter named John Gregory Bourke *(top right)*; and Francis La Flesche *(bottom right)*, a young Omaha Indian. They are called salvage anthropologists, because they salvaged knowledge of cultures they believed were vanishing.

*"Living with my Indian friends I found I was a stranger in my native land. As time went on . . . a change wrought in me. I learned to hear the echoes of a time when every living thing even the sky had a voice. That voice so devoutly heard by the ancient people of America I desire to make audible to others."*

◆

*Alice Fletcher*

**J**ohn Bourke's Paper Medicine ——
Lieutenant Bourke admired and studied the Apache even while he was still fighting them, making notes about their language and customs. Watching Bourke scribbling away, an Apache scout for the army asked if he was "a paper medicine man." The nickname stuck.

**W**hite Mother, Indian Son ——
Alice Fletcher *(above)* taught anthropology to Francis La Flesche *(right)*, her young Omaha assistant. Together they wrote a book and articles about Omaha customs, ceremonies, and dances, and recorded Omaha music on Thomas Edison's new wax cylinders. A spinster, Fletcher adopted La Flesche as her son. "She has been to me like a real mother," he said.

A Dance for the Harvest——

At Zuni Pueblo in New Mexico, dancers celebrate the harvest in this 1879 photograph shot for John Wesley Powell's Bureau of Ethnology. The new bureau lured many would-be ethnologists—teachers, journalists, scientists—eager to do fieldwork. Some began dressing like Indians.

# Gold, Sweat, Death, and Debauchery

"I went to bed and dreamed of riches galore," said George Jackson of the 1859 day that he found gold in Clear Creek, Colorado. "I had struck it rich! There were millions in it." Jackson did not reap millions from his claim, which he soon sold. But his discovery set off a new round of gold and silver rushes that would last for 30 years.

One historian calls these mad rushes "the quintessential frontier experience," because they lured all kinds of people who wanted a better life—preferably in the form of overnight riches. Gold fever struck women as well as men, white and African Americans, Hispanics, Chinese, European immigrants, farmers, merchants, and even teachers.

In the early days, a lucky prospector could make a modest living—and, sometimes, wealth—by panning surface gold. But by the mid-1870s the precious ore usually could be had only by "hard rock" mining, the dangerous work of digging tunnels deep into the earth. By then, too, most good mines belonged to big corporations, whose miners worked for wages of three or four dollars a day. There was also plenty of money to be made in the boom towns by an abundance of saloon keepers and prostitutes, as well as by more respectable merchants.

Working a Surface Claim ——

A woman, perhaps the wife of a miner, brings lunch to three men using a long tom, a trough that functioned somewhat like a miner's pan to wash bits of gold free of sand and gravel. Many prospectors went alone rather than subject their wives to the crude living conditions of the primitive mining camps.

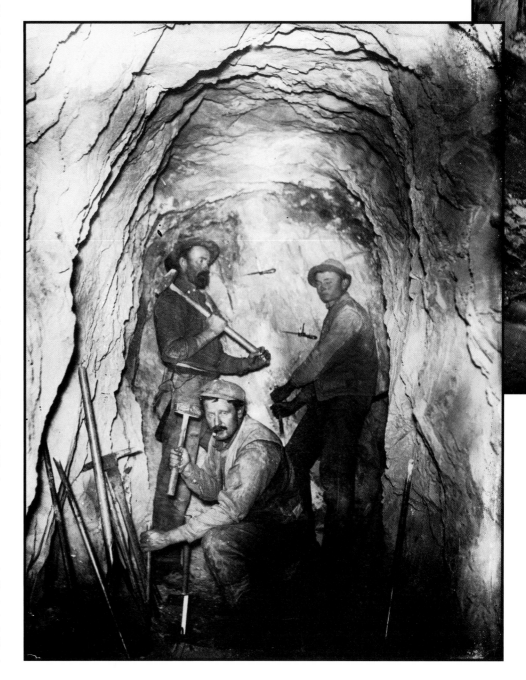

Hard Rock Miners ——

Miners demonstrate how they hammer drills into rock to make holes for blasting powder. Underground mining was grueling—temperatures sometimes reached 120 degrees Fahrenheit—and dangerous. Some 7,500 were killed in frontier mines and about 20,000 maimed.

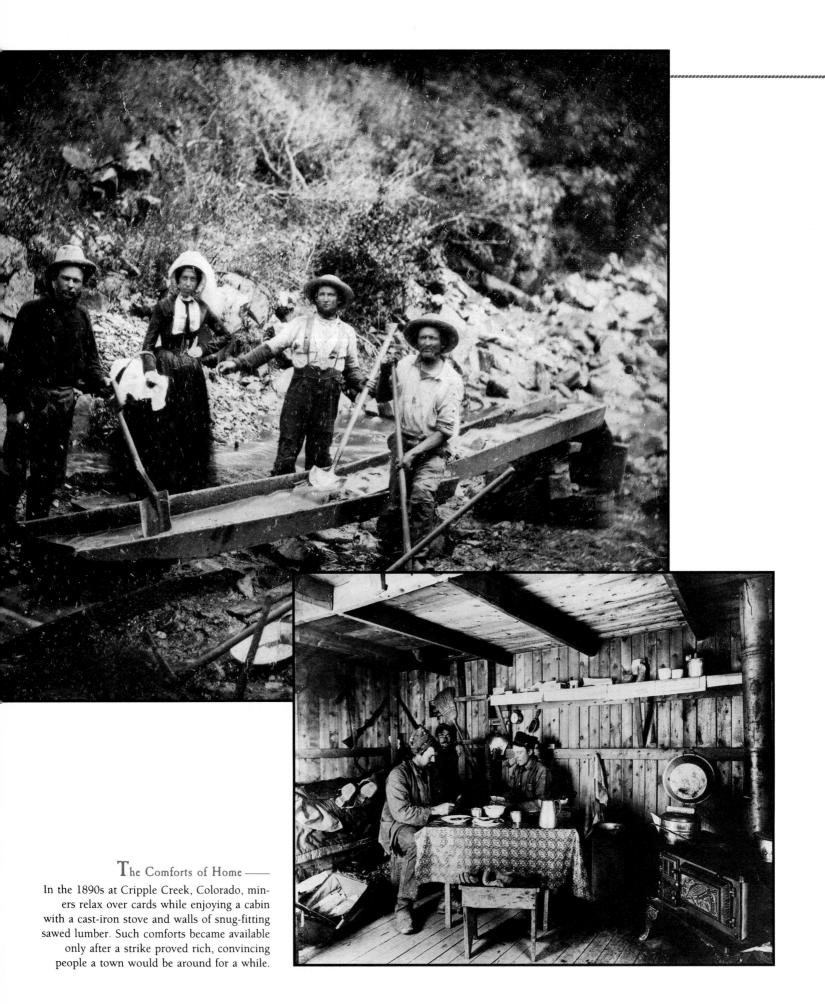

The Comforts of Home
In the 1890s at Cripple Creek, Colorado, miners relax over cards while enjoying a cabin with a cast-iron stove and walls of snug-fitting sawed lumber. Such comforts became available only after a strike proved rich, convincing people a town would be around for a while.

**From Prospector to Scribe**——
William Wright came west to prospect, but after two unlucky years he took a newspaper job in Virginia City, Nevada, so he could send money to his family. He wrote about mining for 31 years, using a pen name, Dan De Quille, for protection against irate readers.

*"It was my first experience of a mining stampede, and I caught the fever at once!"*

◆

*Jim Wardner, who joined rushes in Arizona, Colorado, Idaho, and at Virginia City, Nevada*

A Town of Smoke, Grit, and Riches ———
The tall stacks of the minehead works throw a
smoky pall over Virginia City, which exploded
into being when gold *and* silver—the Comstock Lode—were found there in 1859. By fall
of 1860 the town had 202 businesses.

The Four-Million-Dollar Donkey ———
Idaho children pose with Jack, a donkey credited with the great Coeur d'Alene silver strike.
Owner Noah Kellogg said he found the runaway ass fixated by a silver outcrop. Kellogg
made some four million dollars from the find.

# The Lure of the West's Green Wealth

"Oh! What timber," exclaimed Samuel Wilkeson, a Northern Pacific Railroad agent, on first seeing the forests of the Northwest. "These trees . . . enchain the sense of the grand," he wrote, and "enchant the sense of the beautiful." His interest was more in business than in beauty as he noted that the Western forests surpassed "the woods of all the rest of the globe in the size, quantity and quality of the timber."

In fact, the mighty stands of coast redwood and sequoia, Douglas fir and hemlock, spruce and pine and cedar would produce five times as much lumber per acre as Eastern forests, and the astonishing extent of the area they covered—more than 300,000 square miles—made them a far richer treasure than all the West's silver and gold. It is no surprise that lumbermen swarmed to the region and seized on every new technological development to speed their harvest of trees.

At first, most loggers worked independently or for small outfits. Large companies inevitably took over, but even big business with big machines depended on the energy and bravery of those who worked hard in the face of danger. And as a ditty of the era indicates, they also played as hard as they worked: "My lover was a logger / there's none like him today / If you'd sprinkle whisky on it / he'd eat a bale of hay!"

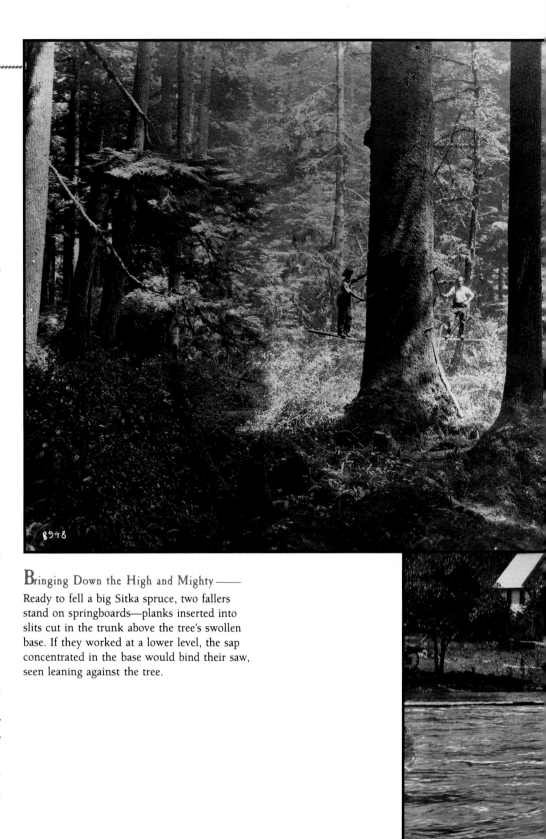

Bringing Down the High and Mighty——
Ready to fell a big Sitka spruce, two fallers stand on springboards—planks inserted into slits cut in the trunk above the tree's swollen base. If they worked at a lower level, the sap concentrated in the base would bind their saw, seen leaning against the tree.

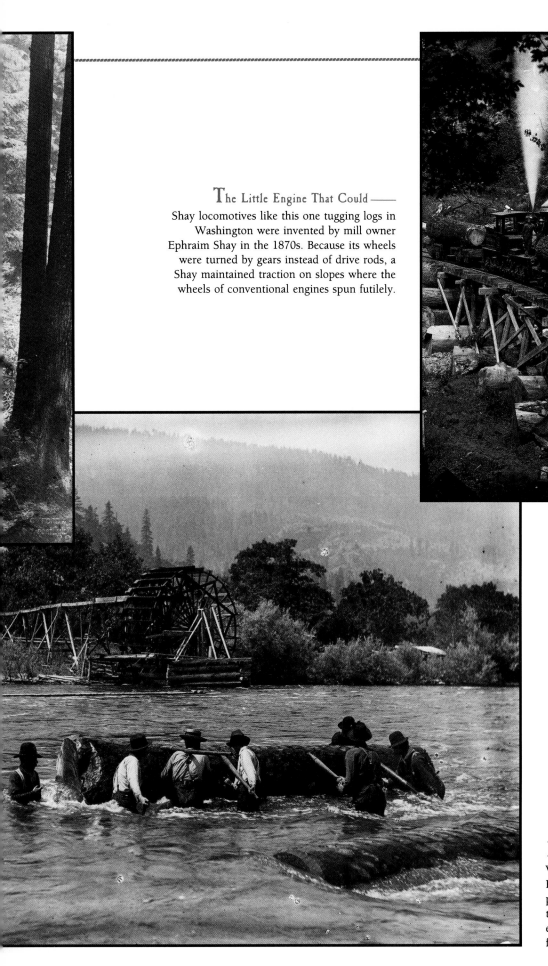

**The Little Engine That Could** ——
Shay locomotives like this one tugging logs in Washington were invented by mill owner Ephraim Shay in the 1870s. Because its wheels were turned by gears instead of drive rods, a Shay maintained traction on slopes where the wheels of conventional engines spun futilely.

**Down the River to the Mill** ——
Waist deep in northern California's Klamath River, workers known as river pigs free a big pine log from a sand bar. The cheapest way to transport logs was to float them. Seagoing tugs even moved huge rafts of logs 1,100 miles from Washington to San Diego.

T̲he Lone Entrepreneur———
Simon Benson (*above*) was one logger who created his own timber empire despite competition from big corporations. The Norwegian immigrant took a $40-a-month job in a lumber camp in 1878; three decades later he was a multimillionaire.

*"If you have faith in yourself you can make good. If you have no goal, if you don't know where you are heading for, you will never reach the port of success."*

◆

*Simon Benson*

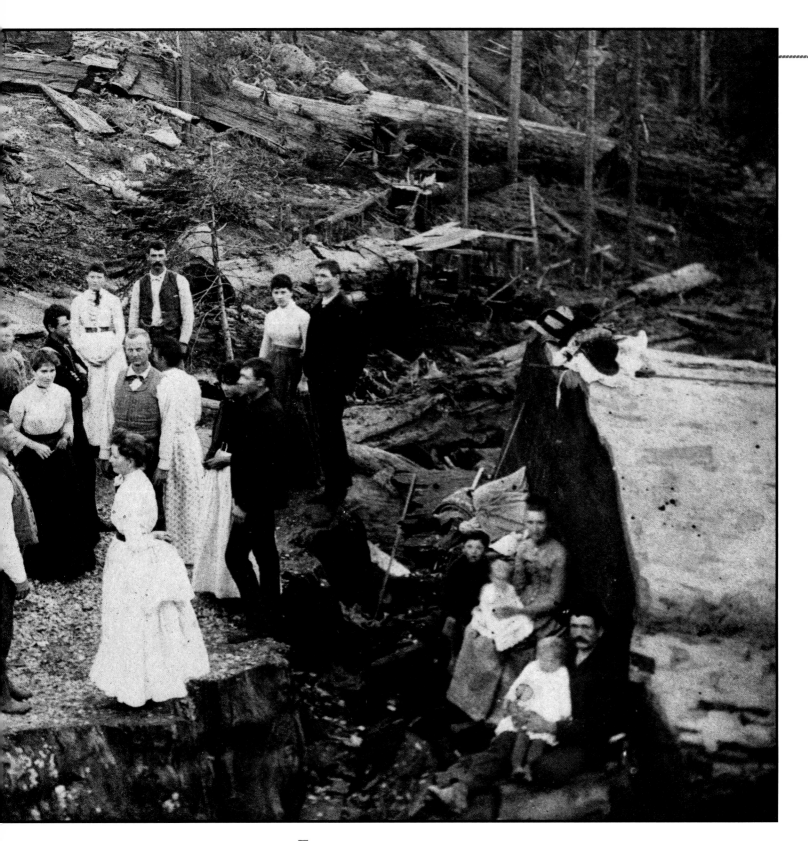

Family Fun at the Logging Camp——
On a giant redwood stump—big enough to
serve as a square-dance floor with room left
over for fiddlers—loggers and their ladies
in Tulare County, California, get ready to do-
si-do. In camps without women, loggers
danced together. Those taking women's roles
tied a bandanna around one arm.

# A Voice Crying for the Wilderness

Loggers were purposeful and thorough. They moved into a stand of timber and felled every tree worth taking, planting no replacements. They ravaged even the giant redwood groves along the coast and in the Sierra Nevada, greedily felling trees thought at the time to be the largest and oldest living things on earth. Never very numerous, these monarchs soared to 350 feet and could weigh more than 1,000 tons. Some were as much as 3,000 years old.

"God has cared for these trees, saved them from drought, disease, avalanches and floods," wrote naturalist John Muir, "but he cannot save them from fools—only Uncle Sam can do that!" Muir's advocacy helped persuade the government to take steps, including creating Yosemite National Park in 1890, to save what was left of the giant trees from total destruction.

The Old Man of the Mountains ——
John Muir (*above*) roamed the mountains he loved for many years. Perhaps his greatest bequest was the powerful Sierra Club he founded in 1892, which carried on his eloquent plea on behalf of wilderness preservation.

*"Tired, nerve shaken, over-civilized people are beginning to find out that going to the mountains is going home; that wilderness is a necessity; and that mountain parks and reservations are useful not only as fountains of timber and irrigating rivers, but as fountains of life."*

◆

*John Muir*

A New Revelation ——
"A view that suddenly breaks upon us in all its glory far and wide and deep," Muir said of Yosemite, "a new revelation in landscape." After its founding, the park was enlarged to protect more trees and now holds 759,000 acres.

Corpses on the Forest Floor ———
Downed sugar pines lie in a tangle of logs and
splinters after a fast and furious clear-cutting
operation that left no usable tree standing.
Such photos fueled public outrage and
strengthened the conservation movement.

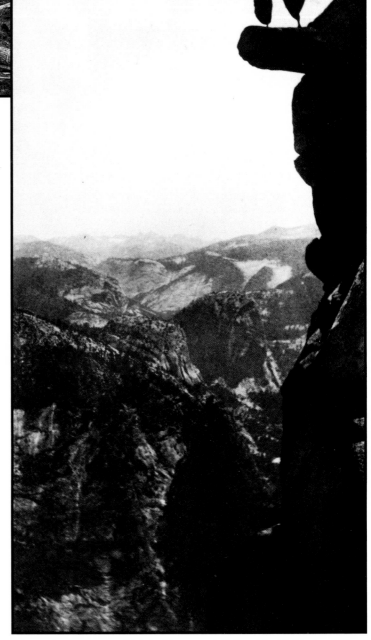

Getting Their Kicks in the Wilderness ———
Two young women dancing on Overhanging
Rock in the 1890s fulfill Muir's wish that
Yosemite be enjoyed. Visitors, who have
thronged to the park since it opened, now
exceed three million a year.

# MYTHMAKERS

# Natural Rock Arch
## Utah

"All men were made by the same Great Spirit. They are all brothers. The earth is the mother of all people, and all people should have equal rights upon it."

*Attributed to Chief Joseph of the Nez Percé, 1877*

# THE LAND

## The Challenge and the Reward

During the early 1800s, the vast territory west of the Mississippi lived in the Eastern imagination as a beckoning dreamscape. Out there—so the stories said—gold littered the ground, mountains of crystal rose to the sky, and rivers flowed between cliffs studded with gemstones. The notion of such a rich, wide-open country was an irresistible lure for anyone infected with the westering fever for freedom, adventure—and profit.

By mid-century, explorers and pioneers had largely pricked the public's bubble of fantasy. The "wide-open country" was in fact home to many well-established and complex Native American cultures, and the land itself posed a truly daunting challenge. To reach the green firs of the Pacific Northwest and the fertile valleys of California one had first to survive the seemingly endless Plains, the sun-scorched desert, and a formidable wall of mountains. But the early journeys also revealed a truth more rewarding than crystal and gold. As the modern-day photographs on the following pages show, this often harsh terrain possessed a powerful beauty. "Description might exaggerate," one enthralled citizen observed in 1872, "but the camera told the truth; and in this case the truth was more remarkable than exaggeration."

# THE WILD WEST

By the Editors of
TIME-LIFE BOOKS

Companion volume to the television miniseries produced by
RATTLESNAKE PRODUCTIONS, INC.
in association with
TELEPICTURES PRODUCTIONS
and
WARNER BROS. DOMESTIC TELEVISION DISTRIBUTION

Foreword by
Dee Brown

Warner Books
A Time Warner Company

# THE WILD WEST ™

## MONUMENT VALLEY
### Arizona

"We seem on the threshold of a destiny higher
and better than any nation has yet fulfilled. And the
great West is to rule us."

*Albert Deane Richardson, frontier reporter, 1867*

# GRASSLANDS
## Colorado

"Like an ocean in its vast extent, in its monotony, and

in its danger. Like the ocean in its romance."

*Anonymous sportsman, 1850s*

# DEATH VALLEY
## California

"Weak and Weary as I am, I would rather go a thousand miles farther than remain in such a desolate and forsaken place as this."

*Anonymous pioneer woman, 1847*

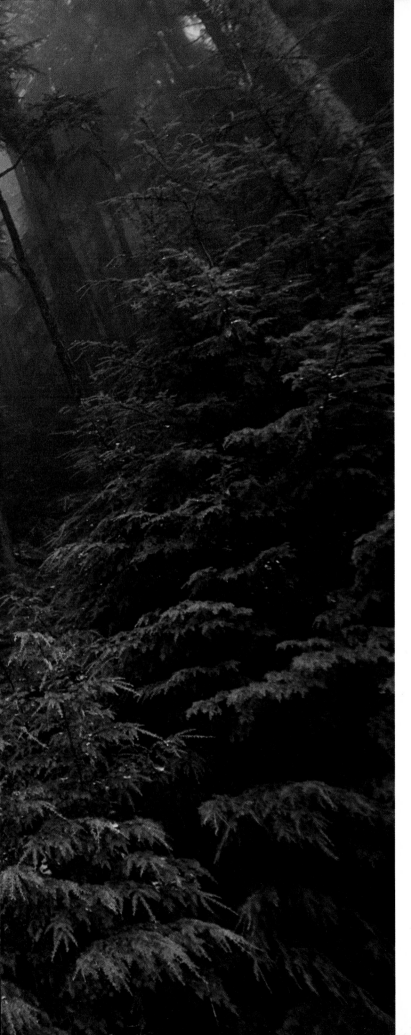

# DOUGLAS FIR
## Washington

"Oh! What timber! These trees—these forests
of trees—so enchain the sense of the grand and
so enchant the sense of the beautiful that I linger
on the theme and am loth to depart . . ."

*Samuel Wilkeson, business agent for Northern Pacific Railroad, 1869*

# GRAND TETONS
## Wyoming

"Since they had no way of knowing that it would later be regarded as one of the truly difficult peaks of North America, they simply went ahead and climbed it. That, in my mind, is the way to climb a mountain."

*William Henry Jackson, photographer, 1872*

# COLORADO RIVER
## Utah

"Your posterity will look back to yours as
the golden age, and envy those who first burst into
this silent splendid nature."

*James Bryce, British lawyer and Western tourist, 1880s*

A vivid 1899 poster shows Indians attacking a wagon train, one of the acts performed in Buffalo Bill Cody's gaudy, long-lived Wild West show

# "Scouts of the Prairie" was, by all accounts, just about the most

atrocious play ever to appear on the American stage. The author, a hack writer who called himself Ned Buntline, admitted he had written it in only four hours—prompting the critic from the *Chicago Times* to wonder, the play being so dreadful, what Buntline "had been doing all that time." Another critic called the drama a piece of "maundering imbecility," while a third said it was "so wonderful in its feebleness that no ordinary intellect can comprehend it."

Despite the acidulous critics, *Scouts of the Prairie* was a raging success. People stormed the theaters to see it—for the simple reason that the hero was played by none other than William F. Cody, already famous as Buffalo Bill. The celebrated chief scout of the Fifth Cavalry was right there in the flesh, and anybody with two bits for a ticket could get in to see him. The play might be claptrap and Cody's acting "execrable," but here was a real blood-and-thunder hero, fresh from a hundred buffalo hunts and battles with Indians, prancing just beyond the flickering footlights, so near he could almost be touched.

Cody was far from being the only plainsman to cash in on the public's fascination with the West. Before long, Wild Bill Hickok joined Cody in another play, alarming audiences by blasting away at the footlights with his six-shooters. Then came frontier markswoman Calamity Jane and even troupes of Indians who preferred appearing in Wild West shows, such as the one Buffalo Bill later ran, to being confined on reservations.

While these real-life folk shot and whooped in person, book publishers produced thousands of cheap, sensational tales about them and other, fictional, Western characters—and even some worthier Western adventure stories as well, such as Owen Wister's classic *The Virginian*. At the same time, artists such as Frederic Remington became wealthy painting pictures that glorified the West's scenery and the derring-do acted out against that magnificent backdrop. Among them these celebrators of life on the frontier created a great myth of the West, an extraordinary mixture of fact and fantasy, truth and bunkum, that before long threatened to overwhelm gritty reality and has colored—even dominated—the public's perceptions about the West ever since.

Fact or myth, the American public ate it all up with enthusiasm. The millions who had never been to the West wanted to live vicariously in what they saw as an exciting, unbridled, dangerous place. But the hunger was deeper than that. People needed heroes to worship, and larger-than-life Westerners such as Cody and Hickok seemed to embody their ideal, to match their dreams and aspirations. Also, after the tragic splitting of the country by the Civil War, Americans were desperately searching for a sense of national unity and purpose. Prophets had trumpeted for decades that it was the nation's manifest destiny to conquer the West and occupy the continent all the way to the Pacific. Increasingly, westward movement seemed to be the nation's fate, its great mission and purpose, and everyone wanted to share in it if only secondhand.

A still more potent appeal of the myth, perhaps, was a longing to escape, at least in the imagination, from the frightening changes being wrought in the older parts of America by the explosive growth of industry that followed the Civil War. Huge new factories were turning cities into dark, smoky infernos crowded with rancid slums. Surely the West was a better, truer, more open and free America. To the working men and women of the East particularly, oppressed by dismal factory jobs and often brutal bosses, the idealized image of the Westerner riding with gun on hip through a vast, uncluttered landscape, utterly his own boss and beholden to nobody, had an intoxicating, mesmerizing appeal.

The West, in short, was transformed by the myth into a land of dreams where men and women were free and brave and, above all, independent. The attraction of the Western Robin Hood who defied corrupt authority became so great, in fact, that a number of bona fide bad guys—bank robbers, horse thieves, and murderers—were elevated to the status of hero. Jesse James's crimes were excused as being the result of beatings he had suffered at the hands of the Federals during the guerrilla fighting that wracked Kansas and Missouri during the Civil War. "We called him an outlaw. But fate made him so," claimed the writer of a novel about James. "When the war closed, Jesse had no home. Proscribed, hunted, shot, driven away from his

Cavalrymen and grizzled scouts fend off an Indian attack in Frederic Remington's *The Last Stand,* a painting that perpetuated a romanticized view of soldiering on the frontier. As it happened, a woodcut of the painting appeared in *Harper's Weekly* 12 days after the cavalry had massacred about 150 Indians, including women and children, at Wounded Knee.

people, a price put on his head—what else could he do?" As for Billy the Kid, this real-life psychopathic killer was transformed into a fair-haired, smiling rebel riding forever into the sunset because he had been shot by a sneaky sheriff in an unfair fight.

The villains more often than not were the Indians. In the pictures and books purveying the myth, they habitually attacked emigrant wagon trains—which in fact they almost never did—and generally came off as barbarians who took savage delight in sneaking up on white settlements to murder women and children. The Sand Creek massacre, Wounded Knee, and the other brutal, wholesale killings of Indians by vigilante groups or the U.S. cavalry got short shrift in accounts that on the whole were more sympathetic to the army. Even when they were portrayed as noble savages following great warrior chiefs such as Red Cloud and Chief Joseph of the Nez Percé, the

Indians—contrary to history—lost every battle. In the myth, the cavalry was always victorious, riding up to rescue the white settlers just in the nick of time.

Indeed, the mythical version of the American West was entirely a white man's invention. Conspicuously missing from the gallery of heroes were Mexicans and African-Americans, although both played vital roles in the real opening of the West. It was a myth invented by the conquerors—and it studiously hid, as did similar sagas of other nations, most of the grim and painful and grubby events that occurred while the conquest was taking place.

Amazingly, this myth was born and elaborated and reached astonishing proportions not when the West it romanticized had become history, but even as the West was in the process of being overtaken by whites. Chiefly responsible for starting the popular craze for things Western was a flood of deceptively innocent-looking little books called dime novels that began to appear as early as the 1860s. Printed on cheap paper, they could be produced by the new rotary steam presses in unlimited quantities. At 10¢ apiece the price was right, the contents were juicy, and they sold by the millions. Ned Buntline helped get the ball rolling, turning out four potboilers that told incredible tall tales about Buffalo Bill even before he had lured Cody onto the stage. Eventually a total of 557 dime novels were written about Cody alone by dozens of different authors, many of whom had never been west of the Missouri River—or of the Hudson for that matter.

The formula of the dime novels was simple. There was usually a square-jawed, clean-shaven Western hero—a sheriff, a scout, or a cowboy—who almost invariably, after many hairsbreadth adventures, found himself rescuing the heroine from dastardly Indians or rustlers. The dialogue was wooden, formulaic, even archaic, but it titillated the reader. "Oh, you wicked wretches! You shall be punished for this! When Seth Culver lays his hands on you, you will suffer!" the heroine would cry. Needless to say, Seth would soon pound up on his lathered horse, guns drawn, and proclaim, "Touch but a hair of her head, and by the Lord that made me, I will bespatter that tree with your brains!"

Dime novels were of course considered disreputable and even sinful by the guardians of public morality. Reading them was said to be an addiction, like smoking opium. There were even congressional investigations. How could working women be happy in the factory after they had read about the dashing "Bandit Queen" Belle Starr? But this made the little books all the more attractive to the public. If the authorities were against them, they had to be good. Nobody cared that the books outrageously blended fact with make-believe. They were terrific reading and provided, as one dime-novel writer recalled, "a thrill per page."

It was Buffalo Bill himself, though, who became the all-time champion purveyor of the myth of the West. After the loopy *Scouts of the Prairie,* he appeared in several more plays. Then, in 1882, he was asked to put on a Fourth of July celebration in North Platte, Nebraska, where he had recently built a home. His show, the "Old Glory Blow-Out," featured shooting, riding, broncobusting, and a supercharged roundup—and it was a sensation. Inspired, Cody soon put together his great Wild West show and took the country by storm. In this extravaganza, the Pony Express dashed across the Plains again, and Indians in war paint and feathers attacked the Deadwood stage, which of course was saved by Buffalo Bill himself. The most expert cowboys Cody could find did trick riding stunts, roped calves, and even tangled with wild buffalo. The consummate trick-shot artist, Annie Oakley, soon joined the cast. And so, for one season, did Chief Sitting Bull. Robbed of his homelands, the great Sioux warrior needed the $50 a week to feed his family. He was also guaranteed all the bowls he wanted of his own favorite dish, oyster stew.

Cody's Wild West crisscrossed America in a special train of 26 white-painted cars, playing to immense crowds. Then it was across the sea to England, where throngs of 30,000 to 40,000 attended each London performance. Even the reclusive Queen Victoria came, and she confided to her diary that she had loved it. The prince of Wales rode shotgun next to Cody on the box of the Deadwood stage while the kings of Greece, Saxony, Denmark, and Belgium rode inside—prompting Cody to note that with four kings and a prince he had a "royal flush." Another European tour took Cody to Paris, Venice, even the Vatican. Once back in the United States, the show went on and on, drawing six million customers at the Chicago World's Fair of 1893 and continuing to be popular until finally, after a series of financial foul-ups, Cody lost control of the enterprise in 1912, five years before his death at age 70 in 1917.

---

Long before that, Bill Cody and his Wild West had become for millions of people the image, the truth, the essence of what the West had really been like, a place almost exclusively devoted to Indian fights, broncobusting, and fancy shooting. The sweat and grime of a real cattle drive, the miserable sod huts and privations of everyday life on the Plains, the true heroism of the emigrants, all these were shoved into the background.

The irony was, of course, that Cody himself had been an authentic Westerner, by the age of 12 a drover on westbound wagon trains, a sure-shot buffalo hunter, and later, an army scout so expert and brave that he was awarded the Congressional Medal of Honor. Nevertheless, Buffalo Bill was also the archpurveyor of the romanticized, mythical West that has remained so stubbornly alive, filling the dreams of millions of Americans, providing the setting of innumerable novels—and flickering across countless movie-theater screens—through all the many years since.

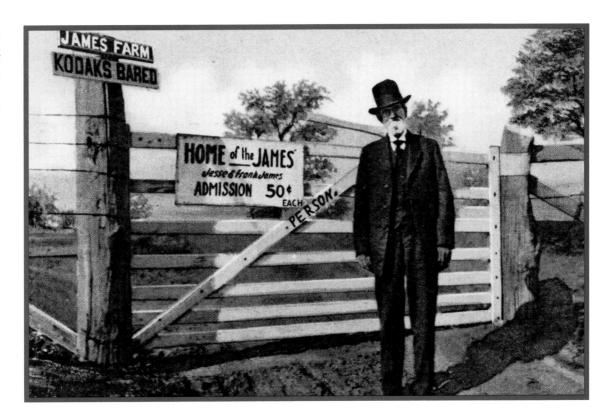

Merchandising his lurid past, former outlaw Frank James, age 70, stands by the gate of his Missouri birthplace in 1910, ready to collect admissions from curious tourists. James also sold pebbles from his brother Jesse's grave.

# TRANSFORMING REALITY INTO POWERFUL LEGEND

Hungry for heroes, 19th-century Americans ravenously consumed the novels, plays, and other shows that glorified the men and women who had dared live their lives in that huge, dangerous expanse beyond the Mississippi. Helping feed the appetite were a number of real Westerners who turned themselves into public figures—and often embroidered on their deeds until truth and fiction became inextricably entwined. One was Wild Bill Hickok, who had been in fact a courageous army scout and the tough sheriff of rough frontier towns. But he was also given to telling lurid tales of his adventures, and it was this Hickok, further mythologized by dime novelists and ordinary folk with a penchant for spinning yarns (below), that became an icon in the popular imagination.

A more shameless self-promotor was Calamity Jane, who claimed to have been the army's only female scout and a doughty Indian fighter. In truth, she was known in the Dakotas as a barroom drunk and occasional prostitute. The leader in mixing fact and fiction, though, was Buffalo Bill Cody, who became an almost surreal amalgam of reality and make-believe. Leaving the cast of a melodrama he was acting in, he rushed west in 1876 to help the army put down an Indian uprising—and went into battle wearing his black velveteen theatrical costume. Then, after he had scalped a Cheyenne named Yellow Hair during the fighting, he carefully saved the bloody topknot and later used it as a prop, waving it onstage when he went back into show business.

*"A hundred pistols were drawn and cocked as Wild Bill fired his first shot. By the time he fired a second time the room was cleared. Alone he cleared the town. . . ."*

◆

Joe McCoy, mayor of Abilene, Kansas

**A Handsome Hero-Sheriff——**
Wild Bill Hickok affects fringed buckskins in a photograph that was probably taken at the time he was appearing onstage with Bill Cody. The victor in a single authentic Western shootout at high noon, he became the archetype of the fast-drawing lawman.

**Fraudulent Western Heroine ——**
Calamity Jane—real name, Martha Jane Cannary—sports the stage costume she wore after a dozen dime novels about her supposed feats had made her famous. Calamity claimed to be Wild Bill's wife and was buried beside him when she died in 1903.

**Epitomes of the Frontier ——**
Buffalo Bill and Sitting Bull pose for a studio portrait in costume in 1885, the year Sitting Bull traveled with Cody's Wild West show. Cody always treated Sitting Bull—as well as the other Indians in his show—with great respect.

# The Making of Buffalo Bill

Ned Buntline, a dime novelist who helped popularize Buffalo Bill, had a name as fraudulent as everything else about him. Born Edward Zane Carroll Judson to an upright New York State family, he ran away at the age of 13 to join the navy, later shot a man who accused him of wife stealing, and was nearly killed in retaliation by a lynch mob. He had five wives, some simultaneously, and called himself Colonel Judson after desultory service in the Civil War—mostly as a deserter.

But this gnomelike liar and ne'er-do-well had a gift for taking a few facts and spinning them into wildly imaginative tales that exactly suited the readers of pulp fiction. Once he had met Bill Cody, he swiftly turned out some of the dime novels that transformed Cody from scout into idol of the nation.

A Man of Make-Believe ——
Decked out in buckskins and bandoleer and holding a handy rifle, Ned Buntline tries to look the part of a scout. Buntline, a heavy drinker, first met the 23-year-old Cody when visiting Colorado's Fort McPherson in 1869 to deliver a temperance lecture. The two men hit it off, although Cody swore mightily in disbelief on reading Buntline's splendidly inaccurate dime novels about him, such as the one at left, which were simply collections of tall tales having little to do with Cody's actual career.

A Backstage Lineup ———
*Scouts of the Prairie,* Ned Buntline's florid drama, starred Buntline himself at left; Bill Cody; Italian dancer Giuseppina Morlacchi, who played the Indian maiden Dove Eye; and Texas Jack Omohundro, a friend of Cody's and a fellow scout who in the play lassoed the band of bloodthirsty Indians.

Immortalizing Cody's Victory ———
A famous painting by Charles Russell depicts Buffalo Bill shooting the Cheyenne chief Yellow Hair with his Winchester during their encounter at Warbonnet Creek. Cody then used his knife to take Yellow Hair's scalp—which he kept for a stage prop in his show.

# The "Grandest Spectacle" Ever

The show was billed as "the grandest, most realistic and overwhelmingly thrilling war spectacle ever seen," and it was in fact nearly that exciting. Buffalo Bill's Wild West not only boasted amazing sharpshooters and the best trick riders but also reenacted Western events—buffalo hunts, Indian attacks on stages or covered wagons, Custer's Last Stand—that then gained their own celebrity. Cody multiplied the show's impact by insisting that everything be genuine. He bought a Concord stagecoach that had been used on the Deadwood run and had herds of real buffalo and Texas steers in the acts. It was this palpable authenticity that attracted huge crowds all over the United States and in 12 foreign countries as well.

Ladies and Gentlemen, the Wild West——
Doffing his big sombrero to the audience *(below)*, Buffalo Bill opens a show in Omaha, Nebraska, by galloping into the arena at the head of his imposing troupes of cowboys, Indians, and other horsemen. By 1908, the probable date of this photograph, the old scout's hair had turned snowy white. At right, scores of soldiers and Indians fight it out amid a din of gun blasts and war whoops on the same afternoon in one of the show's climactic spectacles.

The Wild West crew carried vast amounts of baggage as it traveled from city to city, including hundreds of animals, great canvas backdrops representing the Wyoming Rockies, huge tents for the spectators, and the show's own lighting system for night performances.

## The Rage of the Continent

Cody and four Indians take a gondola ride in Venice during the Wild West show's three-year tour of Europe, following its triumphant trip to England. Beginning in 1889, the show hit France—where the Parisians loved "Annee Oaklee"—then went to Spain, Italy, Austria, and other countries. It was a smash in Germany, where Cody added a new feature, the "Rough Riders of the World," that included Arab and Syrian horsemen and others from France, Germany, Russia, and Britain. The tour ended with more appearances in England before delirious crowds.

**The Star Trick Shooter** ——
Annie Oakley (nee Phoebe Anne Mozee) demonstrates one of her famous tricks—using a mirror to aim at a target behind her. Diminutive and engaging, she would blow kisses to the crowd and miss a shot or two on purpose to gain sympathy. She first showed her skill with guns at age nine by shooting the heads off squirrels to help feed her impoverished Ohio family.

**Shooting on the Run** ——
Taking aim from the back of a galloping horse, Buffalo Bill explodes glass balls flung into the air by an Indian assistant riding next to him. Rumor had it that Cody used a doctored rifle that fired a pattern of bird shot, making the trick easier, but he was nonetheless a genuine marksman.

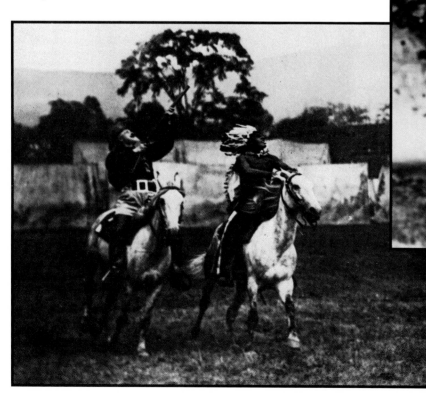

**His Prolonged Farewell** ——
A 1910 poster (*right*) depicts an unrealistically young-looking Buffalo Bill advertising a "farewell shot." Though increasingly tired and ill in his later years, Cody made dozens of "final" appearances to recoup losses from unwise business dealings.

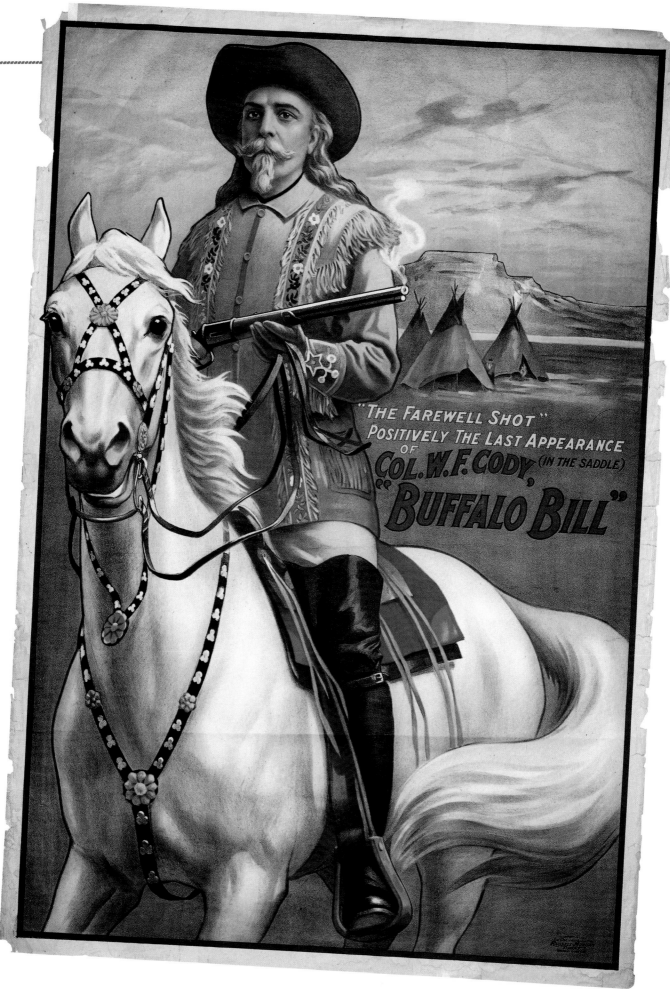

# Perpetuating the Great Myth

A Would-Be Mountain Man——
The 25-year-old Teddy Roosevelt wears a buckskin shirt he had made to show off back East. If his Western adventures helped him politically, Roosevelt also helped the West, promoting the idea of conservation that later led to the National Parks system.

As the frontier receded and then vanished—it was officially declared "closed" in the 1890s—three men especially, all of them Easterners, labored to keep the Wild West, or anyway its myth, alive. One was the masterly artist Frederic Remington. The second was Owen Wister, whose cowboy hero in *The Virginian* summed up the independent, laconic Westerner since seen in countless movies. Third was Theodore Roosevelt, who went west as a young man, fell in love with the place, briefly ran a ranch, and wrote several books that rhapsodized the West's scenic grandeur and rugged people. The publicity he gained through his books plus the fame he acquired leading his Rough Riders—a term he took from Cody's show—in the Spanish-American War were vital in winning him election as president in 1904.

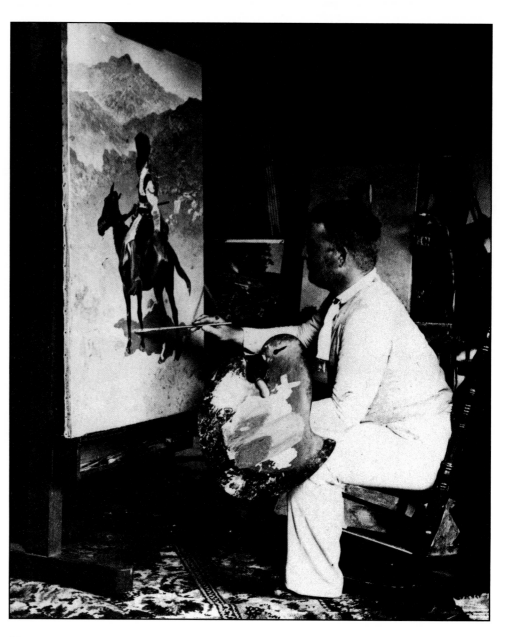

*"I saw men already swarming into the land. . . . I knew the wild riders and the vacant land were about to vanish forever—and the more I considered the subject, the bigger the 'forever' loomed."*

◆

*Frederic Remington, 1905*

Remington at Work——
New Yorker Frederic Remington, seen here applying final touches to *An Indian Trapper* in his studio in 1889, helped to establish an idealized, romantic West in the popular imagination by painting, as he described it, "the West of picturesque and stirring events" and ignoring the mundane lives of most real Western citizens.

The Man behind "the Virginian" ——
Slouching languidly in a chair, Owen Wister
imitates his loose-limbed, lazy-seeming hero,
known only as "the Virginian," seen above
in an illustration of the most famous scene
from Wister's novel. While playing poker, the
hero is cursed by the villain Trampas *(foreground, right)*, who growls, "Your bet, you son
of a . . ." Laying his six-gun carefully on the
table, the Virginian replies with the classic
line, "When you call me that, smile." Wister
himself, a native of Philadelphia who was edu-
cated as a lawyer, went west for his health and
ended up writing *The Virginian* as a paean to
Wyoming's mountains and people.

The West on the Silver Screen——
The earliest known Western movie, called *Cripple Creek Barroom,* featured the saloon scene at right that includes the remains of a card game, a group of seedy and suspicious-looking loungers, a huge crock of raw "Red Eye" whiskey, and a female bartender—actually played by a man—who looks ready and able to bounce any obstreperous customers. The primitive film was made in 1898 and lasted less than a minute, but its creators had already zeroed in on the barroom locale and the characters that would form an integral part of virtually every Western movie made thereafter.

Only five years later Thomas A. Edison's *The Great Train Robbery,* the first full-fledged Western, was a popular sensation and included the other elements of the archetypal horse opera—crime, pursuit, and armed showdown—that would be elaborated endlessly, in hundreds of later movies, keeping the myth of the West alive for generation after generation.

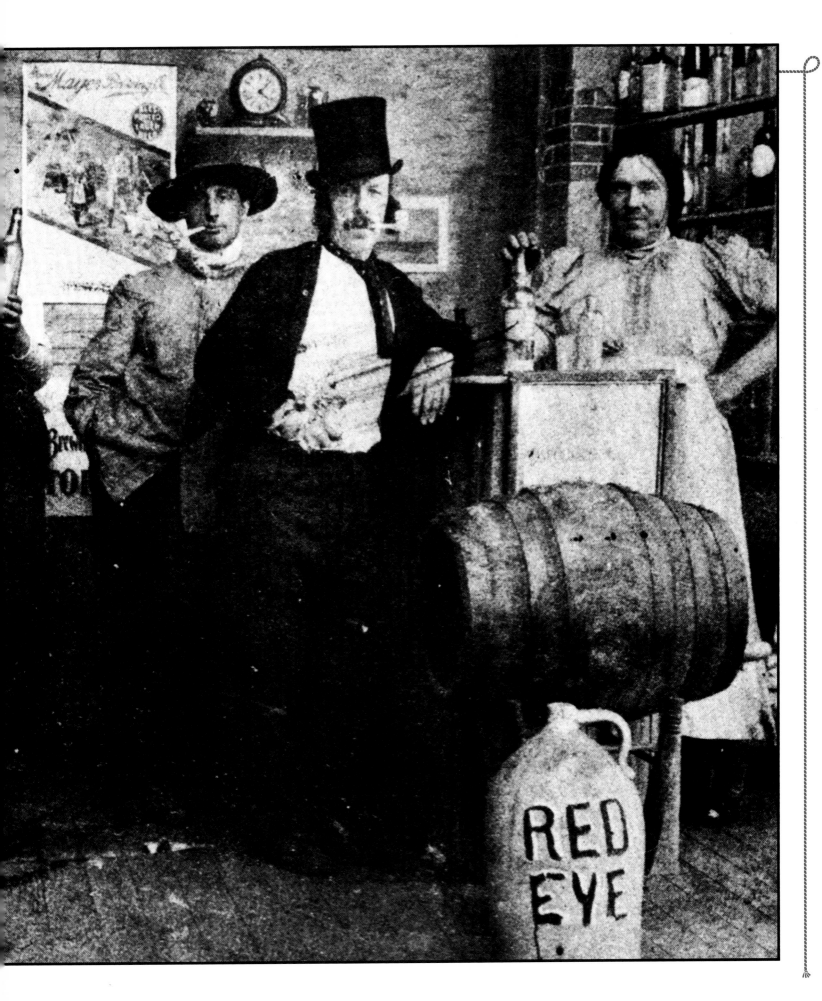

# An Eventful Century

The emigrants from all walks and stations of life who flooded into the western half of the United States were part of an explosive transformation overtaking the country as a whole. In the course of the century, 29 states entered the Union, and the nation's boundaries expanded—often through acts of war—until they touched both the Atlantic and the Pacific.

Meanwhile, as events plotted here and on the following pages reveal, technological advances and social upheavals were changing the pace and fabric of society. The juxtapositions were often bewildering. In 1876, for example, as the country celebrated its 100th birthday, George Armstrong Custer died at the Little Bighorn, Alexander Graham Bell made his first telephone call in Boston, and dim gas lamps on city streets began to give way to bright electric lights. In just a few decades the most efficient way to send a cross-country message went from stagecoach to Pony Express to telegraph to telephone.

By 1890, the year Wyoming became the first state to grant women suffrage, it was no longer possible to draw a line on the map and declare that boundary the "frontier." Nine years later, when Butch Cassidy pulled off his first train robbery, Frontier Day was an established celebration for the nostalgic citizens of Cheyenne, Wyoming. The West of myth and legend was already a thing of the past.

**1803**
President Thomas Jefferson purchases Louisiana Territory from France.

**1820**
Missouri Compromise bans slavery north of 36°30' in Louisiana Purchase.

**1824**
Jedediah Smith discovers South Path through Rocky Mountains.

1803 Ohio    1812 Louisiana    1816 Indiana
1817 Mississippi
1818 Illinois
1819 Alabama
1820 Maine
1821 Missouri
1836 Arkansas
1837 Michigan

## Military & Government

**1817-1825**
Erie Canal built.

## Science & Technology

**1808**
Missouri Fur Company established.

**1814**
Francis Scott Key writes words to "The Star-Spangled Banner."

**1821**
Cherokee alphabet developed by Sequoya.

**1831**
Nat Turner commands slave revolt in Southhampton, Virginia.

## Americana & Social Issues

**1846 -1848**

Mexican War. U.S. wins California, Texas, New Mexico, Utah, Nevada, and Arizona.

**1854**

Kansas-Nebraska Act takes Indian Territory for U.S.

**1861**

• Abraham Lincoln inaugurated as president.
• Civil War begins.

**1862**

• Lincoln issues Emancipation Proclamation.
• Congress passes Transcontinental Railroad Act and Homestead Act.

1845 Florida, Texas
1846 Iowa
  1848 Wisconsin

1850 California

1858 Minnesota
1859 Oregon
1861 Kansas

**1831**

America's first passenger locomotive travels at 20 mph.

**1860**

Pony Express makes its first run.

**1861**

Telegraph service makes Pony Express obsolete.

**1832**

Nathaniel Wyeth brings first emigrants over Oregon Trail.

**1846**

Potato famine in Ireland drives mass emigration to U.S.

**1848**

• First women's-rights convention held, Seneca Falls, New York.
• Gold discovered, Sutter's Mill, California.
• Chinese brought to work in California gold mines.

**1849-1852**

Gold prospectors rush to California.

**1861**

Theodore Judah surveys Sierra Nevada for a transcontinental railroad.

## 1864
- Army massacres Cheyennes at Sand Creek in Colorado Territory.

## 1865
- Lincoln assassinated.
- Civil War ends; Southerners furl Confederate flag in defeat.

## 1866
Sioux massacre Fetterman command at Lodge Ridge Trail, Wyoming.

## 1868
- Seventh Cavalry massacres Cheyennes at Washita in western Oklahoma.
- Government signs treaty with Sioux at Fort Laramie, Wyoming.
- Government signs treaty with Nez Percé — last of 300 Indian treaties in 100 years.
- Ulysses S. Grant narrowly wins presidency.

## 1869
John Wesley Powell explores Colorado River and Grand Canyon.

1863 West Virginia
1864 Nevada

1867 Nebraska

## 1863
- National Academy of Sciences founded in Washington, D.C.
- William Huggins, English astronomer, shows that stars are similar to the sun.

## 1864
- Pennsylvania Railroad starts to use rails made of steel.
- Louis Pasteur develops method for pasteurizing wine that will later be applied to milk.

## 1865
Linus Yale, Jr., invents the cylinder lock.

## 1866
- Henry House develops a 12-horsepower steam automobile.
- American Society for the Prevention of Cruelty to Animals established, New York City.
- Gregor Mendel publishes his laws of heredity.

## 1868
- Air brakes invented by George Westinghouse.
- First practical typewriter invented by Christopher Sholes, Pennsylvania printer.

## 1863
- Construction begins on Central Pacific and Union Pacific railroads.
- Travelers Insurance Co., first company to insure travelers against accidents, founded in Hartford, Connecticut.
- Roller-skating introduced into America.

## 1865
First paid firefighters established in New York City.

## 1866
Long drive of cattle begins from Texas to Kansas and Nebraska railheads.

## 1868
New York Athletic Club holds first annual indoor track-and-field meet.

## 1869
- Central Pacific and Union Pacific joined at Promontory Summit, Utah.
- Cincinnati Red Stockings, first professional baseball team, get regular pay.
- First intercollegiate football game played, New Brunswick, New Jersey.
- Arabella Mansfield, first U.S. woman lawyer, admitted to Iowa bar.

**1870**
Thomas Nast cartoon first to use donkey to symbolize Democratic party.

**1871**
Indian Appropriation Act nullifies all treaties and makes Indians wards of the nation.

**1872**
Yellowstone National Park Reserve established.

**1874**
Nast cartoon first to use elephant to symbolize Republican party.

**1876**
Custer force wiped out at the Little Bighorn.

1876 Colorado

**1871**
German tanners invent technique to turn buffalo hides into usable leather.

**1873**
• Levi Strauss and Jacob Davis patent blue jeans.
• Barbed wire invented independently by Joseph Glidden, I. L. Ellwood, and Jacob Haish.
• Colt issues its classic .45 single-action revolver.

**1876**
• First electric street lighting in U.S.
• Alexander Graham Bell invents the telephone.

**1871**
Chicago devastated by fire.

**1872**
Mark Twain's Roughing It published.

**1875**
Anti-Chinese rioting takes place in San Francisco.

**1885**

Congress prohibits fencing of public lands.

**1886**

Geronimo surrenders to General George Crook in Mexico—only to escape again. He finally surrendered for good after his family was taken prisoner.

**1877**

- Pasteur begins microbe studies that lead to antiseptic surgery and immunization.
- Thomas Edison patents the phonograph.

**1878**

Edison Electric Light Company formed in New York City.

**1880**

- U.S. railroads total 93,671 miles of track.
- U.S. telephones number 50,000.

**1883**

Brooklyn Bridge opened.

**1889**

William Friese-Green invents first motion-picture camera.

**1880**

U.S. population 50,155,783. New York first state to exceed 5 million.

**1881**

- P. T. Barnum and J. A. Bailey create circus known as "The Barnum and Bailey Greatest Show on Earth."
- Gunfight takes place at O.K. Corral in Tombstone, Arizona.
- Billy the Kid killed by Pat Garrett.
- Clara Barton organizes American Red Cross.

**1882**

Jesse James shot and killed by gang member Robert Ford at St. Joseph, Missouri.

**1883**

- First Wild West show formed by Buffalo Bill Cody.
- Cattle barons hold 13 million acres, 23 million cattle.
- Only a few hundred buffalo left on western Plains.
- Theodore Roosevelt makes his first trip west.

**1884**

Belva Lockwood first woman nominated for president.

**1885**

- Kansas becomes Prohibition State.
- Stanford University at Palo Alto, California, chartered.

## 1890
- Indian Territory redefined as Oklahoma Territory.
- Slaughter of Sioux at Wounded Knee marks last major clash between Indians and whites.
- Sitting Bull killed.

## 1891
900,000 acres of Indian land in Oklahoma Territory ceded by Sauk, Fox, and Potawatomi.

## 1892
Crow Indian reservation in Montana, 1.8 million acres, opened to settlers by presidential proclamation.

## 1898
- U.S. wins 3½-month war with Spain; buys Philippines and gains Guam and Puerto Rico.
- U.S. annexes Hawaii.

1889 North Dakota, South Dakota, Montana, Washington
1890 Idaho, Wyoming

1896 Utah

## 1892
George W. G. Ferris designs the Ferris wheel.

## 1893
First open-heart surgery performed by Dr. Daniel Hale Williams.

## 1897
Condensed soup, Jell-O invented; milk sold in glass bottles.

## 1901
Oil discovered at Spindletop, Texas.

## 1903
- Orville Wright makes first manned, powered, and controlled flight at Kitty Hawk, North Carolina.
- Henry Ford organizes Ford Motor Company.

## 1886
- Statue of Liberty dedicated.
- Winter of the "Big Die Up"— hundreds of thousands of cattle die on the open range.

## 1889
Land rush begins in what is now Oklahoma on April 22, on land bought from the Creek and Seminole Indians.

## 1890
- Wyoming first state to grant voting rights to women.
- Census shows population spread has erased the Western "frontier."

## 1892
- First immigrants arrive at Ellis Island.
- John Muir founds Sierra Club.

## 1893
Mormon Temple dedicated in Salt Lake City.

## 1897
First Frontier Day conceived by the citizens of Cheyenne, Wyoming.

## 1899
First train heist pulled off by Butch Cassidy and the Wild Bunch.

## 1901
Butch Cassidy and Sundance Kid escape to South America.

# ACKNOWLEDGMENTS

The Editors gratefully acknowledge the creators of *The Wild West* television production, Rattlesnake Productions. "Cowboys": Producers John Copeland, Jamie L. Smith. "Settlers," "Chroniclers": Producer Steven Manuel, Associate Producer Kellie Flanagan. "Gunfighters," "Soldiers": Producers Ray Herbeck, Jr., Christen Harty-Schaefer. "Searchers," "Townspeople": Producer Dana Millikin, Co-Producer Laura Verklan. "Indians": Producers Kieth W. Merrill, Victoria Westermark. "Dreamers & Wayfarers," "Mythmakers": Producer Rob Wilson, Associate Producer Kathleen Killeen. Music composed and produced by John McEuen. Location photography: Jim Whitefield, Wendel Craighead, Bob Tomer. Camera: Robert Jaye, Chuck Levey, Gordon C. Lonsdale, Mark Parry, Nancy Schreiber. Editors: Lisa M. Citron, David W. Foster, Kathleen Korth, Judy Reidel, Suzanne Sternlicht, George Waite. Historical Consultants: Alan Axelrod, Dee Brown, Gae Whitney Canfield, John E. Carter, Wallace D. Coffey, James M. Cox, Marie C. Cox, Thomas R. Cox, Brian W. Dippie, Jim Dullenty, Bill Gwaltney, Dennis W. Hastings, C. Robert Haywood, Hamlin Hill, Nancy Horn Cloud, George Horse Capture, Paul Andrew Hutton, Professor W. Turrentine Jackson, Alvin M. Josephy, Jr., William Loren Katz, Dr. Howard R. Lamar, Bill Neeley, Peter E. Palmquist, Brian C. Pohanka, Joseph C. Porter, Byron Price, Dr. Glenda Riley, Glenn Shirley, Duane A. Smith, Joseph W. Snell, Lee Stetson, Joanna L. Stratton, Lonn Taylor, Robert M. Utley, Elliott West, Richard B. Williams, Connie Young Yu. Researchers: Joli Ancel, Joy Connelly, Darroch Greer, Jonathan Jerald, Sarah Armstrong Jones, Morgan Sloane. Music Research: Dr. Laurence Ivan Seidman. Rights Clearances: Amy Barraclough. A Rattlesnake Production in association with Telepictures Productions. Produced in cooperation with United Television Productions/Chris-Craft Television Productions.

The Editors also wish to thank Larry D. Ball, History Department, Arkansas State University, Jonesboro; Cynthia Nakamura, Denver Art Museum, Denver; Dr. Glenda Riley, Department of History, Ball State University, Muncie, Indiana; Ray Collins, Brown Brothers, Sterling, Pennsylvania; Billy Plunkett, Harold B. Lee Library, Brigham Young University, Provo, Utah; Harris Andrews, Blaine Marshall, Becky Merson, Lorna Milkovich, and Becky Wheeler, Alexandria, Virginia; Cathey Lomax, Dale Connelly, and Sharon Culley, Still Pictures Branch, National Archives, Washington, D.C.; Inventory of American Paintings and Sculpture, National Museum of American Art, Smithsonian Institution, Washington, D.C.; Elizabeth Holmes, Buffalo Bill Historical Center, Cody, Wyoming; Howard Madaus, Buffalo Bill Museum, Cody, Wyoming.

# PICTURE CREDITS

Historical Society, St. Louis. 70, 71: The Kansas State Historical Society, Topeka. 72, 73: W. D. Johnson/U.S. Geological Survey (157). 74, 75: The Granger Collection, New York. 78: Southern Pacific Transportation Company, San Francisco. 80: *The Coming and Going of the Pony Express,* Frederic Remington, 1900, The Thomas Gilcrease Institute of American History and Art, Tulsa. 82, 83: The Kansas State Historical Society, Topeka; W. H. Jackson/Denver Public Library, Western History Department—California State Railroad Museum, Sacramento, Calif. (SPX5-6). 87: Map by R. R. Donnelley & Sons Company, Cartographic Services Center. 88: De Grummond Children's Literature Research Collection, University of Southern Mississippi, Hattiesburg. 89: Union Pacific Historical Museum, Omaha—courtesy The Oakland Museum. 90, 91: Arizona Historical Society, Tucson (61654)—Wells Fargo Bank History Room, San Francisco; California State Library, Sacramento; Oregon Historical Society, Portland (OrHi4950#1516-A); *We Went Over Mail, Baggage and All,* C. J. Russell, Wells Fargo Bank History Room, San Francisco. 92, 93: L. C. Cooper/State Historical Society of North Dakota, Bismarck; Utah State Historical Society, Salt Lake City. 94, 95: De Grummond Children's Literature Research Collection, University of Southern Mississippi, Hattiesburg—California State Railroad Museum, Sacramento, Calif.; *Men's to Match My Mountain,* Jake Lee, 1965, courtesy Guy Wong, San Francisco; courtesy Connie Young Yu, Los Altos Hills, Calif. 96, 97: The Kansas State Historical Society, Topeka—The Bettmann Archive, New York; courtesy The Oakland Museum. 98, 99: State Historical Society of North Dakota, Bismarck; Smithsonian Institution, OPPS#4586, Washington, D.C.—Monterey History and Art Association, Monterey, Calif.; California State Library, Sacramento; Brigham Young University, Photographic Archives, Provo, Utah. 100: Reprinted with permission from Pinkerton Security and Investigation Services, Pinkerton's Inc., Van Nuys, Calif.—Union Pacific Historical Museum, Omaha. 101: Solomon D. Butcher Collection, Nebraska State Historical Society, Lincoln—*Ambush,* Theodor Kaufmann, 1867, courtesy H. Richard Dietrich, Jr., Philadelphia, copied by Frank Lerner. 102, 103: P. A. Miller and Thomas Croft, courtesy Oklahoma Historical Society, Oklahoma City—D. F. Barry/Denver Public Library, Western History Department; Palmquist Collection, Arcata, Calif.; State Historical Society of Wisconsin, Madison. 104, 105: *Wild Horse Hunters,* Charles M. Russell, 1913, Amon Carter

Museum, Fort Worth, Tex. (1961.209). 109: Courtesy National Cowboy Hall of Fame, Oklahoma City. 110, 111: Courtesy Coffrin's Old West Gallery, Bozeman, Mont. 114: From *We Pointed Them North: Recollections of a Cowpuncher* by E. C. "Teddy Blue" Abbott and Helena Huntington Smith, University of Oklahoma Press, Norman, 1954. 116: Map by R. R. Donnelley & Sons Company, Cartographic Services Center. 118, 119: The Bancroft Library, University of California, Berkeley—Library of Congress; Solomon D. Butcher Collection, Nebraska State Historical Society, Lincoln; *J. A. Ranch, Texas,* 1907, Erwin E. Smith Collection of the Library of Congress on deposit at the Amon Carter Museum, Fort Worth, Tex. 120, 121: *Shoe Bar Ranch, Texas,* 1909, Erwin E. Smith Collection of the Library of Congress on deposit at the Amon Carter Museum, Fort Worth, Tex.—Montana Historical Society, Helena—courtesy Colorado Historical Society, Denver. 122, 123: *Stampede,* Frederic Remington, 1908, The Thomas Gilcrease Institute of American History and Art, Tulsa; courtesy Coffrin's Old West Gallery, Bozeman, Mont.—Wyoming State Museum, Cheyenne. 124, 125: Denver Public Library, Western History Department; Brown Brothers, Sterling, Pa.—The Kansas State Historical Society, Topeka; Montana Historical Society, Helena. 126, 127: *Pouring a Few Drinks in a Room with Colored Wallpaper,* c. 1900-1910, Erwin E. Smith Collection of the Library of Congress on deposit at the Amon Carter Museum, Fort Worth, Tex.—*In Without Knocking,* Charles M. Russell, 1909, Amon Carter Museum, Fort Worth, Tex. (1961.201); *Cowboys Drinking at a Bar, Old Tascoa, Texas,* c. 1908, Erwin E. Smith Collection of the Library of Congress on deposit at the Amon Carter Museum, Fort Worth, Tex. 128, 129: Montana Historical Society, Helena; John B. Riggs Collection, Miles City, Mont.; Library of Congress. 130, 131: Montana Historical Society, Helena. 132, 133: Charles Belden Collection, Buffalo Bill Historical Center, Cody, Wyo.; Archives Division-Texas State Library, Austin. ©, Amon Carter Museum, Ft. Worth, Tex.—Denver Public Library, Western History Department; American Heritage Center, University of Wyoming, Laramie. 134, 135: G. E. Anderson Collection, Brigham Young University, Provo, Utah—American Heritage Center, University of Wyoming, Laramie; Solomon D. Butcher Collection, Nebraska State Historical Society, Lincoln. 136, 137: *When Guns Speak, Death Settles Dispute,* Charles M. Russell, The Thomas Gilcrease Institute of American History and Art,

Tulsa. 140, 141: Buffalo Bill Historical Center, Cody, Wyo., photograph by Ken Kay; Private Collection, photograph by Ken Kay; courtesy Colt Firearms Collection, Museum of Connecticut History, Hartford, photograph by Ken Kay. 142, 143: Reprinted with permission from Pinkerton Security and Investigation Services, Pinkerton's Inc., Van Nuys, Calif. 145: Western History Collections, University of Oklahoma Library, Norman. 148, 149: Courtesy The New-York Historical Society, New York—courtesy Bob McNellis, El Paso, Tex.; The Collection of Barney Hubbs, Pecos, Tex. 150, 151: Museum of New Mexico, Santa Fe (30769); Private Collection. 152: Courtesy S. P. Stevens, San Antonio, Tex. 153: Minnesota Historical Society, St. Paul. 154: Dickinson County Historical Museum, Abilene, Kans. 155: Denver Public Library, Western History Department—D. H. Baldwin/Western History Collections, University of Oklahoma Library, Norman. 156: Boot Hill Museum, Inc., Dodge City, Kans.—The Kansas State Historical Society, Topeka. 157: Archives Division-Texas State Library, Austin (1/102-555); Denver Public Library, Western History Department—Boot Hill Museum, Inc., Dodge City, Kans. 158: Arizona Historical Society, Tucson (1447)—courtesy Glenn G. Boyer, Rodeo, N.Mex.; Arizona Historical Society, Tucson (26793); Arizona Historical Society, Tucson (24740). 160: Arizona Historical Society, Tucson (18346)—Western History Collections, University of Oklahoma Library, Norman; Arizona Historical Society, Tucson (1443); Western History Collections, University of Oklahoma Library, Norman. 161: Western History Collections, University of Oklahoma Library, Norman—Arizona Historical Society, Tucson (24366); Arizona Historical Society, Tucson (24364); Arizona Historical Society, Tucson (24365). 162: Courtesy The Jackson County Historical Society Archives, W. W. Welch Collection, Independence, Mo.; The Kansas State Historical Society, Topeka; courtesy St. Joseph Museum, St. Joseph, Mo. 163: The Kansas State Historical Society, Topeka (2); Centennial Archives, Deadwood Library, Deadwood, S.Dak. 164, 165: The Gerald Peters Gallery, Santa Fe, N.Mex. 166, 167: Montana Historical Society, Helena. 168, 169: The Kansas State Historical Society, Topeka. 170, 171: Denver Public Library, Western History Department. 172, 173: H. R. Farr/Minnesota Historical Society, St. Paul. 174, 175: A. E. Matthews/Solomon D. Butcher Collection, Nebraska State Historical Society, Lincoln. 179: A. P. Swearingen/Western History

Collections, University of Oklahoma Library, Norman. 180: A. P. Swearingen/Western History Collections, University of Oklahoma Library, Norman—The Kansas State Historical Society, Topeka (2). 181: Henry Groskinsky, courtesy Boot Hill Museum, Inc., Dodge City, Kans. 182: Denver Public Library, Western History Department. 183: The Bettmann Archive, New York. 185: Map by R. R. Donnelley & Sons Company, Cartographic Services Center. 186: The Kansas State Historical Society, Topeka. 187: Denver Public Library, Western History Department—Utah State Historical Society, Salt Lake City. 188, 189: Denver Public Library, Western History Department, except bottom left courtesy John A. Carey, Dennis, Mass. 190, 191: Courtesy Eddie Foy III, Burbank, Calif.; Nevada Historical Society, Reno; The Center for American History, The University of Texas at Austin; Montana Historical Society, Helena. 192, 193: Courtesy Colorado Historical Society, Denver (F42,574); Kansas Collection, University of Kansas Libraries, Lawrence—Montana Historical Society, Helena. 194, 195: The Kansas State Historical Society, Topeka; Kansas Collection, University of Kansas Libraries, Lawrence; The Kansas State Historical Society, Topeka; The Center for American History, University of Texas at Austin—The Fred Barton Collection, courtesy Robert C. Ell. 196, 197: Courtesy Colorado Historical Society, Denver (F35,363)—Kansas Collection, University of Kansas Libraries, Lawrence; courtesy John A. Carey, Dennis, Mass. 198, 199: Courtesy Colorado Historical Society, Denver; Kansas Collection, University of Kansas Libraries, Lawrence—Brigham Young University, Photographic Archives, Provo, Utah; courtesy Peter E. Palmquist, Arcata, Calif. 200, 201: Brigham Young University, Photographic Archives, Provo, Utah—Kansas Collection, University of Kansas Libraries, Lawrence (2). 202, 203: *Breaking Through the Line,* Charles Schreyvogel, The Thomas Gilcrease Institute of Art, Tulsa. 205: From *Harper's Weekly,* Aug. 8, 1874, General Research Division, The New York Public Library, Astor, Lenox and Tilden Foundations. 207: National Archives (165-MM-1617); Ken Kay, courtesy West Point Museum, U.S. Military Academy, West Point, N.Y. 208: Buffalo Bill Historical Center, gift of Olin Corporation, Winchester Arms Collection, Cody, Wyo.—Dr. Kenneth O. Leonard Collection, Buffalo Bill Historical Center, Cody, Wyo.; Ken Kay, courtesy West Point Museum, U.S. Military Academy, West Point, N.Y. 209: Dr. Kenneth O. Leonard Collection, Buffalo Bill Historical Cen-

ter, Cody, Wyo.—Denver Art Museum; Dr. Kenneth O. Leonard Collection, Buffalo Bill Historical Center, Cody, Wyo. 211: Paulus Leeser, courtesy West Point Museum, U.S. Military Academy, West Point, N.Y. 212: Denver Public Library, Western History Department; National Archives (64-M-221), copied by Larry Sherer. 213: National Archives (111-SC-93738), copied by Larry Sherer. 215: Map by R. R. Donnelley & Sons Company, Cartographic Services Center. 216, 217: Brigham Young University Photographic Archives, Walter Camp Collection, Provo, Utah; Denver Public Library, Western History Department—from the collection of Charles F. Jepsen, courtesy Sandy Barnard, Terre Haute, Ind. 218, 219: David F. Barry/Denver Public Library, Western History Department—National Archives (111-SC-89498); National Archives (11-SC-83463-8507), copied by Larry Sherer. 220: National Archives (11-SC-83730), copied by Larry Sherer; courtesy Little Big Horn Battlefield National Monument, Crow Agency, Mont. 221: L. A. Huffman/Haynes Foundation Collection, Montana Historical Society, Helena—National Archives (92-F-54-B)—Haynes Foundation Collection, Montana Historical Society, Helena. 222, 223: Seaver Center, Natural History Museum of Los Angeles County; *Guarding the Cañon Pass,* Charles Schreyvogel, from *The Life and Art of Charles Schreyvogel* by James Horan, original painting in the collection of Mr. and Mrs. William Ost. 224, 225: *Attack at Dawn,* Charles Schreyvogel, 1904, The Thomas Gilcrease Institute of American History and Art, Tulsa; National Archives (111-SC-85709). 226, 227: Little Big Horn Battlefield National Monument, Crow Agency, Mont.; *Custer's Last Stand,* Edgar S. Paxson, 1899, Buffalo Bill Historical Center, Cody, Wyo. 228, 229: Arizona Historical Society, Tucson (19775)—from the collection of Kenneth Wiggins Porter, Eugene, Oreg.; *Lieutenant Ross's Attack,* Frederic Remington, courtesy The New-York Historical Society, New York. 230, 231: National Archives (111-SC-89534)—The Bettmann Archive, New York; Smithsonian Institution, National Anthropological Archives (2575-T). 232, 233: Nebraska State Historical Society, Lincoln; Library of Congress (LC-62-11786). 234, 235: *Indian Encampment at Sunset,* Albert Bierstadt, 1872, © Collection of the Eiteljorg Museum of American Indian and Western Art, Indianapolis. 240, 241: The Thomas Gilcrease Institute of American History and Art, Tulsa; *Buffalo Hunting,* Charles M. Russell, 1894, Amon Carter Museum, Fort Worth, Tex. (1961.211)—Peabody Museum

at Harvard University, photograph by Hillel Burger. 243: Map by R. R. Donnelley & Sons Company, Cartographic Services Center. 245: National Museum of the American Indian, Smithsonian Institution; Smithsonian Institution OPPS#55299, Washington, D.C. 246: Charles Phillips, courtesy Smithsonian Institution, Washington, D.C. 248: Denver Public Library, Western History Department; Smithsonian Institution, National Anthropological Archives—Seaver Center, Natural History Museum of Los Angeles County. 250: John A. Anderson/Nebraska State Historical Society, Lincoln; The Huntington Library, San Marino, Calif. 251: *The Medicine Man,* Charles M. Russell, 1908, Amon Carter Museum, Fort Worth, Tex. (1961.171)—*Catching the Wild Horse,* George Catlin, The Thomas Gilcrease Institute of American History and Art, Tulsa. 252, 253: Archives Division-Texas State Library, Austin (1/104-214)—National Museum of American Art, Washington, D.C./Art Resource, New York; Smithsonian Institution, National Anthropological Archives (41106-B). 254: *Running Fight Between Crees and Blackfeet,* Charles M. Russell, 1895, Amon Carter Museum, Fort Worth, Tex. (1961.174)—Henry Beville/Smithsonian Institution, National Anthropological Archives. 255: Benschneider, courtesy National Park Service, Dept. of the Interior—Otto Nelson/Denver Art Museum; Field Museum of Natural History, Chicago (A111348-C); Paulus Leeser, courtesy Panhandle-Plains Historical Museum, Canyon, Tex. 256: Seaver Center, Natural History Museum of Los Angeles County—courtesy Coffrin's Old West Gallery, Bozeman, Mont.—Denver Public Library, Western History Department. 257: Charles Phillips, courtesy Smithsonian Institution—Smithsonian Institution, National Anthropological Archives. 258, 259: Smithsonian Institution, National Anthropological Archives (3179-C)—Cumberland County Historical Society, Carlisle, Pa.; National Archives, Brady Collection (111-B-4669). 260, 261: Library of Congress (LC-USZ62-49148); B. F. Upton/Minnesota Historical Society, St. Paul; Smithsonian Institution OPPS#43305, Washington, D.C.—Smithsonian Institution OPPS#56630-B, Washington, D.C.; Nevada Historical Society, Reno. 262, 263: Courtesy Texas Collections, Baylor University, Waco, Tex.; The Thomas Gilcrease Institute of American History and Art, Tulsa (2 at center); Smithsonian Institution, National Anthropological Archives (1746-A-2). 264, 265: *The Scouting Party,* William Tylee Ranney, 1851, Thyssen-Bornemisza Collection. 266, 267: Courtesy Colorado Historical Society, Denver (F17954); The Huntington Library, San Marino, Calif.—Southern Oregon Historical Society, Medford (747); *Trappers at Fault, Looking for Trail,* Arthur Fitzwilliam Tait, Denver Art Museum. 268: The Kansas State Historical Society, Topeka; Smithsonian Institution, National Anthropological Archives. 269: *The Old Scout's Tale,* William Tylee Ranney, The Thomas Gilcrease Institute of American History and Art, Tulsa—Arizona Historical Society, Tucson (58683); courtesy Colorado Historical Society, Denver; Arizona Historical Society, Gatewood Collection, Tucson (19505). 270: Nebraska State Historical Society, Lincoln; The Kansas State Historical Society, Tucson. 271: *Rounded-Up,* Frederic Remington, 1901, oil on canvas, courtesy Sid Richardson Collection of Western Art, Fort Worth, Tex.—Museum of New Mexico, Santa Fe (9855); Arizona Historical Society, Tucson (15738); Museum of New Mexico, Santa Fe (7151). 272, 273: *Sierra Nevada Morning,* Albert Bierstadt, 1870, The Thomas Gilcrease Institute of American History and Art, Tulsa. 275: Courtesy The Mark Twain Project, The Bancroft Library, University of California, Berkeley. 277: The Kansas State Historical Society, Topeka. 278: W. H. Jackson/Denver Public Library, Western History Department; Smithsonian Institution, OPPS#Hayden-1, Washington, D.C. 279: Courtesy Weston and Mary Naef, photograph by Paulus Leeser; W. H. Jackson/Denver Public Library, Western History Department. 280: The National Portrait Gallery, Washington, D.C. (NPG-76-106). 283: Library of Congress (LC-USZ62-43469). 284: The Kansas State Historical Society, Topeka. 286, 287: *Indian Village, Shoshone Encampment,* Alfred Bierstadt, 1860, courtesy The New-York Historical Society, New York; *Tower Falls,* Thomas Moran, 1872, The Thomas Gilcrease Institute of American History and Art, Tulsa. 288, 289: *Grand Canyon of the Yellowstone,* Thomas Moran, 1872, National Museum of American Art, Washington, D.C./Art Resource, New York; *The Great Hot Springs, Yellowstone Park,* Thomas Moran, 1893, The Thomas Gilcrease Institute of American History and Art, Tulsa. 290, 291: Courtesy Colorado Historical Society, Denver—W. H. Jackson/U.S. Geological Survey (3076); Library of Congress (LC-USZ62-56180). 292, 293: Courtesy Solomon D. Butcher Collection, Nebraska State Historical Society, Lincoln. 294, 295: Courtesy Frank Woods Picture Bank, Alexandria, Va. 296, 297: *A Dash for the Timber,* Frederic Remington, 1889, Amon Carter Museum, Fort Worth, Tex. (1961.381).

298, 299: *Three Generations,* Charles M. Russell, 1899, courtesy R. W. Norton Art Gallery, Shreveport, La.; *Chief Crowfoot,* Charles M. Russell, c. 1880-1, courtesy R. W. Norton Art Gallery, Shreveport, La.—*Self-Portrait,* Charles M. Russell, 1899, courtesy R. W. Norton Art Gallery, Shreveport, La. 300, 301: *Chasm of the Colorado,* Thomas Moran, National Museum of American Art, Washington, D.C./Art Resource, New York. 304: National Archives/U.S. Geological Survey (52-HS-1111). 308, 309: John Zimmerman, courtesy Fort Humboldt State Historic Park, California Dept. of Parks and Recreation, Eureka, Calif. 310: Smithsonian Institution, OPPS#1784, Washington, D.C. 311: Smithsonian Institution, OPPS#1791-A, Washington, D.C.—Smithsonian Institution, OPPS#1837-B, Washington, D.C.; Smithsonian Institution, OPPS#2232-A, Washington, D.C. 313: Map by R. R. Donnelley & Sons Company, Cartographic Services Center. 314, 315: International Museum of Photography at George Eastman House, Rochester, N.Y.; National Archives (77-WA-23), copied by Larry Sherer; Library of Congress (LC-02347). 316, 317: Smithsonian Institution, National Anthropological Archives (36-B); International Museum of Photography at George Eastman House, Rochester, N.Y.; U.S. Geological Survey/National Archives (57-PS-431-A)—Haynes Foundation Collection, Montana Historical Society, Helena; National Archives (57-PE-50), copied by Larry Sherer. 318, 319: U.S.M.A. Library/Special Collections, Cadet Photograph Collection, West Point, N.Y.—Smithsonian Institution, OPPS#55375, Washington, D.C.—Smithsonian Institution, OPPS#3939-A12, Washington, D.C.; Smithsonian Institution, OPPS#2267-P, Washington, D.C. 320, 321: Amon Carter Museum, Fort Worth, Tex.; C. E. Watkins/California State Library, Sacramento, Calif.—McClure/Denver Public Library, Western History Collection. 322, 323: From *The Big Bonanza* by Dan De Quille, Alfred A. Knopf, New York, 1947; C. E. Watkins/California State Library, Sacramento, Calif.; Museum of North Idaho, Coeur d'Alene, Idaho. 324, 325: Angelus Collection (T386), Special Collections, Knight Library, University of Oregon, Eugene; Angelus Collection (T169), Special Collections, Knight Library, University of Oregon, Eugene—C. L. Goddard, courtesy The Bancroft Library, University of California, Berkeley. 326, 327: Courtesy Oregon Historical Society, Portland (OrHi48559); The Bancroft Library, University of California, Berkeley. 328: Library of Congress (LC-USZ62-53148); National

Archives (200-JH-10), copied by Larry Sherer. 329: H. C. Tibbitts, courtesy Time Inc. Magazines Picture Collection—Yosemite National Park Research Library, Harpers Ferry, W.Va. 330, 331: Library of Congress. 334: *The Last Stand,* Frederic Remington, Woolarec Museum, Bartlesville, Okla. 337: State Historical Society of Missouri, Columbia. 338: Western History Collections, University of Oklahoma Library, Norman. 339: The Kansas State Historical Society, Topeka—Buffalo Bill Historical Center, Cody, Wyo. 340: Buffalo Bill Historical Center, Cody, Wyo.—Library of Congress (PZ3-J92BUL). 341: Vincent Mercaldo Collection, Buffalo Bill Historical Center, Cody, Wyo.—*Buffalo Bill's Duel with Yellowhand,* Charles M. Russell, 1917, oil on canvas, Sid Richardson Collection of Western Art, Fort Worth, Tex. (SWR 79). 342, 343: Courtesy Wyoming State Museum, Cheyenne (2); The Denver Public Library, Western History Department. 344: Courtesy John and Mabel Ringling Museum of Art, Sarasota, Fla.; Vincent Mercaldo Collection, Buffalo Bill Historical Center, Cody, Wyo. 345: Buffalo Bill Historical Center, Cody, Wyo. 346: The Kansas State Historical Society, Topeka. 347: Library of Congress (LC-46198-US262-23232); Henry Groskinsky, courtesy General Research Division, The New York Public Library, Astor, Lenox and Tilden Foundations—American Heritage Center, University of Wyoming, Laramie. 348, 349: Courtesy William Everson, New York. 350: *Thomas Jefferson at the Natural Bridge,* Caleb Boyle, c. 1801, Kirby College of Historical Paintings, Lafayette College, Easton, Pa.—*Entering the Lock,* E. L. Henry, 1899, gift of Catherine Gansevoort Lansing, from the Collection of the Albany Institute of History and Art—Museum of the Cherokee Indian, Cherokee, N.C.; Culver Pictures, New York. 351: Archives Division-Texas State Library, Austin (1992/23-23)—The Bettmann Archive, New York—*Placerville Mining,* Albertis Del Orient Browere, The National Cowboy Hall of Fame, Oklahoma City. 352: *Furling the Flag,* R. N. Brooke, West Point Museum, U.S. Military Academy, West Point, N.Y. 353: The Bettmann Archive, New York—Culver Pictures, New York. 354: Library of Congress (LC-USZ62-11624)—Culver Pictures, New York. 355: Spindletop/Gladys City Boomtown Museum, Beaumont, Tex.; Library of Congress (LC-USZ62-6166A)—The Granger Collection, New York; Library of Congress (LC-USZ62-2235); from the collections of Henry Ford Museum and Greenfield Village (188-10187).

# BIBLIOGRAPHY

## BOOKS

Abbott, E. C. ("Teddy Blue"), and Helena Huntington Smith, *We Pointed Them North: Recollections of a Cowpuncher*. Norman: University of Oklahoma Press, 1939.

Abdill, George B., *Pacific Slope Railroads: From 1854 to 1900*. New York: Bonanza Books, 1959.

Allen, Alice Benson, *Simon Benson: Northwest Lumber King*. Portland, Oreg.: Binford and Mort, 1971.

*American Heritage History of the Great West, The*. New York: American Heritage, 1965.

Axelrod, Alan, ed., *American Frontier Life: Early Western Painting and Prints*. New York: Abbeville Press, 1987.

Baigell, Matthew, *Albert Bierstadt*. New York: Watson-Guptill, 1981.

Barnard, Edward S., ed., *Story of the Great American West*. Pleasantville, N.Y.: Reader's Digest Association, 1977.

Bartlett, Richard A., *Great Surveys of the American West*. Norman: University of Oklahoma Press, 1962.

Beebe, Lucius, *The Central Pacific & the Southern Pacific Railroads*. Berkeley, Calif.: Howell-North, 1963.

Best, Gerald M., *Iron Horses to Promontory*. San Marino, Calif.: Golden West Books, 1969.

Billington, Ray Allen, *Westward Expansion: A History of the American Frontier*. New York: Macmillan, 1967.

Blacker, Irwin R., *The Old West in Fact*. New York: Ivan Obolensky, 1962.

Bowman, John S., ed., *The World Almanac of the American West*. New York: Pharos Books, 1986.

Boyer, Glenn G., ed., *I Married Wyatt Earp: The Recollections of Josephine Sarah Marcus Earp*. Tucson: University of Arizona Press, 1976.

Breihan, Carl W., *Lawmen and Robbers*. Caldwell, Idaho: Caxton Printers, 1986.

Brown, Dee, *Bury My Heart at Wounded Knee*. New York: Henry Holt and Company, 1970.

Brown, Mark H., and W. R. Felton, *Before Barbed Wire: L. A. Huffman, Photographer on Horseback*. New York: Bramhall House, 1961.

Brown, Ronald C., *Hard-Rock Miners: The Intermountain West, 1860-1920*. College Station: Texas A&M University Press, 1979.

Brown, William L., III, *The Army Called It Home: Military Interiors of the 19th Century*. Gettysburg, Pa.: Thomas Publications, 1992.

Capps, Benjamin, and the Editors of Time-Life Books:

*The Great Chiefs*. (The Old West series). Alexandria, Va.: Time-Life Books, 1975.
*The Indians* (The Old West series). Alexandria, Va.: Time-Life Books, 1973.

Carroll, John Alexander, ed., *Reflections of Western Historians*. Tucson: The University of Arizona Press, 1969.

Carroll, John M., ed.:

*The Black Military Experience in the American West*. New York: Liveright Publishing Corporation, 1971.
*Ten Years with General Custer among the American Indians*. Brian, Tex.: John M. Carroll, 1980.

Clarke, James Mitchell, *The Life and Adventures of John Muir*. San Diego: The Word Shop Publications, 1979.

Clemens, Samuel Langhorne (Mark Twain), *Roughing It* (2 vols.). New York: Harper & Row, 1913.

Cody, William F., *The Life of Hon. William F. Cody—Known as Buffalo Bill*. Lincoln: University of Nebraska Press, 1878.

Coffman, Edward M., *The Old Army: A Portrait of the American Army in Peacetime, 1784-1898*. New York: Oxford University Press, 1986.

Combs, Barry B., *Westward to Promontory: Building the Union Pacific across the Plains and Mountains*. Palo Alto, Calif.: American West, 1969.

Connelly, William Elsey, *Wild Bill and His Era*. New York: Press of the Pioneers, 1933.

Creigh, Dorothy Weyer, *Nebraska: A Bicentennial History*. New York: W. W. Norton, 1977.

Current, Karen, *Photography and the Old West*. New York: Harry N. Abrams, 1978.

Custer, Elizabeth B., *Boots and Saddles or Life in Dakota with General Custer*. New York: Harper & Brothers, 1885.

Cutright, Paul Russell, *Theodore Roosevelt: The Making of a Conservationist*. Urbana, Ill.: University of Illinois Press, 1985.

Davis, Kenneth S., *Kansas: A Bicentennial History*. New York: W. W. Norton, 1976.

Davis, William C., and the Editors of Time-Life Books, *Brother Against Brother* (The Civil War series). Alexandria, Va.: Time-Life Books, 1983.

Dick, Everett, *The Sod-House Frontier: 1854-1890*. Lincoln, Nebr.: Johnsen, 1954.

Dillon, Richard H., *North American Indian Wars*. New York: Gallery Books, 1983.

Dimsdale, Thomas Josiah, *The Vigilantes of Montana*. Ann Arbor, Mich.: University Microfilms, 1966. (Reprint of 1866 edition.)

Dobie, J. Frank, *Cow People*. Boston: Little, Brown, 1964.

Dykstra, Robert R., *The Cattle Towns*. New York: Alfred A. Knopf, 1968.

Easter, Deborah, ed., *Myth of the West*. New York: Rizzoli, 1990.

Editors of Time-Life Books:

*The Gamblers* (The Old West series). Alexandria, Va.: Time-Life Books, 1978.
*The Old West*. New York: Prentice Hall Press, 1990.
*Prelude: 1870-1900* (This Fabulous Century series). New York: Time-Life Books, 1970.
*Spies, Scouts and Raiders* (The Civil War series). Alexandria, Va.: Time-Life Books, 1985.
*The United States* (Library of Nations series). Amsterdam: Time-Life Books, 1984.

Ellis, Anne, *The Life of an Ordinary Woman*. Boston: Houghton Mifflin, 1929.

Ewers, John C., *Artists of the Old West*. Garden City, N.Y.: Doubleday, 1986.

Farr, William E., and K. Ross Toole, *Montana: Images of the Past*. Boulder, Colo.: Pruett, 1978.

Faulk, Odie B., *Dodge City: The Most Western Town of All*. New York: Oxford University Press, 1977.

Ferris, Robert G., ed., *Soldier and Brave*. Washington, D.C.: United States Department of the Interior National Park Service, 1971.

Fielder, Mildred, *Wild Bill and Deadwood*. New York: Bonanza Books, 1965.

Forbis, William H., and the Editors of Time-Life Books, *The Cowboys* (The Old West series). Alexandria, Va.: Time-Life Books, 1973.

Fowler, Don D., *Myself in the Water: The Western Photographs of John K. Hillers*. Washington, D.C.: Smithsonian Institution Press, 1989.

Gaines, Ann, *John Wesley Powell and the Great Surveys of the American West*. New York: Chelsea House, 1991.

Garrett, Wilbur E., ed., *Historical Atlas of the United States*. Washington, D.C.: National Geographic Society, 1988.

Getlein, Frank, and the Editors of Country Beautiful, *The Lure of the Great West*. Waukesha, Wis.: Country Beautiful, 1973.

Gilbert, Bil, and the Editors of Time-Life Books, *The Trailblazers* (The Old West series). Alexandria, Va.: Time-Life Books, 1973.

Goetzmann, William H., and William N. Goetzmann, *The West of the Imagination*. New York: W. W. Norton, 1986.

Hassrick, Peter H., *Artists of the American Frontier: The Way West*. New York: Promontory Press, 1988.

Hendricks, Gordon, *Albert Bierstadt: Painter of the American West.* New York: Harry N. Abrams, 1973.

Hillerman, Tony, ed., *The Best of the West: An Anthology of Classic Writing from the American West.* New York: Harper Collins, 1991.

Hine, Robert V., *The American West: An Interpretive History.* Boston: Little, Brown, 1973.

Hogg, Garry, *Union Pacific: The Building of the First Transcontinental Railroad.* New York: Walker, 1967.

Hoig, Stan. *The Battle of the Washita.* Garden City, N.Y.: Doubleday, 1976.

Honig, Donald, *In the Days of the Cowboy.* New York: Random House, 1970.

Hook, Jason, *American Indian Warrior Chiefs.* Dorset, England: Firebird Books, 1990.

Horan, James D.:
*The Gunfighters: The Authentic Wild West.* New York: Crown, 1976.
*The Lawmen: The Authentic Wild West.* New York: Crown, 1980.
*The Outlaws: The Authentic Wild West.* New York: Crown, 1977.

Horn, Huston, and the Editors of Time-Life Books, *The Pioneers* (The Old West series). Alexandria, Va.: Time-Life Books, 1974.

Hunt, Frazier, and Robert Hunt, *I Fought with Custer.* Lincoln: University of Nebraska Press, 1947.

Hutton, Paul Andrew, ed., *Soldiers West: Biographies from the Military Frontier.* Lincoln: University of Nebraska Press, 1987.

Jackson, Clarence S., *Picture Maker of the Old West: William H. Jackson.* New York: Charles Scribner's Sons, 1947.

Jackson, William Henry, *Time Exposure: The Autobiography of William Henry Jackson.* New York: G. P. Putnam's Sons, 1940.

James, Will, *Lone Cowboy: My Life Story.* New York: Charles Scribner's Sons, 1930.

Jensen, Oliver, *The American Heritage History of Railroads in America.* New York: American Heritage, 1975.

Johnson, William Weber, and the Editors of Time-Life Books, *The Forty-Niners* (The Old West series). Alexandria, Va.: Time-Life Books, 1974.

Katz, William Loren, *The Black West.* Seattle, Wash.: Open Hand, 1987.

Keating, Bern, *An Illustrated History of the Texas Rangers.* Chicago: Rand McNally, 1975.

Kraus, George, *High Road to Promontory.* Palo Alto, Calif.: American West, 1969.

Laubin, Reginald, and Gladys Laubin, *The Indian Tipi: Its History, Construction, and Use.* Norman: University of Oklahoma Press, 1957.

Lavender, David, *The Way to the Western Sea: Lewis and Clark across the Continent.* New York: Harper & Row, 1988.

Lummis, Charles Fletcher, *Dateline Fort Bowie: Charles Fletcher Lummis Reports on an Apache War.* Norman: University of Oklahoma Press, 1979.

McCracken, Harold:
*The American Cowboy.* Garden City, N.Y.: Doubleday, 1973.
*Great Painters and Illustrators of the Old West.* New York: Dover Publications, Inc., 1988.

McPherson, James M., *Battle Cry of Freedom.* New York: Oxford University Press, 1988.

Mark, Joan, *A Stranger in Her Native Land: Alice Fletcher and the American Indians.* Lincoln: University of Nebraska Press, 1988.

May, Robin, *The Story of the Wild West.* London: Hamlyn, 1978.

Miles, Nelson A., *Personal Recollections and Observations of General Nelson A. Miles.* New York: Da Capo Press, 1969.

Miller, Don C., *Ghost Towns of Montana.* Boulder, Colo.: Pruett, 1974.

Mills, Anson, *My Story.* Washington, D.C.: Byron S. Adams, 1921.

Milton, John, *South Dakota: A Bicentennial History.* New York: W. W. Norton, 1977.

Morris, John W., Charles R. Goins, and Edwin C. McReynolds, *Historical Atlas of Oklahoma.* Norman: University of Oklahoma Press, 1986.

Mouquin, Wayne, and Charles Van Doren, eds., *Great Documents in American Indian History.* New York: Praeger, 1973.

Muir, John, *Our National Parks.* Boston: Houghton Mifflin, 1901.

Naef, Weston J., *Era of Exploration.* Boston: New York Graphic Society, 1975.

Nankivell, John H., ed., *The History of the Twenty-Fifth Regiment United States Infantry, 1869-1926.* Ft. Collins, Colo.: The Old Army Press, 1972.

Nevin, David, and the Editors of Time-Life Books:
*The Expressmen* (The Old West series). Alexandria, Va.: Time-Life Books, 1974.
*The Mexican War* (The Old West series). Alexandria, Va.: Time-Life Books, 1978.
*The Soldiers* (The Old West series). Alexandria, Va.: Time-Life Books, 1974.

*New York Public Library Desk Reference.* New York: Prentice Hall General Reference, 1989.

Newman, Joseph, ed., *200 Years: A Bicentennial History of the United States* (2 vols.). Washington, D.C.: U.S. News & World Report, 1973.

O'Connor, Richard, *Iron Wheels and Broken Men: The Railroad Barons and the Plunder of the West.* New York: G. P. Putnam's Sons, 1973.

O'Neil, Paul, and the Editors of Time-Life Books:
*The End and the Myth* (The Old West series). Alexandria, Va.: Time-Life Books, 1979.
*The Rivermen* (The Old West series). Alexandria, Va.: Time-Life Books, 1975.

Paullin, Charles O., *Atlas of the Historical Geography of the United States.* Washington, D.C., and New York: Carnegie Institution of Washington and American Geographical Society of New York, 1932.

Pohanka, Brian C., ed., *Nelson A. Miles: A Documentary Biography of His Military Career, 1861-1903.* Glendale, Calif.: Arthur H. Clark, 1985.

Porter, Joseph C., *Paper Medicine Man.* Norman and London: University of Oklahoma Press, 1986.

Powell, John Wesley, *First through the Grand Canyon.* New York: Macmillan, 1925.

Prucha, Francis Paul, *Atlas of American Indian Affairs.* Lincoln and London: University of Nebraska Press, 1990.

Reiter, Joan Swallow, and the Editors of Time-Life Books. *The Women* (The Old West series). Alexandria, Va.: Time-Life Books, 1978.

Remington, Frederic, *Frederic Remington's Own West.* New York: Dial Press, 1960.

Renner, Frederic G.:
*Charles M. Russell: Paintings, Drawings, and Sculpture in the Amon G. Carter Collection.* Austin and London: University of Texas Press, 1966.
*Charles M. Russell: Paintings, Drawings, and Sculpture in the Amon Carter Museum.* New York: Harry N. Abrams, 1974.

Rennert, Jack, *100 Posters of Buffalo Bill's Wild West.* New York: Darien House, 1976.

Rennert, Vincent Paul, *Western Outlaws.* New York: Crowell-Collier Press, 1968.

Rickey, Don, Jr., *Forty Miles a Day on Beans and Hay: The Enlisted Soldier Fighting the Indian Wars.* Norman: University of Oklahoma Press, 1963.

Riegel, Robert E., and Robert G. Athearn, *America Moves West.* New York: Holt, Rinehart and Winston, 1971.

Rochlin, Harriet, and Fred Rochlin, *Pioneer Jews.* Boston: Houghton Mifflin, 1984.

Roosevelt, Theodore, *Theodore Roosevelt's Ranch Life and the Hunting-Trail.* New York: Bonanza

Books, 1978.

Rosa, Joseph G., *They Called Him Wild Bill.* Norman: University of Oklahoma Press, 1989.

Rosa, Joseph G., and Robin May, *Buffalo Bill and His Wild West: A Pictorial Biography.* Lawrence: University Press of Kansas, 1989.

Rossi, Paul A., and David C. Hunt, *The Art of the Old West.* New York: Alfred A. Knopf, 1973.

Sandler, Martin W., *American Image: Photographing One Hundred Fifty Years in the Life of a Nation.* Chicago: Contemporary Books, 1989.

Schmitt, Martin F., and Dee Brown, *The Settlers' West.* New York: Bonanza Books, 1955.

Schoenberger, Dale T., *The Gunfighters.* Caldwell, Idaho: Caxton Printers, 1971.

Scott, John Anthony, *The Story of America.* Washington, D.C.: National Geographic Society, 1984.

Shapiro, Michael Edward, and Peter H. Hassrick, *Frederic Remington: The Masterworks.* New York: Harry N. Abrams, 1988.

Stands in Timber, John, and Margot Liberty (with the assistance of Robert M. Utley), *Cheyenne Memories.* New Haven: Yale University Press, 1967.

Sturtevant, William C., ed., *Handbook of North American Indians.* Washington, D.C.: Smithsonian Institution, 1979.

Tanner, Ogden, and the Editors of Time-Life Books, *The Ranchers* (The Old West series). Alexandria, Va.: Time-Life Books, 1977.

Terrell, John Upton, *The Man Who Rediscovered America: A Biography of John Wesley Powell.* New York: Weybright and Talley, 1969.

Thrapp, Dan L., *General Crook and the Sierra Madre Adventure.* Norman: University of Oklahoma Press, 1972.

Towell, Emily, *Covered Wagon Women* (Vol. 10). Spokane: Arthur H. Clark, 1991.

Trachtman, Paul, and the Editors of Time-Life Books, *The Gunfighters* (The Old West series). Alexandria, Va.: Time-Life Books, 1974.

Turner, Frederick, *Rediscovering America.* New York: Viking Penguin, 1985.

*Utah: A Guide to the State.* New York: Hastings House, 1954.

Utley, Robert M.:

*Cavalier in Buckskin: George Armstrong Custer and the Western Military Frontier.* Norman and London: University of Oklahoma Press, 1988.
*Frontier Regulars: The United States Army and the Indian, 1866-1891.* New York: Macmillan, 1973.

Utley, Robert M., ed., *Life in Custer's Cavalry.* New Haven: Yale University Press, 1977.

Utley, Robert M., and Wilcomb E. Washburn,

*History of the Indian Wars.* New York: American Heritage, 1977.

Vanderwerth, W. C., *Indian Oratory.* Norman: University of Oklahoma, 1971.

Viola, Herman J., *Exploring the West.* Washington, D.C.: Smithsonian Books, 1987.

Waite, M. D. "Bud", and B. D. Ernst, *Trapdoor Springfield.* North Hollywood, Calif.: Beinfeld, 1980.

Wallace, Robert, and the Editors of Time-Life Books, *The Miners* (The Old West series). New York: Time-Life Books, 1976.

Wardner, Jim, *Jim Wardner of Wardner, Idaho.* New York: Anglo-American Publishing Corporation, 1900.

Weinstein, Allen, and Frank Otto Gatell, *Freedom and Crisis: An American History* (Vol. 2, 3d ed.). New York: Random House, 1981.

Wellman, Paul I., *A Dynasty of Western Outlaws.* New York: Bonanza Books, 1961.

Wheeler, Keith:

*The Chroniclers* (The Old West series). Alexandria, Va.: Time-Life Books, 1976.
*The Railroaders* (The Old West series). Alexandria, Va.: Time-Life Books, 1973.
*The Scouts* (The Old West series). Alexandria, Va.: Time-Life Books, 1978.
*The Townsmen* (The Old West series). Alexandria, Va.: Time-Life Books, 1975.

White, Richard, *"It's Your Misfortune and None of My Own": A History of the American West.* Norman and London: University of Oklahoma Press, 1991.

Wilkins, Robert P., and Wynona Huchette Wilkins, *North Dakota: A Bicentennial History.* New York: W. W. Norton, 1977.

Wilkins, Thurman, *Thomas Moran: Artist of the Mountains.* Norman: University of Oklahoma Press, 1966.

Williams, Richard L., and the Editors of Time-Life Books, *The Loggers* (The Old West series). Alexandria, Va.: Time-Life Books, 1976.

Wolle, Muriel Sibell, *Montana Pay Dirt: A Guide to the Mining Camps of the Treasure State.* Denver: Sage Books, 1963.

Wright, Robert M., *Dodge City: The Cowboy Capital.* Wichita, Kans.: Wichita Eagle Press, 1913.

Yenne, Bill, *The Encyclopedia of North American Indian Tribes.* New York: Arch Cape Press, 1986.

## PERIODICALS

Bowen, Don R., "Guerrilla War in Western Missouri, 1862-1865." *Comparative Studies in Soci-*

*ety and History,* April 1977.

Bourke, John G., "General Crook in the Indian Country." *Century Magazine,* March 1891.

Bright, Abbie, "Roughing it on her Kansas Claim: The Diary of Abbie Bright." *Kansas Historical Quarterly,* Autumn and Winter 1971.

Castel, Albert, "Men behind the Masks: The James Brothers." *American History,* June 1982.

Hunt, Frazier, "The Last Frontier—The Biography of Ad Spaugh, Cowman." *Country Gentleman,* December 1939.

Judah, Anna, Personal Correspondence. *Themis,* December 14, 1889.

McGinty, Brian, "John Wesley Hardin: Gentleman of Guns." *American History,* June 1982.

Maraniss, David, "Due Recognition and Reward." *Washington Post Magazine,* January 20, 1991.

Nimmo, Joseph, Jr., "The American Cowboy." *Harper's New Monthly Magazine,* November 1886.

Palmquist, Peter E., "Pioneer Women Photographers in Nineteenth-Century California." *California History* (Journal of California Historical Society), Spring 1992.

Pohanka, Brian C., "Their Shots Quit Coming." *Military History Magazine,* 1984.

"Regulars in a Trap." *Chicago Herald,* April 16, 1892.

Remington, Frederic, "A Few Words from Mr. Remington." *Colliers Weekly,* March 18, 1905.

West, Elliott, "Wicked Dodge City." *American History,* June 1982.

## OTHER SOURCES

Batten, Derek James, *From the Bottom Up: Life for the Enlisted Soldier in the U.S. Army on the Western Frontier, 1865-1890* (dissertation). Manchester, England: University of Manchester, 1991.

Lyon, Mary. Written recollection. Burlingame Hills, Calif.: Lilla Day Monroe Collection/Joanna Stratton, n.d.

Newcomb, Samuel P., and Susan E. Newcomb. Personal diaries. Austin: University of Texas, Center for American History, n.d.

Parnham, Delbert. Written recollection. Burlingame Hills, Calif.: Lilla Day Monroe Collection/Joanna Stratton, n.d.

Singleton, Benjamin. "News from Kansas" (circular). Topeka: Kansas State Historical Society, Negro Immigration Files, Singleton Scrapbook, March 19, 1877.

*Southern Pacific's First Century* (booklet). San Francisco: Southern Pacific, 1955.

# INDEX